The
Plagiarism
Plague

A Resource Guide and CD-ROM Tutorial
for Educators and Librarians

Edited by

Vibiana Bowman

Neal- Schuman Publishers, Inc.
New York   London

Published by Neal-Schuman Publishers, Inc.
100 William St., Suite 2004
New York, NY 10038

The paper used in this publication meets the minimum requirements of American National Standard for Information Sciences—Permanence of Paper for Printed Library Materials, ANSI Z39.48-1992. ∞

Printed and bound in the United States of America.

Library of Congress Cataloging-in-Publication Data
Bowman, Vibiana, 1953–
    The plagiarism plague: a resource guide and CD-ROM tutorial for educators and librarians / edited by Vibiana Bowman.
        p. cm.

    Includes bibliographical references and index.

    ISBN 1-55570-501-4 (alk. paper)
    1. Plagiarism. I. Title.

PN167.B68 2004
808-dc22   2004050448

Table of Contents

Table of Contents

Table of Contents

List of Figures

Preface

Plagiarism is a plague—it is infectious, pervasive, and rapidly spreading.

- A 1991 study finds that the most frequent kind of cheating was the "failure to footnote sources in written work," while next in frequency was "collaboration on assignments when the instructor specifically asked for individual work." (McCabe 1991.)
- A 1999 finding shows that one third of the one thousand faculty members surveyed who were aware of student cheating in their classes did nothing about it. (Center for Academic Integrity.)
- A 2001 survey from Rutgers University indicated that three out of four high school students stated that they had cheated on a test at least once during that academic year, and the same number confessed to handing in another person's written work (Sohn 2001.)

Conquering this ethical epidemic requires preventative steps. Today's students need a clear understanding of intellectual dishonesty. They must understand why it is wrong, whom it hurts, how it hurts them, and how it can be easily avoided. Today's instructors need a commitment to a new form of education—one that incorporates ethics, vigilance, collaboration, and technology.

The Plagiarism Plague: A Resource Guide and CD-ROM Tutorial for Educators and Librarians offers real-world examples and lessons of how to teach students the structure and code of scholarly writing. In this book, a diverse group of expert contributors share their experiences of what has worked, what they have learned, and what they feel must be passed on to other educators. *The Plagiarism Plague* approaches the subject holistically, providing ample background information, Web resources, sample exercises, multiple perspectives, and an interactive CD-ROM.

In Part I: "Understanding the Problem: Background and Overview" four chapters cover the crisis: What is it? How did it start? How is it challenged? What are the legal ramifications? Chapter 1, "Teaching Intellectual Honesty in a Tragically Hip World: A Pop-Culture Perspective," unravels the complications that technology, word processing, and pop culture have brought upon scholarly writing. Chapter 2, "The Onus of Originality: Innovation, Imitation, and Other Problems of Writing," explores the complexities and challenges that students encounter when deriving original material from the existing body of knowledge. Chapter 3, "The Dark Side of the Web: Where to Go to Buy a Paper," familiarizes educators with the rise of paper mills (centers for exchange, sale, and collection of papers) and their effect on students' decisions. Chapter 4,

"It's a Small World?: Cross-Cultural Perspectives and ESL Considerations," illuminates several of the special considerations for ESL students and plausible solutions for educators.

"Part II: Finding Remedies: Proven Faculty, Departmental, and Institutional Strategies," presents instructional advice, recent findings, and policy examples from a wide variety of institutions and levels of education. Chapter 5, "Intellectual Honesty: Selling It!," offers new and inventive ways to market tutorials to students and faculty. Chapter 6, "Cite it Right: A Tutorial," walks readers through the conception, planning, design, implementation, marketing, and assessment of the Rutgers University Web resource as an example of an effective educational tool. Chapter 7, "Teach Your Children Well: The High School Research Experience," Chapter 8, "Communicating Honesty: Building on the Student/Teacher Relationship," and Chapter 9, "Encouraging Excellence: A Departmental Approach," are real stories of how plagiarism is addressed from the perspectives of a high school teacher, an instructor of undergraduate courses, and a university department chair, respectively. Chapter 10, "Academic Remedies: A Survey of Universities' Policies on Intellectual Honesty," compiles policies and procedures from a variety of colleges and universities and is an especially valuable resource for those looking to develop effective and proven statements of their own.

The six chapters of "Part III: A Practitioner's Toolkit," collect the resources and important issues instructors can share with students and faculty. Chapter 11, "Read the Fine Print: Legal Issues Related to Student Plagiarism," details copyright, legal, and administrative issues associated with intellectual property. Chapter 12, "Call the Pros: Professional Organizations' Recommendations on Intellectual Honesty," gathers the responses of professional organizations in the humanities, social sciences, education and libraries, and science and engineering to help address questions across the disciplines. Chapter 13, "Plagiarism Busters: Free (and Not-So-Free) Web Resources for Plagiarism Detection," and Chapter 14, "Where to Go For What They Need to Know: Style Sheets, Guides, and Other Resources," reveal new technology tools for instructors and students to detect fake papers and learn proper citation, research, and writing skills. Chapter 15, "High- Tech and Low- Tech: Materials for Teaching Intellectual Honesty," evaluates the effectiveness of technology tools for instruction. Chapter 16, "And in the End: An Annotated Bibliography of Resources, Media, and Other Teaching Tools," is an ideal resource for posting to Web pages, circulating among faculty and staff, or incorporating into class instruction.

Ethical issues are nothing new to the academic community, but today's widespread disregard for originality is new and requires the type of intervention that *The Plagiarism Plague: A Resource Guide and CD-ROM Tutorial for Educators and Librarians* can help provide. In each of these chapters, the authors provide their best advice and suggestions for curing the plagiarism plague. Their recommended antidotes—education and information—are just as infectious, pervasive, and rapidly spreading as the epidemic it remedies.

Works Cited

Center for Academic Integrity. 2003. "CAI Research." Available: http://www.academicintegrity .org/cai_research.asp.

McCabe, Donald L. August 1 992. "The Influence of Situation Ethics on Cheating among College Students." Sociological Inquiry (August) 62 : 365-74.

Sohn, Emily. 21 May 2001. "The Young and the Virtueless." U.S. News & World Report 130, no. 20: 51.

Acknowledgments

A sincere thank you to the following groups of kind people who made this project possible:

- The Neal-Schuman team for their mentoring and professional guidance; with a special thank you to Michael G. Kelley, my editor, and Corrina Moss for her care and attention in preparing the manuscript for publication.
- The faculty and staff of the Paul Robeson Library for all their help, advice, and support with a special tip of the hat to John Maxymuk, John Gibson, Julie Still, and Dr. Gary Golden.
- The contributing authors for their hard work and diligence.

Love and thanks to my dear husband and terrific children for putting up with me through the process of writing and editing this book.

The titles of Chapters 7 and 16 make allusion to songs by Crobsy, Stills, Nash, and Young and The Beatles respectively.

Understanding the Problem: Background and Overview

Many, *many* years ago, when I was an editor for my high school newspaper, our faculty advisor taught us that a good news story should tell the reader who, what, when, where, and why. For maximum effectiveness, the news story should tell that to the reader up front and with clarity. I would suggest that the same advice holds true for all nonfiction writing, including scholarly writing. With this in mind, Part I of this book is designed to answer the who, what, when, where, and why regarding the plagiarism plague that is facing education today.

The "who," of course, is our students—high school and college young adults. Chapter 1 examines their attitudes and habits with regard to information, most especially the information that they have access to on the World Wide Web. Chapter 4 contains special considerations for educators about that "who," with regard to students from different cultures and students whose first language is not English. A statement of "what" and "why" (i.e., a statement of the problem of plagiarism and why it is so prevalent) is found throughout Part I. Chapter 2 contains a specific discussion of the problems of teasing out what "originality" is in a complex, information-oriented society. The "where" and "when" of plagiarism are outlined in Chapter 3, which includes an in-depth discussion of the "paper mills" that students use—the origin of these mills and how they work.

With modern advances in communications technology, the citizen of the twenty-first century seems constantly connected to and constantly bombarded with information. The ability to sort through this information, analyze it, verify it, and use it in an appropriate manner are the skills that an information-literate person needs. The Association of College and Research Libraries provides an excellent resource for standards, guidelines, and definitions regarding information literacy in "Information Literacy Competency Standards for Higher Education" (available: www.ala.org/ala/acrl/acrlstandards/informationliteracy-competency.htm). In the section that follows, my colleagues and I attempt to outline the problems facing educators in preparing an information-literate citizenry specifically with regard to the issue of plagiarism.

CHAPTER 1

Teaching Intellectual Honesty in a Tragically Hip World: A Pop-Culture Perspective

Vibiana Bowman

Introduction: Some Thoughts about Plagiarism

In 2002, historian Doris Kearns Goodwin was involved in some academic unpleasantness—specifically, charges of plagiarism. An accusation of plagiarism is damaging for any scholar, but especially one of Goodwin's standing. Goodwin has impeccable credentials: bestselling author, recipient of the Pulitzer Prize for History, and member of various prestigious societies, such as the Harvard Board of Overseers, the Society of American Historians, and the American Academy of Arts and Sciences (Academy of Achievement, 2003). The problem arose when critics noticed that portions of her book *The Fitzgeralds and the Kennedys* (1987) bore a remarkable resemblance to passages from Lynne McTaggart's work *Kathleen Kennedy: Her Life and Times* (1983). Goodwin publicly apologized for the error. She explained that she had done copious research but had neglected to footnote properly her source material and that this lapse in scholarly protocol was a source of professional embarrassment: "What made this incident particularly hard for me was the fact that I take great pride in the depth of my research and the extensiveness of my citations" (Goodwin, 2002: 69).

Goodwin's woes were exacerbated by the fact that the incident came quick on the heels of accusations of plagiarism for another popular and well-respected historian, Stephen Ambrose. Ambrose was criticized for using whole passages from Thomas Childers's work *The Wings of Morning* (1995) in his book *The Wild Blue* (2002). Critics were harder on Ambrose than Goodwin mainly because his apology seemed cavalier and self-serving. Ambrose told the press that although he may have had lapses in scholarly procedure by failing to use quotation marks around direct quotes, he did indicate source materials through the use of notes in the work (Tolson, 2002: 6). Jay Tolson of *US News & World Report* called this remark a "mea sorta culpa" and noted that few university professors would have accepted this excuse from an undergraduate student caught in the same situation.

I think that these incidents involving Goodwin and Ambrose are illustrative of the high stakes involved in the art of good scholarship: the stress and pressure to meet deadline dates versus the time and discipline required to maintain academic integrity. The troubles of Goodwin and Ambrose served to increase my sympathy for the plight of the undergraduate student. If eminent scholars can become overwhelmed by the detail work required for scholarly writing, what of the poor novice? It occurred to me that educators need to be concerned with not only teaching students the mechanics of good scholarship, such as using footnotes to credit properly another person's intellectual property, but also with giving students a clear understanding of the ethics and meaning behind these seemingly arcane academic practices.

There are some sobering statistics and studies about undergraduates that give educators pause. In response to a recent Rutgers University survey, three out of four high school students stated that they have cheated on a test at least once during that academic year, and the same number confessed to handing in another person's written work (Sohn, 2001). The ease with which student papers can be purchased is disconcerting. Plagiarism.org, the Web site that hosts the plagiarism-buster service Turnitin.com, reports that hundreds of "paper mills" exist that offer hundreds of thousands of academic papers for sale:

The fact that many of these sites have become profitable ventures (complete with paid advertising!) only attests to the unfortunate truth that plagiarism has become a booming industry (Plagiarism.org, 2003).

At the other end of the spectrum, faculty and administrators feel at a loss at how to address appropriately the issue of academic honesty or what to do when confronted with situations in which student cheating is apparent. In a national survey of psychology professors, 71% of the respondents reported that "dealing with instances of academic dishonesty was among the most onerous aspects of their profession" (Keith-Speigel et al., 1998: 215). Literature in scholarly journals underscores the concern and a sense of urgency for understanding and dealing with a seeming erosion of academic integrity:

Most students want to be honest; dishonesty is not innate; it is learned. Preemptive instruction, role modeling, and rewards must precede the learning of cheating (Petress, 2003: 624).

On a personal note, I have worked with undergraduate students for more than 10 years. I believe that most do not set out to cheat or plagiarize deliberately. Rather, most are unaware and uncertain about how to go about writing an appropriate, scholarly paper. We should keep in mind that our students (i.e., those young adults in their late teens and early twenties) have very different cultural attitudes and perspectives than educators (especially those of use who are in the thirty-something-on-up category.) In order to teach our students about intellectual *honesty*, it is important to understand this generational divide in background experience toward research and toward the concept of intellectual *ownership*.

Plagiarism and Technology

Though personal computing dates back to the 1970s, the rise of PCs as the recognizable household device that we know today began in the early 1980s with the introduction of affordable, easy-to-use IBM products (Long, 2003). The early 1980s is also when our undergrads were being born. This demographic group can be thought of as the "PC generation." These children grew up with computing technology, analogous to the way baby boomers grew up with television. It is one of their defining popular culture influences. According to recent census data, more than 69% of American teenagers (children between the ages of 12 and 17 years) have access to a home computer. Of those children, more than 47% have access to the Internet (U.S. Bureau of the Census, 2000). Finally, a recent survey indicates that teenagers now spend more time on the Internet than watching TV. Teenagers spend an average of 17 hours per week online contrasted to 14 hours of watching television (Reuters, 2003).

For teenagers, personal computers are a source of entertainment and communication; they are devices to download "free" movies and "free" music. Such ease of access does not foster much consideration regarding copyright or ownership of artistic material. The current crackdown by the music industry (e.g., the lawsuits brought against individuals by the RIAA) is intended to alter significantly these attitudes. The problem is that there exists a deeply ingrained sensibility that if it is on the Net, it is free:

> …the convenience and anonymity of file sharing have made it a remarkably guilt-free form of plunder. In effect, the masses of Americans have joined the previously small chorus of hard-core hackers in chanting the credo "Information want to be free" (Terrell and Rosen, 2003: 43).

5

Add to this mix the fact that our students have grown up gathering information from the World Wide Web. It, therefore, becomes a daunting task for educators to help their students to differentiate between the "infotainment" and commercial purposes of the Web that they use daily and the scholarly resources that they are expected to use, and use correctly.

Gloria J. Leckie (Graduate School of Library and Information Science, University of Western Ontario) did an analysis of the undergraduate research process. She concluded that undergraduates gather information for college-level research papers according to the strategies that they have used for previous projects and papers. This would include using public libraries and asking family and friends for information. "They are also likely to use whatever sources are most familiar...even if they are not appropriate" (Leckie, 1996: 204). Among those familiar resources, I would suggest, are the Internet sites and Web search engines that students are accustomed to using on a day-to-day basis.

By the time they reach college, most undergraduates have spent a lot of time surfing the Web and consider themselves to be very computer savvy. For the most part, this is true. As freshmen, they arrive with many skills essential for computer literacy: a facility for keyboarding, a familiarity with a number of software packages, knowledge of chat software and instant messaging, and a background experience in navigating the World Wide Web. However, skill at using personal computers and familiarity with searching the Internet do not equate with research skills or knowledge of standard research practices. This differentiation of skills should be part of our educational objective in teaching students about the research process.

Word Processing and Scholarly Writing

In addition to a familiarity with Internet searching, the PC generation has grown up using word-processing software to write their research papers. Word-processing software has become a ubiquitous office tool, and many of us take it for granted. There is a school of thought that holds that the act of word processing, including the software tools it uses and the ease with which the words appear on the screen, is influencing the way that we as a society think and write (Heim, 1999). Scholars from various fields (e.g., psychology, linguistics, and literary criticism) are concerned with this question (Norris, 1989: 277).

Prolific author Stephen King has also commented on the phenomenon of the relationship of writing tool to writing style. King wrote his early bestsellers on a typewriter, moved to word processing, and then reverted to writing in longhand after his near-fatal accident in 1999. In a recent interview, he stated that writing on a computer is like ice-skating and writing in longhand is like swimming. In the former, you glide across the surface, and in the latter, you are totally immersed in the process (Baker, 2003).

From personal observation and experience, I know that high school and undergraduate students will usually begin a research project by browsing the Internet for source material on a topic. They will next cut and paste the material that they need for their paper into the document on which they are working. It is in the subsequent steps, reworking the material into their own words, using quotations for exact quotes, and citing the material that is not their original intellectual property, where students typically run into problems. The act of cutting and pasting material from one source to another is a wonderful tool, but it is one that needs to be used with caution. The ease with which a writer can physically transfer the written word is offset by the burden of keeping good records of what came from where and what needs to be properly credited. Goodwin noted, in her apologia, that she lost track of her source material in her final book manuscript through the process of cutting and pasting from her notes (Goodwin, 2002). I reiterate that if a professional writer can get into trouble via technology, how much more vulnerable to mistakes is the student researcher?

Plagiarism and Popular Culture

For educators and students to have a shared value about what constitutes plagiarism, they must also assume a shared understanding regarding what constitutes an individual's right to ownership to an intellectual or an artistic concept. Social critics are positing that there has been a generational shift of attitude with regard to the ideas of ownership. First, there is an emerging construct that all information and ideas are data and should flow freely in the intellectual community (Anestopoulou, 2001). Second, in popular culture, there has been an increasing tendency to reference or "sample" previous works, be they musical, written, or visual. Allusion to other cultural phenomenon, or quotationalism, has been called "the dominant trend of thought of the twentieth century" (Matheson, 2001: 123). Referencing, or sampling, has become so prevalent that it is hard to tell where homage stops and rip-off starts.

One area where referencing is prominent and which has gained a lot of media attention is in popular music, most particularly with hip-hop artists. Though hip-hop has a complex history, it is safe to say that it erupted on the popular consciousness in the mid-1970s and started to gain real prominence in the mid-1980s. The trajectory of hip-hop music is roughly analogous to that of the rise of the PC. Hip-hop culture is now de rigueur and it deeply influences all popular media including film, music videos, and literature. Sampling music, a staple of hip-hop DJs, has heavily been influenced by technology. As the technology got better, the sampling became easier to do and used more by artists. Of the current popular music scene, philosophy scholar Carl Matheson writes: "The musical world is a hodge-podge of quotations of styles where often the original music being quoted is simply sampled and re-processed" (Matheson, 2001: 118). Some artists, such as M.C. Hammer, give proper credit (and royalties) to the creator of the material that is sampled. Hammer paid an appropriate licensing fee to Rick James (albeit after much controversy) for use of material from James' song "Super Freak" (1981) in the Hammer hit "U Can't Touch This" (1990) (Anonymous, 1992). Other artists consider sampling to be a political statement—one that is both in defiance of a corporate, capitalist culture and a direct, cultural descendent of the oral traditions of the African diasporic tradition (Bartlett, 1994).

Evidence of referencing, quotationalism, or plagiarism (depending on your philosophical perspective) can be found in all aspects of popular culture and not just music. Couturier Nicolas Ghesquiere of the House of Balenciaga recently admitted to "borrowing" designs from a San Francisco designer, Mr. Wong, for his spring collection for 2002. Wong, who died in 1990, was little known but had a cult following that included Ghesquiere. The similarity was noted in a column at the fashion Web site Hintmag.com (Silva and Widdicombe, 2002). When interviewed about the similarities, Ghesquiere freely admitted to "referencing" Wong; however he gave no credit—neither verbal nor written—to Wong as the source of his inspiration when the collection debuted. In an article in *The New York Times*, fashion writer Cathy Horyn posed the question whether copying another's work is plagiarism or just part of the creative process. Horyn quotes Metropolitan Museum of Art costume curator Harold Koda regarding Ghesquiere's designs:

> I think that it is a phase of our time. Part of it is post-Warhol.
> It's just rummaging through extant material culture and jux-
> taposing it with other things to create something different.
> Postmodernism has really pervaded our culture (Horyn, 2002:
> B10).

In recent literature, a whimsical foray into pop culture is the postmodern, allusion-riddled novel *Gilligan's Wake* (2003) by Tom Carson. The premise is that each character from the "classic" 1960s sitcom *Gilligan's Island* tells his (or her) life story. Each narrative is somehow intertwined with important cultural or political figures and events à la *Forrest Gump*. Ginger has a liaison with Frank Sinatra. Skipper served on a PT boat with JFK in World War II. The playful interplay between real and imaginary people and events, drawn from high-, low-, and middle-brow sources, makes the novel a poster child for the ironic brand of comedy so prevalent in late twentieth/early twenty-first century America.

Some Thoughts and Conclusions

I would like to share some personal thoughts about our postmodern, self-cannibalizing popular culture and what we educators assume to be a shared

American popular culture literacy. The first has to do with two of my favorite television shows, *The Simpsons* and *South Park*. Both shows rely heavily on allusion for humor. Each references dozens of movies, novels, and television shows, often so quickly that it is difficult to catch all the references in one sitting. Matheson notes that in just one *Simpsons* episode, "A Streetcar Named Marge," the writers manage to squeeze in visual and verbal references to a Tennessee Williams play, Ayn Rand's *Fountainhead*, the movie *The Great Escape*, and Hitchcock's *The Birds* (Matheson, 2001). Matheson finds the multitudinous use of references, this "hyper-irony," culturally significant: "I think that, given a crisis of authority, hyper-ironism is the most suitable form of comedy" (Matheson, 2001: 119). Deconstructionist humor for a deconstructed world. *South Park* takes the hyper-irony to even greater heights. In one surreal episode, the *South Park* characters become *The Simpsons* characters, thus referencing the ultimate reference.

As I watch these shows with my teenage children, I realize that they are being bombarded with cultural allusions from the 1950s through to the present. Matt Groening was born in 1954. Trey Parker and Matt Stone were born in 1969 and 1971, respectively. Because these creators draw heavily upon the cultural icons from their formative years, as the runs of the shows continue, the pop-culture reference points get further and further away from the younger members of the viewing audience. Eventually, the audience, now separated by a gulf of 20 to 40 years from the childhood experiences of Groening or Parker/Stone, will relate to these allusions, not as allusions, but as original material from the shows that they are watching. Case in point: *The Simpsons Halloween Specials* frequently allude to old *Twilight Zone* or *Alfred Hitchcock Presents* episodes. My teenagers, when they see the originals on cable, are frequently amused ("Hey! This was on *The Simpsons*!"). They had no clue up to that point that *The Simpsons* were doing a parody. The exposure to the original adds to their understanding and appreciation of the cartoon the next time that they see the parody episode.

This strikes me as being significant when it comes to teaching students about plagiarism. We educators assume a common cultural understanding that is decreasing with each new batch of freshman. Philosopher and pop-critic William Irwin writes:

> Cultural literacy is essential for successful communication and comprehension as is clear in condensing allusions (Irwin, 2001: 87).

If a phrase, an idea, or some other item of intellectual property has embedded itself deeply into pop culture, students might be totally unaware of its origin or the fact that it needs to be referenced in a scholarly work. In an increasingly hip and ironic world, students are becoming farther removed from cultural source material. We need to be aware of this gap in order to be effective teachers.

A recent incident drove home to me how far apart a baby boomer, like me, can be in her cultural reference points from a member of the PC generation. I was preparing some instructional material for teaching critical thinking skills, especially as they pertain to evaluating materials on the Web. I mocked-up a visual joke to include in my presentation. Using Adobe Photoshop, I transposed the head of Shaggy from the *Scooby Doo* cartoon series onto the famous photograph of Lee Harvey Oswald. I am referring to the photo that shows Oswald holding a newspaper and the gun that was purportedly used to assassinate President Kennedy. The point of the doctored photo was to illustrate the point that you cannot trust everything that you find on the Internet. I tested the page, unscientifically, on about 20 students ranging in age from about 17 to 30 years. Not one recognized the photo of Lee Harvey Oswald. Most did not know who Lee Harvey Oswald was. This particular attempt at humor failed due to a total lack of a shared cultural background. A photograph that was iconic to me was meaningless to my younger audience. I abandoned the illustration and developed a new respect for the subjectivity of humor.

Educators need to be aware of our own assumptions and reference points and how these differ from our students. Good scholarship requires good work ethics, a working knowledge of accepted procedures, and the ability to recognize and keep track of the origins of numerous pieces of information. These we can teach. Our cultural, technological, and philosophical touchstones may be very different than those of our students. Still, we can effectively communicate if we approach them with an open mind, sensitivity, and a respect for their differing background knowledge and experiences.

Works Cited

Academy of Achievement. "Doris Kearns Goodwin: Biography" (2003). Available: www.achievement.org/autodoc/page/goo0bio-1.

Anestopoulou, Maria. 2001. "Challenging Intellectual Property Law in the Internet: An Overview of the Legal Implications of the MP3 Technology." *Information & Communications Technology Law* 10, no. 3 (October): 319–337.

Anonymous. 1992. "A New Spin on Music Sampling: A Case for Fair Pay." *Harvard Law Review* 105, no. 726 (January): 726.

Baker, Dorie. "Best-Selling Author Stephen King Says Everyday Life Inspires Him." *Yale Bulletin and Calendar* (2 May 2003). Available: www.yale.edu/opa/v31.n28/story4.html.

Bartlett, Andrew. 1994. "Airshafts, Loudspeakers, and the Hip-hop Sample: Contexts and African American Musical Aesthetics." *African American* Review 28, no. 4 (Winter): 639–642.

Goodwin, Doris Kearns. "How I Caused That Story." *Time* 59, no. 5 (4 February 2002): 69.

Heim, Michael. 1999. *Electric Language*. New Haven: Yale University Press.

Horyn, Cathy. "Is Copying Really Part of the Creative Process?" *The New York Times* (9 April 2002): B10.

Irwin, William, and J.R. Lombardo. 2001. "The Simpsons and Allusion: 'Worst Essay Ever!'" In *The Simpsons and Philosophy: The D'oh of Homer*, edited by William Irwin, Mark T. Conrad, and Aeon J. Skoble. Chicago: Open Court.

Keith-Speigel, Patricia, Barbara G. Tabachnick, Bernard E. Whitley, and Jennifer Washburn. 1998. "Why Professors Ignore Cheating: Opinions of a National Sample of Psychology Instructors." *Ethics and Behavior* 8, no. 3: 215–227.

Leckie, Gloria J. 1996. "Desperately Seeking Citations: Uncovering Faculty Assumptions about the Undergraduate Research Process." *Journal of Academic Librarianship* 1996: 201–208.

Long, Major Dale J. "A Brief History of Personal Computing, Part 1" (2003). Available: www.chips.navy.mil/archives/02_summer/authors/index2_files/briefhistory.htm.

Matheson, Carl. 2001. "The Simpsons, Hyper-Irony, and the Meaning of Life." *In The Simpsons and Philosophy: The D'oh of Homer*, edited by William Irwin, Mark T. Conrad, and Aeon J. Skoble. Chicago: Open Court.

Norris, Christopher. 1989. "Review Essay—'Electric Language: A Philosophical Study of Word Processing by Michael Heim.'" *Comparative Literature* 41, no. 3 (Summer): 270–277.

Petress, Kenneth. 2003. "Academic Dishonesty: A Plague on our Profession." Education 123, no. 3 (Spring): 624–627.

Plagiarism.org. "Plagiarism Today" (2003). Available: www.plagiarism.org.

Reuters. 2003. "Youth Spend More Time on Web then TV—Study." July 24.

Silva, Horacio, and Ben Widdicombe. "Chic Happens." Hintmag.com (27 March 2002). Available: www.hintmag.com/archives/archives.php.

Sohn, Emily. 2001. "The Young and the Virtueless." *US News & World Report* 130, no. 20 (21 May): 51.

Terrell, Kenneth, and Seth Rosen. 2003. "A Nation of Pirates." *US News & World Report* 135, no. 1 (14 July): 40–45.

Tolson, Jay. 2002. "Whose Own Words?" *US News & World Report* 132, no. 2 (21 January): 52.

U.S. Bureau of the Census. "Children's Access to Home Computer and Use of the Internet at Home: 2000." Series P23–107. Available: http://govcensus.doc.us.

CHAPTER 2

The Onus of Originality: Innovation, Imitation, and Other Problems of Writing

Laura B. Spencer

Introduction

What has been is what will be, and what has been done is what will be done; and there is nothing new under the sun.

—Ecclesiastes 1:9, Revised Standard Version

Just what is an original idea? In my freshman year of college, I told my English professor that I did not believe there was any such thing. At home, I had heard the above Old Testament verse recited or paraphrased often enough for it to have sunk in and significantly influence my thinking. At college, I was starting to learn how much human knowledge already existed. Any time I opened a book, I discovered yet another century in which writers had grappled with problems similar to those of my own time and came upon solutions as good as or better than my own. I thus despaired of producing original work myself and doubted that anybody else could either, because I strongly suspected that somebody, somewhere, had addressed the question or problem already.

The follower of scientific or technological developments might rightly observe that new things arrive under the sun all the time, from the combustion engine to the microchip. Although the scientific principles behind such inventions might have been discovered in ancient Rome or seventeenth-century

Europe, the application of those principles, combined with the discovery of new ones, bring about inventions that clearly are new. Originality in science, at least, is most certainly possible; it would be absurd to suggest it is not, even while observing that innovations owe a debt to previous work. In the discussion that follows, I explore how closely bound together are the new and the familiar, the original and the derivative, the innovative and the traditional. It appears that we cannot have the one without the other.

In his *Stolen Words*, Thomas Mallon writes:

> Originality—not just innocence of plagiarism but the making of something really and truly new—set itself down as a cardinal literary virtue sometime in the middle of the eighteenth century and has never since gotten up (Mallon, 1989: 24).

Originality, as newness unfettered by tradition, is an idea but a few centuries old. The idea that tradition is nothing to escape from, but rather something to embrace and follow, is a good bit older. As an undergraduate, I found that the notion of the "cardinal literary virtue" of newness was at odds with my own sense of the difficulty in achieving that newness. The readings I was assigned in philosophy and literature reinforced my doubts that I, or anybody else, could add anything new and worthwhile. Since then, I have discovered that I am not alone in this doubt. Indeed, I have much company—from the author of Ecclesiastes in the third century B.C. to Samuel Johnson in the eighteenth century A.D. As Thomas L. Jeffers, Associate Professor of English at Marquette University, put it: "There is something annoyingly unoriginal about harping on the impossibility of originality" (Jeffers, 2002).

Originality may be possible, but it is certainly paradoxical. A writer must blend the familiar with the new; the challenge and the difficulty is in how this blend is accomplished. Thomas McFarland observed in his *Originality and Imagination* that this paradox "stems from the larger paradox of human existence" in which "our social natures on the one hand and our individual natures on the other" are ever in conflict (McFarland, 1985: 31). An individual is at once an autonomous self and a member of a community. The autonomous selfhood and the community membership exist in tension with one another, in a paradoxical and complementary relationship. At any given time, within a single society, one will be stronger or more ascendant than the other. That ascendancy of the one is not permanent. The struggle between the two, however, is. "Neither individuality nor communality can be felt without the other, although each strains against its complement" (McFarland, 1985: 1). As our social and individual natures strain against each other, while yet remaining bound together, so in a similar manner do the original and derivative aspects of our work (e.g., written papers) struggle together. They must both exist, in all their tension and paradox. "Any attempt to resolve the paradox is unsuccessful" (McFarland, 1985: 1). The trouble comes when we do not agree on how best to balance the two.

That disagreeing "we" can be society as a whole, fighting over how to balance personal autonomy with communal responsibility, or simply a teacher and student discussing how well the latter wrote her paper. Did the student fail to credit her sources? Did she dutifully credit her sources, but rely on them too heavily, thus drowning out her own voice or masking the fact that she had not developed one yet? Relying overmuch on sources might or might not be plagiarism, but it certainly can be a sign of poor writing or insufficient thinking. Our cardinal rule requires that student writers put matters in their own words. We want our students to have thought through what they have read so that when they write about it, they understand the material enough to use words that come more or less naturally to them; to use their own unique voice.

I think this is the heart of the matter: to have read and thought and digested well enough and carefully enough to have made the material enough your own to say it your way, yet simultaneously and scrupulously to maintain the distinction between "yours" and "theirs." This creates a tense paradox. Keeping that distinction is very difficult for beginners whose own voices are not yet well developed. It takes time and practice to strike the right balance. In a culture that values speed and efficiency as much as ours does, taking one's time is often punished. Even an instructor who advocates the taking of time has only 16 weeks in which to inculcate this value.

I am not certain that a clear, fat, and bright line can always and easily be drawn between acceptable borrowing and unacceptable theft or between original and derivative prose. My view of the territory between "original" and "derivative" is that they are two areas on a continuum, and it is not always clear when one bleeds into the other. Incorporation of properly credited sources into one's own work can certainly be indulged in overmuch, but determining when quantities exceed acceptable limits is not a simple, straightforward calculation of a constant, nonnegotiable value. This discussion attempts to shed light upon the terrain where the original and the derivative mingle and rub elbows and asks us to think about the implications of that mingling. The sources of that light are from laboratory science, marketing, and music.

Students want their lessons to be relevant with "relevant" defined as "interesting to me" or "helps me to get a good-paying job." Believers in the value of a well-rounded liberal arts education might groan inwardly at this seemingly narrow definition, but the definition is by no means a new one. T.S. Eliot observed a similar taste for relevance in his 1932 essay, *Modern Education and the Classics*: "The individual wants more education, not as an aid to the acquisition of wisdom, but in order to get on" (Eliot, 1950: 452–453). "Getting on" with one's life, family, and career is a perfectly legitimate endeavor, however, and one's education need not be a hindrance to it. Wisdom can be fun and useful, although it cannot reliably be counted upon to fetch a high fee on the open market. Technical skills for "getting on" tend to pay better, which accounts for their perennial popularity. One way or another, an education, whether in the liberal arts or a technical field, is intended to prepare students for life in the real world. But how much of that world should intrude into the classroom culture? Hamilton College Professor of History Maurice Isserman writes that a mission of colleges and universities is to help students "to develop their own voices and establish ownership of the words they use. And, if and when we in higher education stop doing that, we have pretty well abandoned our justification for existence" (Isserman, 2003).

The increasing concern about plagiarism in academia suggests such abandonment is not imminent. Educators want students to write using their own words, not somebody else's, no matter how articulate that somebody else is. Plagiarism, simply put, is the taking of words that do not belong to you. It is wrong because it is theft, but it is also wrong because it circumvents the learning process. Cutting and pasting large chunks of text—even with proper attribution—is a shortcut that short-circuits learning. Students, since time out of mind, have probably wished for some way to sleep with their books underneath their pillows, so that the information contained within would seep into their brains overnight. The electronic form in which much information now appears makes that wish almost come true. It is now exceedingly easy to assemble a finished product that, in its superficial aspects, is pretty close to what the teacher asked for. In a world that values speed, efficiency, and streamlined work flows, persuading its future workers to embark upon a lengthy, inefficient, and messy process when a short and tidy one is available with a few mouse clicks is a hard sell. It looks like advocacy of an outrageous waste of time and energy.

Yet, in order to produce a literate and intelligent workforce, such an exercise is a necessary part of the educational process in order to teach the voice development and word ownership Isserman refers to above, as well as critical thinking skills. However, the culture of the business world, which is product based, conflicts with the culture of the educational world, which also emphasizes process. Although the research and development divisions of major corporations might have their share of trial-and-error mistakes, the experimental techniques and research methods of its workers meet professional standards. If not, the workers would very likely be looking for new jobs. It should be remembered that these researchers learned their good techniques in their laboratory science classes, over a period of time, back when they were undergraduates.

What, if anything, do concepts such as "originality" and "creativity" mean in a laboratory science class? In the section that follows, Dr. Karen Winey, Associate Professor of Materials Science at the University of Pennsylvania, describes the difference between "original" and "derivative" science using the example of what a typical undergraduate in a laboratory science class might be expected to accomplish. The author is indebted to Dr. Winey for her comments and insights. Any errors in this section are the author's and not hers.

In the Science Lab

When a student runs an experiment in a laboratory at school, there is evidence that work has been done because supplies have been used. In fact, the person running the lab has usually witnessed that the student has done this work and used these supplies. Labs, unlike remotely accessible databases and books checked out to the student, are not available 24/7 or out of sight of faculty, teaching assistants, and other overseers. When a professor has a student look through an electron microscope, the student will be looking at known images. The professor, indeed the entire the profession, already knows what the student will see. The student needs to learn how to see these images and identify them; the professor will evaluate how well she does so. The exercise is to evaluate the student's experimental technique, not her capacity for "original" research.

Professional scientists do not get ahead in their fields by repeating experiments already performed; they must publish new, "original" findings. Undergraduates may replicate an experiment, however, because experiment replication is one of the ways necessary skills and competencies are acquired and refined. Such replication also serves as necessary, preliminary work for a student's or professional scientist's original project. Though an undergraduate's lab work will usually be derivative, the student still must collect the data herself and write-up her results with *her* findings, even if her values are identical to the known values from the prior study. She is still obliged to use the data that she herself collected (Winey, 2003). If she has conducted her experiment well, then her findings will in fact be the same as the known values. She cannot report the values "in her own words" the way a student in the humanities is expected to put the results of his research in his own words. For the science student, original effort, rather than original expression, is the key to doing a good job. How she conducts her experiment, not what findings she reports, is the parallel to "putting it in your own words."

Trade Dress at CVS

The plagiarism that angers us most, I suspect, is when the writer deliberately intends to deceive. Our society values truth and candor; readers, like

17

consumers, do not like to be fooled by appearances. In the marketplace, one way to distinguish one company's goods from another is with distinctive trademarks and a distinctive packaging that is called "trade dress." Trade dress is defined as "a product's physical appearance, including its size, shape, color, design, and texture," and it can "also refer to the manner in which a product is packaged, wrapped, labeled, presented, promoted, or advertised" (West Group, 1998: 106).

Thou shalt not deceive—or confuse—thy customer base. The purpose of trademarks, trade dress, and logos is to distinguish the product from that of a competitor—to brand it—so that customers immediately think of a particular product when they see a particular label. Companies are very aware of the value of brand recognition and work to distinguish their brands from their competitors. An exception to this practice appears to occur in the packaging of over-the-counter (OTC) store-brand drugs.

CVS Pharmacy is a chain store that sells prescription drugs, OTC medicines, and health-care products such as vitamins and first-aid supplies. At CVS, the store-brand OTC drugs are placed directly beside a national brand. The store-brand product is referred to as an "equivalent" of the national brand and is usually significantly cheaper. If you read the contents of both the name brand and the store brand, you will notice that the list of ingredients is very similar, and the active ingredients are often identical in both kind and amount. The package design is often very similar in color and shape. A national brand of cough syrup, Whitehall-Robins' Robitussin CF, for example, is packaged in a white, green, and pink box. CVS's Tussin CF is likewise packaged in a white, green, and pink box.

CVS does not, of course, use packaging identical to those of the name brands for any of its products. A closer look reveals that there are horizontal white pinstripes in the green and pink areas of the Robitussin and there are not in the store-brand equivalent. The green and pink areas are square or rectangular on the Robitussin. On CVS's brand, those areas have a wavy, rather than straight, top edge. A look at several other OTC products, from plastic bandages to pain relievers, reveals that the labels on the CVS brands usually have that wavy top edge, thus creating a characteristic CVS trade dress. CVS distinguishes its packaging in other ways. For instance, plastic bandages from Johnson & Johnson are pictured horizontally, against a background of dark blue and light blue. CVS plastic bandages are displayed vertically, against a hazy blue background (with wavy top edge) with reddish elements. Is that different enough or is CVS "plagiarizing?"

This practice of similar trade dress is a common one and not limited to CVS. Most major supermarket and drug store chains have store-brand products. The names and packaging of these products frequently mimic the names and packaging of a well-known brand. When the major brand finds the similarity too close, suits are filed and changes are made. A manufacturer and packager of many store-brand OTC pharmaceuticals, including CVS's, is Michigan-based Perrigo Co. Perrigo has been the subject of several suits. Schering-Plough, a maker of allergy tablets, nasal spray, and other products, sued Perrigo in federal court in 1984, alleging that Perrigo's packaging was "confusingly similar" to Schering-Plough's. They wanted Perrigo to stop and sued for "triple damages, recovery of Perrigo's profit from those products' sales and legal fees and expenses" (*Wall Street Journal*, 1984). Perrigo agreed to stop and settled with Schering-Plough for $125,000 (*Wall Street Journal*, 1985). On the topic of trade dress, Perrigo's chairman and CEO, Michael J. Jandernoa, stated that

> ...the challenge is not getting too close, to where you're copying the packaging, which raises the legal issue of trade dress ...our focus...is on being similar but not being the same (Stern, 1993).

In the interests of full disclosure: I buy equivalents all the time. I do not mean to cast aspersions on Perrigo or similar companies. I use them as an example because the practice of creating a similar trade dress for a lesser known product sheds a light on the issue of deliberate plagiarism by students. Sometimes, the store-brand packaging explicitly instructs the consumer to compare the product inside with the national brand of which it is an equivalent. I think that this is analogous to the student who uses a well-known scholar's entire framework of thought in a paper and footnotes a single quote from the source. In both cases, you know what the sources are. Like that student's paper, the store-brand's packaging is piggybacking off the hard work (and marketing money) that went into establishing the national brand. The store-brand marketers are completely conscious of what they are doing. We need to wonder if that student is aware that plagiarism is not just stealing exact words but also ideas and carefully researched trains of thoughts. Sometimes "putting it in your own words" is simply not enough, and more credit needs to be given in the paper.

On the other hand, much of good scholarship is derived from following the established procedure and canonized literature of a particular discipline. Laboratory science students demonstrate good technique by measuring characteristics of a metal and getting the same results as the experts have established to be correct. Humanities students demonstrate familiarity with material by writing about it in such a way to make it obvious that they have done a close reading of the material. They need to be ready to demonstrate that they have really read it for style and meaning and not just passed their eyes over the pages or dragged their mouse over the text to copy and paste it into their own paper. This familiarity is accomplished in part by citing or quoting the material, of course, and also by more or less restating it—freshly, and in their own words. Here is a troublesome, paradoxical area. An undergraduate need not be expected to break new ground in the discipline, because he is too inexperienced, but neither is he permitted to merely parrot the authorities in the field.

The undergraduate, like the rest of us, must inhabit a region that combines the old with the new, the derivative with the original. Negotiating the terrain requires acknowledging the authorities in the field without being subservient to them. Subservience in this instance would be repeating mindlessly what they wrote. The plagiaristic technique of cutting and pasting huge chunks of text without attribution is, ironically enough, a kind of subservience. Students do not see it in these terms; to them this technique of quickly assembling papers is a kind of freedom. But to writers in the English Renaissance, copying was viewed as slavish and subservient, and they frowned upon it (White, 1935). The modern day equivalent, cutting-and-pasting, is frowned upon as well.

Yet, a good student cannot defiantly ignore the authorities in his field. To present a well-informed argument, a student needs authoritative source materials. He cannot rely solely on his own knowledge to write his term paper, even if his conclusions concur with the established authorities in the field. He must consult and cite them, at the very least to support his own views. This can be exasperating to the bright, impatient student, who feels dragged down by what feels like petty pedantry. Our culture does not suffer authorities gladly; our egalitarianism often encourages us to doubt "they" know more than "we" do about any but the most technical of subjects. Our drive to focus on "results" makes us impatient with mere "process." These cultural tendencies are at odds with the classroom requirements for proper research and writing methods.

The successful writer will be neither wholly slave nor wholly rebel but draw upon authorities as needed for support or insight. Perhaps she will present them in a fresh way, or find a new relevance, or come up with a new or intelligent critique. She will not escape the paradox of needing to be at once both familiar and new. Neither will the laboratory scientist, the marketing executive, nor, as we will shortly see, the musician.

A Hip-Hop Sample Example

Hip-hop recording artists live the paradox of innovation and tradition when they engage in the practice known as sampling, "a technique of extracting a recorded passage from a previous musical work and inserting that passage into a new recording" (Warshavsky, 2002). Although sampling is hardly a new phenomenon, its use in popular music has increased especially with the rise of hip-hop, which uses it heavily. The issue of sampling arises repeatedly in discussions related to fair use of copyrighted materials and intellectual ownership.

On a personal note, I did not grow up listening to hip-hop or the other genres of music that employ sampling techniques. The whole notion of what sampling meant occurred to me one day when I first found myself humming a melody I knew well while listening to a song I had never heard before in my life. I realized that my humming went right along with what I was hearing on the radio and I was puzzled. I then realized that the new song on the radio had sampled the old song with which I was well familiar but had transformed it into something different. Once I understood that, my puzzlement turned to curiosity. Why would a musician choose to insert somebody else's work into his own, rather than compose a wholly new piece that was in his heart or head or soul? Was it, I wondered, an acknowledgment that true originality was so difficult, onerous, or impossible, that recording artists have no choice but to incorporate older works into their own in order to have any new work at all? Had modern popular music proved that I was right at 18, that there is no such thing as a truly original idea? This seemed unlikely.

Why does a writer, whether student or professional, quote a source in the first place? She quotes because it supports her argument; because the quotation sheds light or is phrased superbly; or because the source is an established authority with a stellar reputation. Sections of musical pieces are sampled, I suspect, for comparable reasons. With sampling, authority is about good music, rather than solid scholarship. It is about the listener being moved. Christopher "DJ Premier" Martin describes sampling as "repeating a part of a record that grabs you." "Sampling is all about placement, where it emotionally grabs you and makes your head nod" (Mitchell, 2000). The sampled piece lends an emotional power to the new recording, just as a quote lends scholarly power to the research paper.

In both the sound recording and the research paper, the quality of the final product is enhanced. As Rick James, who has "made millions from musicians sampling his tracks" (Taraska, 1998), puts it:

> "Yes, it's their rap," he says. But it's our fucking music. [People] have danced to it, made love to it. If [these musicians] think their rap is what's really getting it over, try playing it without our shit" (Taraska, 1998: 13).

Here is an argument for the vital power of the sampled pieces and the cachet or authority they bring to the new recording that incorporates them. One can sample well or badly. One way to sample badly is to neglect to pay royalties to the copyright owner of the work sampled. Copyright owners have been aggressive in enforcing the law, to the point that compliance is now more the rule than the exception (Bessman, 2003).

Another way to sample badly is to do so in a haphazard way. Plagiarists who think their term papers will read well if they crib from various sources by rearranging the paragraphs of published articles and altering some phrases should consider hip-hop DJ Edward "Eddie F." Ferrell's observation on the art of good sampling: "If you don't really fine-tune what you're doing and are just trying to throw something together, it won't sound good" (Mitchell, 2000). The attentive ear will be able to hear the difference between a good sample and a bad one. Digital technology makes sampling easy; it does not necessarily make it good. Individual judgment, talent, and expertise make sampling good and make money (the real-world version of getting an A) for both the sampler and the sampled.

Likewise, the attentive eye will be able to read the difference between a good borrowing from sources and a bad one. In a 1920 essay on the Elizabethan playwright Philip Massinger, T.S. Eliot wrote:

> Immature poets imitate, mature poets steal; bad poets deface
> what they take, and good poets make it into something better,
> or at least something different (Eliot, 1950: 182).

Serious listeners to hip-hop and other musical genres that employ sampling techniques will recognize the parallels between Eliot's good poets and their good musicians.

Student writers will, in one way or another, incorporate what they read into what they write. Educators want them to do so properly, whether by correct footnoting techniques or by the thorough reading and hard thinking that are the necessary preludes to putting matters in their own words. Educators today might not wish to use Eliot's terminology of stealing and theft, lest their students be confused over when stealing is right and when it is wrong. On the other hand, however, the stark terminology might get the attention of students, a necessary prerequisite for both students and educators to perform the hard work of thinking about the close and dynamic relationship between honest writing and plagiaristic writing; between being properly influenced and improperly enriched by one's sources; between the kind of taking that makes material your own through intimacy with it, and the kind of taking that prevents it, by keeping the taken material at too great a distance.

Conclusion

I sought parallels in the "real world" to the problems students face and the techniques they employ when they write their papers. I found that for undergraduates in laboratory science, original effort is usually more feasible than original expression. This is not completely opposite to what undergraduates' term papers in the humanities should strive to be, but the difference might be worth thinking about. Though our business culture tends to stress innovation as the key to success and profits, we have seen that sometimes a close imitation can benefit a company. Originality, in store-brand packaging at least, is likely to be a liability. The plagiarist who is tempted to take to heart this observation might want to consider that there is more here than is readily apparent; as it takes art, effort, and skill to record a quality song that incorporates samples, so also it takes art, effort, and skill to package a product that does not attract the attention of clever lawyers in the pay of large, powerful companies. If the plagiarist is interested in time- and energy-saving shortcuts, she might want to consider the possibility that it would actually take *less* art, effort, and skill to sit down and write a more thoroughly original piece in the first place. Now *there's* a paradox for us.

Works Cited

Bessman, Jim. 2003. "In a Decade, Music Publishers Have Gone from Litigating to Actively Promoting the Use of Their Copyrights—For a Price." *Billboard* 115, no. 24 (14 June): 43–44.

Eliot, T.S. 1950. *Selected Essays.* New York: Harcourt Brace.

Isserman, Maurice. 2003. "Plagiarism: A Lie of the Mind." *Chronicle of Higher Education* 48, no. 34 (2 May): B12–13.

Jeffers, Thomas L. 2002. "Plagiarism High and Low." *Commentary 114*, no. 3 (October): 54–60.

Mallon, Thomas. 1989. *Stolen Words: Forays into the Origins and Ravages of Plagiarism.* New York: Ticknor and Fields.

McFarland, Thomas. 1985. *Originality and Imagination.* Baltimore and London: Johns Hopkins University Press.

Mitchell, Gail. 2000. "Where'd You Get That? The Further Evolution of Sampling." *Billboard* (9 December): 56.

Stern, Gabriella. 1993. "Cheap Imitation: Perrigo's Knockoffs of Name-Brand Drugs Turn Into Big Sellers—Its Versions of Advil, Listerine Are Sold as Stores' Own at Rock Bottom Prices—'Pink Bismuth' for Indigestion." *Wall Street Journal*, Eastern edition (15 July): A1. Available: http://factiva.com.

Taraska, Julie. 1998. "Sampling Remains Prevalent Despite Legal Uncertainties." *Billboard* (14 November): 12–13.

Wall Street Journal, Eastern edition. 1984. "Schering-Plough Unit Files Trademark Suit." 12 April. Available: http://factiva.com.

Wall Street Journal, Eastern edition. 1985. "Schering-Plough's Suit Against Perrigo Is Settled." 6 February. Available: http://factiva.com.

Warshavsky, Oren. "Will Case Change Law on Sampling?" 2002. *National Law Journal* 24, no. 56 (14 October): C1.

West Group. 1998. "Trade Dress." In *West's Encyclopedia of American Law*, Vol. 10, 106–107. St. Paul, MN: West Group.

White, Harold Ogden. [1935] 1965. *Plagiarism and Imitation During the English Renaissance: A Study in Critical Distinctions*. New York: Octagon Books.

Winey, Karen. 2003. Conversation with author. Philadelphia, PA (23 November).

CHAPTER 3

The Dark Side of the Web: Where to Go to Buy a Paper

Nick Cvetkovic

Introduction

There is a plethora of sites on the World Wide Web that provide papers for sale. The purpose of this chapter is twofold: first, to instruct the instructors where these sites are and how the students find them; second, to provide links to these sites as a resource to teachers to use in exposing plagiarized papers. Sample paper requests and links are included on the CD supplied with this book.

"Paper mill" is a term used to describe an Internet Web site that students can access in order obtain a term paper on any topic. Some students do not even think that obtaining a paper in this manner is plagiarism, but it is given the definition of plagiarism: "stealing somebody's work or idea: copying what somebody else has written or taking somebody's else's idea and trying to pass it off as original" (*MSN Encarta World English Dictionary*). Paper mills are the logical progression of the old fraternity term-paper files carried to an extreme thanks to the power of the Internet.

Paper mills began on the Internet very shortly after the Internet itself was born, possibly right after that driving force of technological change acceptance, pornography. This chapter looks at the origin and history of paper mills on the Internet, how to find them, and the three distinct types of paper mills. Paper mills all contain a disclaimer that states that their papers are only "models" and not for direct submission for academic credit.

The Origin and History of Paper Mills

The very first paper mill on the Internet is not generally known. It is widely agreed that Schoolsucks.com was instrumental in raising the awareness and popularity of paper mills. Schoolsucks.com was founded by Kenny Sahr. Sahr gained a lot of attention by circulating the following e-mail to a large number of fraternities and sororities in June of 1996 (Leland, 2003):

Dear Frat or Sorority:

Greetings from Miami, Florida!

www.SchoolSucks.Com

School Sucks is a new web site which will no doubt interest you. It is the Internet collection of College Term Papers. All papers are organized by topic (i.e. College of Arts and Sciences, etc.).

School Sucks is a FREE service, allowing college students (all of whom have free Internet access across the globe) to DOWNLOAD THEIR WORKLOAD.

School Sucks has been asked more than once, "How can we HELP School Sucks grow? Start a campaign to encourage students to submit papers they've written. IMAGINE MILLIONS OF STUDENTS WITH MILLIONS OF PAPERS. What a library!

As School Sucks is new, we need submissions. They can be sent to termpapers@schoolsucks.com. Students built the Internet and now it's their turn to benefit from it.

School Sucks needs any links, attention or articles than you can provide. It will ALWAYS remain free. It is sitting on a T1 line (1,500k) and the owners will gladly hire students to work on it when enough papers are submitted!

Next time you have a paper to write, it may have already been written. At least you'll be able to use someone else's sources or see how OTHER students attacked the problem!

School Sucks is run by Kenny Sahr. Kenny currently lives in Miami and spent seven years in Israel (three in Israel Defense Forces) working as a journalist. His Jordan Travel Guide was the first Hebrew language travel guide about that nation.

www.SchoolSucks.Com

(Sahr. Letter reprinted with permission.)

Schoolsucks.com has grown by leaps and bounds to this day to the point of getting 10,000 unique visitors per day.

The evolution of paper mills has reached the point were they have become very sophisticated. Paper mills generally fall into one of three broad categories: free; for-a-fee for an existing paper; custom written. Today one is most likely to find sites that combine the features of the three distinct types. This seems to be to appeal to as broad an audience as possible with some sites now paying contributors to attract ever more papers. Before we go into the detailed workings of specific sites, let us take a look at how students typically find the paper mills on the Internet.

Finding Paper Mills

There are many ways to find a paper mill on the Internet. Just entering "term paper" on any of the popular search engines such as www.google.com will produce, literally, hundreds of thousands of hits. In addition to "term paper," students can search on the sites by subject area and/or enter key words to find papers that relate to the topics for which they are searching. Google will recognize most searches for paper mill sites and present advertiser sites on the right-hand side of each and every result page. Instead of trying to guess at key words, there are easier ways to find a suitable term paper as explored in the next two sections.

Specific Resources

The easiest way to find a number of sites is to look for "directory list" Web pages. There are many of these available. The most highly regarded, most comprehensive and useful list for the various types of paper mills can be found at www.coastal.edu/library/mills2.htm. This resource is maintained and updated twice a year by Margaret Fain, Reference Librarian at Kimbel Library at Coastal Carolina University, located in Conway, South Carolina. When she started the list, barely 4 years ago, it had 35 sites on it: it now contains more than 250 sites.

Ms. Fain also maintains a subject-specific list of more than 70 sites at www.coastal.edu/library/mills5.htm. Neither of these lists is exhaustive, but they are a very good starting point for finding the sites students are most likely to have used. Mills.htm is referenced by almost 500 other sites (Google search, March 2004).

The paper mill business is very dynamic with sites springing up and folding quite regularly, so no list can be kept totally accurate. There is a valuable cross-reference site for paper mills located at www.thejournal.com/magazine/mcmurtry/. This cross reference uses a check list of attributes to allow one to find what one is looking for quickly. These attributes include:

- Whether the site is free.
- Is the submission of a paper required to gain access to all papers?
- Whether the site uses variable pricing.
- Sites at specific per-page price ranges of $5.95 or $8.95 per page or $19.97 per essay.
- Custom essays at specific price points such as $18.95 per page or $10.00 for the first page and $20.00 per page or true custom pricing specific to the requested paper; prices vary.
- Sites with a charge, such as $9.95 for full access to all term papers.

A Journey Through the Search Engines

Knowing how search engines "work" can make using the returned results more satisfying. For example, Google uses a proprietary search algorithm expanded from their original PageRank™ mechanism (Craven, 2004) to determine popularity, and as of February 2004, these were the most popular sites:

CheatHouse.com (www.cheathouse.com/): This site contains a library of essays, term papers, and book reports for high school and college that are categorized with comments and ratings.

Genius Papers (www.geniuspapers.com/): Service provides students with access to a database of term papers, book reports, and essays.

GetPapers (www.getpapers.net/): Student can order prewritten and custom essays on a variety of literature topics.

More information about Google's patented search algorithm as well as an explanation of PageRank can be found at www.webworkshop.net/pagerank.html#how_is_pagerank_calculated (Craven 2004).

Searching on the popular "information" site www.about.com for "+term +papers" using the About Network dropdown yields a long list of paper mill-related sites as well as many sponsored (e.g., advertising) links. The "on the web" portion of the results shows 1,644,738 pages with those two search terms. About.com, though, orders the list to show only real paper mills for the first dozen or so pages. Other aggregations of paper mills can be found at Term Papers (Open Directory) and Term Papers (Yahoo).

How students proceed from this point will vary greatly depending whether they want a free paper or are prepared to pay. Most sites now offer different types of papers, but, generally, there are three fundamental types of paper mill sites, which are explained in depth in the sections that follow.

The Three Basic Types of Paper Mills

As has been explained, paper mills could originally be easily classified into one of three major types: free, per page and custom. During the years, many paper mill sites have evolved to try and be a "one size fits all" site by being a blend of all three types. However, it is still useful to look at the three distinct underlying types.

Free Paper Mills

These claim to be the purest form of paper mill, with a direct lineage back to the old fraternity paper files. Though these sites are free, some require uploading papers in order to obtain downloading credits. Some of the better known free paper mill sites are listed below.

- All Free Essays (http://allfreeessays.com/): Essays are readily available. No registration required. One can submit an essay to be added to the database.
- Cyber Essays (www.cyberessays.com/): "Relies on students to submit their own paper" (from the site).
- Essayworld.com (www.essayworld.com/): Contains "over 8,000 essays online."
- GradeSaver (www.gradesaver.com/classic/ClassicNotes.html): "Free literature summaries and analysis."
- Killer Essays (www.killer-essays.com/): The site contains the disclaimer: "We care for you the student; so please do not copy, steal, or plagiarize our essays because cheating is wrong and teachers know about this website."
- Genius Papers' Term Papers, Essays, Book Reports (www.geniuspapers.com/): Where "a one-time fee of $19.95 gives you a full year of unlimited access to thousands of term papers" (from the site).
- OPPapers.com (www.oppapers.com/): "Other People's Papers. Free. Site asks for donation of papers. Provides links to Top 25, 50, and 100 Essay Sites" (from the site).
- Term Papers Term Papers (www.termpapers-termpapers.com/): Advertises, "Free papers and term papers library for college students."

- WowEssays (www.wowessays.com/dbase/ac2/index.shtml): WowEssays describes itself as the "premier source of free essays, book reports and cliff notes on all subjects."

For Fee: Existing Papers

These sites require payment to obtain any of their many term papers. The fee structure varies with some sites requiring a flat membership fee, either lifetime or per month, and others charging fees depending on various attributes of the requested paper.

The sites with fixed fees for unlimited access tend to be very much like the free sites with a larger selection of slightly better papers. Unlimited access fees can be as little as $9.95 for a lifetime membership up to $19.95 per month and even higher. Looking at these sites, one generally gets what one is paying for, with the higher priced sites providing higher quality papers.

Some of the sites in this category charge a fee for each paper. The fee varies from a fixed amount per paper to an amount per page. The fixed amount per paper will vary with the complexity of the paper as will the amount per page. Some of the more popular for-fee sites are listed below.

- 12,000 Papers.com (www.12000papers.com/): Claims to have the largest number of prewritten papers on the Web. Cost is $9.95 per page. "The Paper Store, Inc. is committed to doing all we possibly can to uphold high standards of academic integrity worldwide."
- CheatHouse.com (www.cheathouse.com/): Prices range from $3.95 for 1 week, $14.95 for 1 month, to $49.95 for 1 year.
- Essays International (www.jerryeden.com/esa/): One essay costs $5; two essays $7.50; three for $10. Lifetime access for $50.
- Genius Papers (www.geniuspapers.com/): Annual fee of $19.95 provides a year's worth of access to available papers.
- Lazy Students.com (www.lazystudents.com/): For $24.95, "unlimited lifetime access to more than 50,000 free term papers, research papers, theses and dissertations written by graduate and undergraduate students as well as professors."

For Fee: Custom Papers

This last category of term paper sites claims that they write each particular paper on a "custom" basis based on strict specifications supplied by the purchaser. The fee structure is generally for a fixed amount per page. The sites charge significant surcharges for papers that are requested with a tight deadline. Many sites advertise on their sites that their papers are written by actual school teachers or college professors who are moonlighting. Though obviously more expensive, these custom paper sites will provide the closest thing to a real paper that a student might create on his or her own. There is no way to verify that these custom papers actually are written totally anew for each requestor. Some of the more prominent sites for custom papers are listed below.

- Accepted Term Papers (www.acceptedpapers.com/): Custom papers $14.95 per page; more if rush.
- Itchy Brains (www.itchybrainscentral.com/): Custom-written papers are $29.95 per page. The site states: "Itchy Brains never plagiarizes. Many other companies that promote research material in the form of papers, recycle pre-written papers. We use professional writers who provide custom-written papers, guaranteed."
- Papers Inn (www.papersinn.com/): $12.95 per page; more if rush.
- Term Papers Highway (www.papershighway.com/): Custom papers with prices that range from $14.55 to $18.00 per page. References and bibliography free. "Team of professionals hold Masters Degree in their respective field(s)." This site includes a statement about plagiarism.
- A1 Termpaper (www.a1-termpaper.com/): The site states: "All work offered is for research purposes only."

Paper Mills: The Current Trend

Term paper sites continue to evolve. Either they turn into a blend of the three previous types or they specialize in some specific area or areas, such as a particular subject area or level of paper. The umbrella sites are trying to offer a "one-stop" shopping experience, hoping to draw in as many customers as possible. Many of these sites advertise on Google and other places on the Internet to try and draw as much traffic as possible to their sites.

One of the better-known combination sites current as of this writing is Cyber Essays: Free, High-quality Term Papers, Essays, and Reports on All Subjects (www.cyberessays.com).

Specialty sites try to reach a particular target audience with specific services such as a certain subject area. Some sites now even claim to offer full dissertations for graduate study.

Some of the better known combination sites current as of this writing are listed below.

- ACI Writing Assistance Center: Thesis and Dissertation Help (www.aci-plus.com/graduate.htm): Minimum fee for any job, editing or custom research, is $500. "The editing services we provide are given with the understanding that the student has the approval of the appropriate authorities to receive this assistance."

- Associated Writers (http://associatedwriters.com/): "Confidential, professional writing service for doctoral and masters candidates with needs in the areas of writing, research, and editing."
- Dissertations and Theses: Custom Research (www.dissertationsandtheses.com/customreports.html): Five page minimum and "accepts orders up to 500 pages." Cost is $19.95 per page. A Paper Store Enterprises site.
- Graduate Papers (www.graduatepapers.com/index.html): Online papers $8.95 per page. "Custom research and writing of a thesis or dissertation for only $18.95 a page."
- Thesis Writing and Research Services (www.thesiswriting.net/): "Can write, rewrite, or edit all or part of your work." Cost is $38 for original work per page.
  Specialty sites offering term papers by subject include the following.
- Africanlit.com: Essays on African Literature (www.africanlit.com/): $9.95 for papers in database with free bibliographies/works cited. Custom work is $19.95 per page.
- Aristotle Papers (www.aristotlepapers.com/): Prewritten papers are $9.95 per page; custom papers are $19.95 per page.
- China Research Papers (www.china-research-papers.com/): Prewritten papers are $9.95 per page; custom papers are $19.95 per page.
- EthicsPapers.com (www.ethicspapers.com/): $9.95 prewritten; $19.95 custom.
- Jane-Austen-Essays.com (www.jane-austen-essays.com/): Owned by Paper Store Enterprises, this site charges $9.95 per page for papers on file; $19.95 per page for custom work.
- Literature Papers (www.literaturepapers.com/): Cost is $7.95 per page unless rush. "We guarantee that our term papers will not be available in any database online. All orders are custom made and confidential."
- Philosophypapers.com (www.philosophypapers.com/): $9.95 per page for on-file papers; custom papers $19.95 per page.

"We Don't Encourage or Condone Plagiarism"

Virtually all paper mills contain disclaimers disavowing any intent to encourage or even condone any form of plagiarism using the materials available on their sites. Though some of the disclaimers are minimal, some are informative and very direct in terms of what they tell the students. Some example text from Web sites in the form of specific disclaimers and FAQs (frequently asked questions) are quoted here with permission of the respective sites.

From the Cyber Essays site, in answer to "Can I get some information about Cyber Essays?" Answer: "Cyber Essays is a completely free service that provides students with papers on a specified topic. Although we support education and feel it is a priceless commodity, we also feel it cannot be attained by teachers giving the same assignments year after year that only force the student to lose sleep—not to make him or her think. Cyber Essays is here to challenge the lazy teacher into helping her students and give assignments from which the students can learn. Mark Twain once said, 'Never let schooling get in the way of your education.' This is even more true today."

A questions that appears on the Term Papers on File: "Can I turn your paper in to my teacher as my own?" Answer: "ABSOLUTELY NOT! It is both unethical and illegal to submit someone else's work as your own for academic credit. Most students use our research as model examples—just like when you have a friend who took the same course as you a year before—If that friend got an "A" on the class term paper, you'd probably want to see their paper to get a feel for how yours should look. The same idea applies here....The Paper Store Enterprises Inc., or its affiliates will NEVER sell a model paper to ANY student giving us ANY reason to believe that (s)he will submit our work, either in whole or part, for academic credit at any institution in their own name. IF YOU QUOTE FROM OUR WORK, YOU MUST CITE OUR PAPER AS ONE OF YOUR SOURCES. The Paper Store does not engage nor participate in any transactions for the purpose of assisting students in committing academic fraud." (Term Papers on File; available: www.termpapers-on-file.com/faq.htm. Quoted with permission.)

Conclusion

A recent article in the online magazine Slate examined term paper mills. Some paper mills were tried and the returned papers graded, including custom ones. Slate came to the following conclusions. For the prewritten papers, the author states that this is "not a bad strategy" for a "smart but horribly lazy student." His review of the custom paper was: "When the custom paper came back, it was all I'd dreamed" (Stevenson, 2001). Thus, it is very clear that paper mill Web sites continue to flourish and to grow as long as students believe that there is no downside to using them. There is a strong trend to raise awareness levels among students and faculty alike that there is rampant plagiarism being made feasible through the use of papers obtained from the various paper mills.

A number of factors conspire to assure students can still turn in these papers little changed as their own work. These include overly large classes and faculty too busy to do the extra work required to check for plagiarism or those who refuse to believe their own students would resort to plagiarism in light of honor codes and other mechanisms in place to prevent it. By being aware of these sites and how complete a solution they provide, faculty will be better equipped to attack the problem of plagiarism on many fronts.

Works Cited

Craven, Phil. "How Page Range Is Calculated." Web Work Shop. (2004) Available: www.web-workshop.net/pagerank.html#how_is_pagerank_calculated.

Leland, Bruce. "Plagiarism and the Web." Western Illinois University, Macomb, Illinois. (2003) Available: www.wiu.edu/users/mfbhl/wiu/plagiarism.htm.

MSN Encarta World English Dictionary. Available: http://encarta.msn.com/encnet/features/diction-ary/dictionaryhome.aspx.

Sahr, Kenny. School Sucks. (1996–2004) Available: http://schoolsucks.com.

Stevenson, Seth. "Adventures in Cheating: A Guide to Buying Term Papers Online." Slate.com. (December 11, 2001) Available: http://slate.msn.com/?id=2059540.

CHAPTER 4

It's a Small World?: Cross-Cultural Perspectives and ESL Considerations

Robert J. Lackie

and

Michele D'Angelo-Long

Introduction: Some Historical Context

All language learning is to some extent a process of borrowing others' words.
        —*Alastair Pennycook (1996: 227)*

Though all students need collaboration and direction when they are learning to write, special challenges exist for English as a second language (ESL) students. Average American students may have limited experience with academic writing and so may require specific direction, but they have awareness of American diction, syntax, and certainly basic vocabulary. That is often not the case for ESL students. Not only will foreign-born ESL students tend to rely on rhetorical patterns and cognitive style they learned (or perhaps did not learn) in their native country, but they are also more likely to exhibit particular homage to authority in their writing. The issue of plagiarism becomes much more complex when dealing with students who do not have a grasp of general vocabulary and rhetorical patterns and who have difficulty with punctuation, grammar, and general mechanical correctness. They are more likely to imitate and, at times,

35

"steal" in an effort to complete assignments that often require higher level abilities than they possess. Teachers of ESL students need to help their students find and create their own voices. This chapter will expound on issues and challenges that ESL students and teachers face and provide plausible solutions to combat this unacceptable, unethical form of conscious—or unconscious—cheating.

Robert Harris, Ph.D., noted writer and educator on plagiarism, details on his VirtualSalt Web site why students sometimes plagiarize. He states that many students are "natural economizers" or procrastinators and may resort to plagiarism possibly because of their "poor time management and planning skills" (Harris, 2002). Essentially, they make bad choices and do not allow themselves enough time to do all of the necessary recursive writing and research required. Though this seems to be the case for many plagiarizers in American high schools and colleges, communicating in another language is very difficult, and often this difficulty drives a student's paper. Students may make statements that they do not believe because this gives them the opportunity to rely on the author's structure and vocabulary to advance their point. It is quite plausible that these two (i.e., poor planning and poor English writing skills) can become an equation for plagiarism.

In addition to the personality profile previously suggested by Harris coupled with an L2 (second language) deficiency, there is a cultural variable that enters into the equation of plagiarism. For instance, in many Asian, Middle Eastern, African, and First Nation cultures, ideas and words expressing those ideas are not considered the sole property of the originators. Countries like Italy and China, for example, according to TESL (Teaching English as a Second Language) expert Jim Hu, Ph.D., are more concerned with content and less with form and do not wage war on plagiarism. "As Pennycook (1996) observed, 'writing in one's own words' was not something that the students in Hong Kong (and most other places) could do in English, for the students seemed to feel that they had no ownership over English" (Hu, 2001: 54).

Additionally, plagiarism is a relatively new concept. Historically speaking, repeating one's work was grounded in the oral tradition and encouraged throughout the centuries. In fact, repetition of one's stories was not only encouraged but also necessary if customs and traditions were to be passed down. Imitation was the ultimate compliment. "This view was grounded in the belief that knowledge of the human condition should be shared by everyone, not owned or hoarded. The notion of individual authorship was much less important than it is today" (Hansen, 2003: 782).

In their 1997 book *The Appearance of Impropriety*, Morgan and Reynolds agree that "even before the development of written language, poets and bards raided one another's work." They further state that "even after written language became well-established, originality was not at a premium: Aristotle, Socrates, Aristophanes and Plato borrowed heavily from earlier works." Classical "writers strove, even consciously, to imitate earlier great works" (Morgan and Reynolds, 1997: 140). Moder and Halleck advance this point further when they argue that in traditional African cultures, "originality was a function of manner rather than of matter. Hearing a well-told story was a more satisfying esthetic experience than hearing a new story badly told. It was crucial that the storyteller as he traveled from place to place, as his audience changed in terms of age or status, adapted his material for relevance, and his stylistic devices for pleasure and conviction, but it did not matter from where he derived his materials" (Moder and Halleck, 1995: 16). Dick Feldman further explains, "…in many countries, it is considered sufficient for students to show that they understand what the experts in their fields have written. In their written papers, students show that they have mastered the experts' ideas, and they can restate or synthesize those ideas coherently" (Feldman, 1989: 160–161).

In cultures outside of America and Western Europe, the imitation and replication of ideas solidifies one's work and is highly praised. Ideas and words are not owned the way we stipulate in America, for example. According to Bowden, for many Asian students in composition classes, proper acknowledgment of the language and ideas of others is a very difficult concept to understand, much less master. Additionally, our concepts of language ownership and property can be correlated with our sense of political and economic determinism in the West. "There is a strong connection between ownership and selfhood, with [the] implication that whatever one owns (language included) makes up one's personal identity" (Bowden, 1996: 13).

Evans and Youmans assert "that definitions of plagiarism vary somewhat from culture to culture, [and that] cultural issues beyond mere definitions were at the root of students' beliefs and attitudes toward plagiarism." They found in their research that "due to the academic environments and cultures from other countries, plagiarism has become a necessary norm" (Evans and Youmans, 2000: 57). They cite examples from interviews with students who relate the necessity of cheating to survive in European lecture halls and to students who felt forced to resort to bribery of their tutors in order to pass their examinations in Russia and Iran.

In our English composition classes, we have both encountered ESL students who claimed that using some expert's words or works was a "sign of the utmost respect" in their country. We have had to teach our students that in our country, directly quoting or paraphrasing someone's work without using quotations or citations is plagiarism. Students who come from a country where plagiarism definitions differ, or where it is supposedly not addressed at all, have a lot of catching up to do. We need to teach them that in America, words are the currency of academia and that we can no more steal them than steal a person's lawnmower, for instance, without getting into trouble. Teaching someone to piece together sentences and paragraphs from others' works—without properly acknowledging their contributions—is the wrong way to teach ESL students to write. Every student must eventually learn when and how to cite properly when borrowing words or ideas.

Plagiarism has increased because of changes in our educational system as well as cultural shifts of information dissemination and the idea of what constitutes appropriate collaboration. Collaboration is required and validated today in business and educational settings. For instance, in higher education, there is now more emphasis on collaborative and group learning and team building. Consequently, students today often have less face-to-face contact with faculty, who now teach using electronic forms of communication, albeit with that same faculty (i.e., distance learning, partner and group collaboration, and so forth) (Ashworth and Bannister, 1997). Information technologies assume a more integral role in student learning and contribute to the plagiarism sinkhole.

Special Considerations for ESL Students: Vocabulary, Rhetorical Patterns, and Mechanics

In Middle East and Pacific Rim countries, there is a particular emphasis placed on cooperative learning outside the classroom. These cultures, which are founded on the teachings of Confucius, "value memorization and imitation as the mark of an educated person" (Moder, 1995). In China, for example, "scholars learn to write by memorizing classical texts. It is assumed that this results in an internalization of the principles of good writing. Scholars can quote verbatim from these texts without the necessity of citing their sources, because any educated person would recognize the quotation" (Moder and Halleck, 1995: 16). Imitation of text in one's own primary language does not prepare one for the arduous task of creating meaning in a second language. In addition, according to Silva, studies repeatedly show that "people trying to write in a second language are less fluent, make more errors, do not have an 'ear' for what 'sounds' good, are less able to paraphrase, and have more difficulty reading background text" (Silva, 1993: 670). Moreover, we agree with Hyland (2001) when she says that developing one's own voice is difficult if one does not have an accepted vocabulary. We have found that there is a general lack of understanding on the part of the L2 user about which words are simple common usage that need no attribution and which are sophisticated, complex phrases/ideas whose source must be quoted or acknowledged. A general lack of vocabulary leaves L2 writers without a base from which to express their ideas.

Furthermore, from our combined experience (20 years) in our respective classrooms, we have observed that Asian students, in particular, rely on asking questions. American writing conventions necessitate turning those questions into statements to effectuate argument while discussing the relative strengths and weaknesses. In addition, ESL students often have difficulty envisioning a U.S. audience, which results in vague papers. They tend to believe that the audience knows to what they are referring, and we know this not to be the case. Because of this, authors, titles, and quotations are often missing from their writing. In America, for instance, we expect students to frame their writing by referring to time and place and to setting the stage, if you will, with an author's background. We often tell composition students to consider their audience as their peers or even academics in a given discipline. We tell them not to take anything for granted in their writing presentation, and certainly this frame of reference needs to be communicated to L2 writers, particularly in higher education.

In addition, some ESL students have difficulty ascertaining an effective translation of a native phrase into English because they lack knowledge of the correct vocabulary, syntax, and rhetorical patterns. In order to bring a more academic style or sophistication into their writing, some ESL students resort to translation Web sites/search engines. Although we do not believe it is necessarily a bad thing to use one of these search engines or Web sites initially to change a particular foreign phrase into English, we do believe that when ESL students rely too heavily on these rough translations or quote them verbatim, trouble will follow. Because ESL students are often not proficient consumers of English, they cannot make informed decisions regarding the proper vocabulary and syntax, especially where idiomatic expressions are concerned. For example, some major search engines do provide limited translation services; however, these are rough translations and often miss essential syntax and meaning. For instance, although Google Language Tools (www.google.com/language_tools) offers translation interfaces in a variety of authentic languages, such as German, Spanish, French, and Italian, it also includes: Elmer Fudd, Klingon, and Pig Latin. Clearly, there is an ironic reference that perhaps only L1 (first language) writers would initially get. We need not entertain the potential pitfalls of using Elmer Fudd as a translation interface!

As we mentioned earlier, the translation technologies associated with free sections of professional translation sites and general search engines are powerful and useful to a degree. However, these free translation tools are not perfect by any means. For instance, typing the sentence "Robert and Michele won't have a leg to stand on if they cannot produce a good translation Web site" into Google's Language Tools Translation section to be translated into Spanish produces the following: "Roberto y Michele no tendrán una pierna a estar parada encendido si no pueden producir un buen Web site de la traducción." Taking this machine translation (literal translation) and placing it back into Google's Translation section and asking it to translate it back into English gives us this: "Roberto and Michele will not have a leg to be ignited shutdown if they cannot produce a good Web site of the translation." Doing the same type of English-Spanish-English translation at the FreeTranslation (www.freetranslation.com) site produces the translation: "Roberto and Michele will not have a leg to be on stop if cannot produce a good Web site of the translation."

Of course, the FreeTranslation site states that this "free translation is ideal for instant, draft-quality results. It is a 'gisted' translation, providing a basic understanding of the original text." They recommend their Edited or Premium translation services for those interested in obtaining higher quality translations, for a fee. Some of the better, well-known free Web sites/online translators besides Google and FreeTranslation that we believe may be useful to ESL students, as long as they understand their limitations and pitfalls, are AltaVista's Babel Fish Translation (http://world.altavista.com/), Smart Link's PROMPT-Online Translation (http://translation2.paralink.com/), SYSTRAN 4.0 (www.systransoft .com/), WorldLingo's Online Translator (www.worldlingo.com/products_ services/worldlingo_translator.html), and Lexico's Dictionary.com Translator (http://dictionary.reference.com/translate/text.html). And, finally, if you are looking to read some very funny "botched" automatic translations (English-foreign language-English) dealing with politics, advertising, fast food, and more, visit Recksieck's Automated Translations pages at the Shtick site (http://shtick.org/Translation/). They are amusing and will perhaps drive our point squarely home!

Special Considerations for ESL Students: Paraphrasing

Though vocabulary acquisition requires its own strategies and learning curve as we mentioned previously, the same may be said of paraphrasing. Though paraphrasing is difficult for everyone because it necessitates knowledge of vocabulary, rhetorical stance, and mechanical correctness, inferential thinking presents additional challenges for students trying to effectuate the acquisition of honest prose. In other words, it makes it exponentially more difficult. Students have to be able to take those skills to a higher level, reprocess the work, and deliver it back to us in their own words.

Yamada (2003) points out that paraphrasing is difficult for native speakers as well as L2 learners. Colleges vary widely on the topic of what are accepted norms of paraphrasing. Because ESL speakers lack not only the appropriate vocabulary but also the requisite schemata to accompany the formulation of ideas in a second language, they are foiled as they begin the process of idea generation. None of us can write if ideas are not readily available to us—unless of course, we plagiarize! "Paraphrasing is arguably the highest and most synthetic language skill of all," notes Sharon Myers, Associate Professor and Director of the Academic English as a Second Language Program at Texas Tech University. "Not only does the student have to possess a large and sophisticated vocabulary, but [he or she] OR [the student] must also recognize (so as not to repeat) sometimes very subtle stylistic features of writing" (Myers, 1998: 9).

The Dilemma

As you can imagine, students from foreign countries often encounter serious conflicts with our ideas of plagiarism. Hyland writes that instructor "sensitivity" to students' feelings and the inclination to understand cultural differences prevent "the instructors from efficiently pointing out to students infelicities in their essay that may be judged as plagiarism" (Hyland, 2001: 381). In addition, she points out that this is a developmental problem that should be addressed as such. Certainly, developing one's own voice is difficult if one does not have an accepted vocabulary. Yamada concludes that "over-sensitivity to [cultural and ideological] issues prevents effective teaching of the skills ESL/EFL [English as a foreign language] writers need to avoid committing plagiarism" (Yamada, 2003: 255). In other words, our understanding and appreciation of cultural differences is not a substitute or an even exchange for violations of plagiarism rules.

Moreover, there are differences in the scope and range of linguistic competence mandated in various disciplines. According to Leki and Carson (1997), writing classes emphasize linguistic and rhetorical forms; content classes emphasize the content of papers—not form. There is a notable distinction and resulting conflict. Though it is incorrect to say that content can never be wrong in a writing class, it is seldom the focus of the paper grader. Form resonates more. Issues of unity and coherence weigh more heavily, and "how" often takes precedence over "what." Actually, we can argue that the form of writing becomes the content in writing classes. Thus, a teacher's tendency to sympathize with cultural idiosyncrasies favoring plagiarism may combine with the discipline's inherent emphasis on form. The unhappy result is that telltale signs of plagiarism are ignored or inadvertently overlooked.

Plausible Solutions/Considerations

So far, we have covered the background history, special cultural considerations, and the basic dilemma associated with ESL writers. Are there plausible solutions and/or considerations that we as teachers and librarians can implement and discuss to assist ESL students in becoming better academic writers? Glenn Deckert's considerable experience teaching composition courses in Hong Kong to Chinese ESL undergraduate students led to his conclusion that most "overuse source material through an innocent and ingrained habit of giving back information exactly as they find it" (Deckert, 1993: 133). How do we as instructors and librarians best teach L2 writers to "make the transition to a different standard" (Deckert, 1993: 142)? Our experience and research confirm that several seemingly opposing viewpoints exist: (1) incrementally adjusting expectations, (2) modeling, (3) revising traditional notions of intellectual property, and (4) teaching boundaries of acceptable practice.

Incrementally Adjusted Expectations: Patchwriting

Traditional definitions of plagiarism fail to recognize the difficulty of constructing meaning from text in a foreign language and assimilating those ideas into an accepted academic construct (i.e., appropriately attributed writing). Writing is a developmental process for all writers, not just L2 writers. But Hu (2001) believes that instructors should have lower expectations for newcomers to English and allow patchwriting in the early stages. Patchwriting can have positive academic value, according to Hu, because it allows a type of modeling for L2 writers. Patchwriting involves copying sentences and deleting words and substituting synonyms and altering grammatical structures. Hu continues that it is not whether an L2 writer should use others' words but how those words should be used. Hu concludes his article by arguing, "if academics are serious about inducting inexperienced ESL students into their discourse community, they must permit students in the transitional stage prior to becoming full academic community participants to imitate their language to a certain extent with the intention to learn" (Hu, 2001: 59).

Ultimately, it seems that Hu is saying that many ESL students are going to plagiarize when they are becoming literate in English and that the only fair way of dealing with that is to lower standards and model coherent English expression. We feel such practice this could be a dangerous precedent to set. How are neophyte L2 writers supposed to successfully negotiate the transition from patchwriting to the acquisition of honest prose? Our own experience as professionals writing this chapter repeatedly offered somewhat confusing situations of source attributions. Our collaboration process, though it enhanced our research, writing, and thinking, also contributed to this confusion. Learning a new form of documentation (*The Chicago Manual of Style*, 15th edition) and relying on two separate files of attributed, paraphrased notes increased our anxiety about plagiarism infractions, extending the revision time frame for the chapter—and we are fluent L1 speakers and writers!

Clearly, Hu is willing to initiate conventional standards of plagiarism only after L2 learners have had ample opportunity to assimilate their language usage. We wonder what the tenure of this patchwriting process is and how one graduates from it. Our concern is that many ESL students never fully acquire conventions of language usage and source attribution and that they are then set out into the academic community without continued support and monitoring. As has been our experience with L1 and L2 writers, if correction of patchwriting papers is not strongly and immediately given, our inexperienced writers may assume that patchwriting is acceptable within our composition classes and other courses, in general. We must teach them to authenticate their writing through appropriate source attribution. However, just adding the quotation marks and parenthetical citations does not a paper make. So, although we agree with Hu that patchwriting can be a form of modeling and that modeling is a very effective way to help all neophyte writers, it can be a slippery slope to plagiarism. We caution against the over reliance on patchwriting as we believe it will exacerbate plagiarism.

Modeling

Campbell's 1987 study considered how L1 and L2 university students used background information in their writing. For example, issues of explaining, summarizing, paraphrasing, and quoting were examined, and the results showed that L2 students were more likely to copy, almost verbatim, from the text significantly more and more often than L1 students. In addition, it showed that L2 students' vocabulary lacked sophistication. Furthermore, Campbell's study indicated that more assignments requiring the use of specific background source materials would promote and support the development of academic language by L2 students. She points out that "composition instructors need to direct students' attention to how academicians reference their sources, when they provide quotations rather than paraphrases or summaries of information and, probably most importantly, how these references support rather than govern the writer's content" (Campbell, 1987: 36).

We agree with Campbell's assessment that high school and college L2 students would benefit from using a textbook and other appropriate background text sources. In our own composition and rhetoric courses, however, we found that most L2 students initially learned to write in English by writing about personal experiences and interests, rather than using a text of any kind. Just as we teach native speakers to write simple stories and scenarios in their journals when they are neophyte writers, L2 learners likewise benefit. However, writing a short paper based on a required reading gives L2, and any student for that matter, more experience in summarizing, paraphrasing, and quoting, as well as an opportunity to discuss plagiarism and how to acknowledge correctly the writing of others. We also believe that the initial use of limited background materials makes it easier for the L2 student by providing specific appropriate textual models and, likewise, assists the teacher in detecting any plagiarism from those materials and in providing immediate feedback.

East Meets West: Revise Traditional Notions of Intellectual Property

ESL students need to be given explicit instruction on Western notions of plagiarism and significant opportunities to process text. According to Hu (2001), plagiarism becomes a highly charged emotional issue because in many places in the world, plagiarism, as we know it, is quintessentially a foreign concept. Besides discussing the differing opinions of what constitutes plagiarism between Eastern and Western cultures, will we as composition instructors or librarians, assisting L2 writers with proper paraphrasing or quoting, be willing to address the complex and apparently inconsistent practice within Western cultures of proper acknowledgment of words and/or ideas?

Deckert brings up some interesting examples of acceptable practice that emerging L2 writers might seriously argue conflict with our professed value of originality and attribution. For instance, he writes that "it is acceptable for persons in political office to rely heavily upon professional speech writers without giving credit or…for company executives to sign their names to communications drafted by various assistants" (Deckert, 1993: 132). This seeming contradiction or accepted irregularity certainly does make it a bit more difficult for us to impress upon L2 students the necessity of avoiding improper use of source materials. We need to communicate emphatically to our students that the conventions within popular culture are not necessarily applicable to academia.

Teach Boundaries of Acceptable Practice

How do we best teach L2 writers about the boundaries of acceptable practice concerning research and writing conventions? Being consistent is important with both detection of and consequences for infractions. Most schools have handbooks and official policies detailing academic dishonesty, but the problem results from lip service to the procedures or at least perceived incongruence in effectuated policies. Perhaps follow-through with infractions will become as important as designing the ideals and even teaching the protocols. Statements of academic honesty detailing ownership of submitted work as well as agreeing to take the consequences of submitting plagiarized work are prolific on college campuses. Faculty need to get to the place where they realize and accept that detecting plagiarism is part of their job description and thus work toward limiting it and responding appropriately to it.

Of course, we probably cannot expect that L2 students will be interested in respecting the intellectual property rights of authors unless teachers provide ample reason, time, and resources for the L2 writers to practice appropriate citing and quoting of supporting documentation, whether directly quoted or paraphrased. Our experience shows us that one of the best antiplagiarism strategies is to discuss initially with our students the beneficial aspects of proper attribution of source material within their papers, an idea we believe is even more essential when dealing with L2 students. For instance, citing material from professional magazines and Web sites and scholarly journals and books can provide just the expert testimony needed to solidify and support their points or opinions stated within their papers. Unfortunately, as Harris explains, "many students do not seem to realize that whenever they cite a source, they are strengthening their writing.... [He adds that,] in a nutshell, citing helps make the essay stronger and sounder and will probably result in a better grade" (Harris, 2002).

Providing compelling reasons for appropriately documenting sources is not enough, though, for L2 students to improve their writing. Providing resources and the time to practice writing in English for L2 students is paramount. Fortunately, there are excellent online resources that provide ample explanations, tutorials, and exercises that can assist L2 writers attempting to make the transition to more sophisticated academic writing. Of course, teachers must be willing to accommodate their L2 students by providing sufficient time for them to practice with these online resources, inside and outside of the classroom. Some of our favorites are listed below.

- Dave's ESL Café (www.eslcafe.com/): This is a favorite ESL site on the Web. It is a frequently cited award-winning site brought to us by Dave Sperling, teacher, author, and Internet and ESL/EFL consultant.
- English as a Second Language (ESL) Resources, Handouts and Exercises (http://owl.english.purdue.edu/handouts/esl/index.html): The Online Writing Lab (OWL) at Purdue University offers ESL students and teachers a wealth of free information and assistance at their Web site.
- English as a Second Language (www.rong-chang.com/): This often-cited and frequently updated ESL Web site is brought to us by Rongchang Li, Ph.D.
- The Internet TESL Journal (http://iteslj.org/): This monthly online journal is meant for ESL teachers, as it provides articles, research papers, lesson plans, and handouts, but it also has a great "Activities for ESL Students" section, among other useful and interesting ESL items.
- Antimoon.com: Learn English Effectively (www.antimoon.com/): This is a fairly unique and memorable ESL/EFL resource site. Creators Szynalski and Wojcik (prior ESL students, now English teachers) explain their dis-

tinct, motivational "philosophy of learning English, based on [their] successful experiences as English learners." They stress studying and practicing pronunciation combined with other language-building activities, rather than taking formal classes or completing grammar exercises.

To find excellent annotations and reviews for our above recommended ESL sites for teachers and students as well as other evaluated and recommended ESL directories and Web sites, we recommend frequently visiting the following Web sites.

- Librarians Index to the Internet (http://lii.org/): Type ESL into the search block to obtain this authoritative online directory's annotated listing of ESL sites.
- About (http://esl.about.com/index.htm): This is their ESL section, brought to us by About Guide Kenneth Beare; click onto a subject link, such as ESL/EFL Sites, to see Ken's picks in those areas.
- Blue Web'n (www.blueWebn.com/wired/blueWebn/): SBC Knowledge Network Explorer's award-winning online library, choose their Foreign Language content area and then click on the English as a Second Language (ESL) subsection for their annotated listing of quality ESL sites.
- Education World (www.education-world.com/awards/past/): This valued and respected free resource site for educators provides us with detailed reviews of some of the best ESL sites found on the Web; choose the Language Arts section from their Site Review Center Archives and then click onto the ESL subsection link to view their staff's ESL selections.

Conclusion and Final Thoughts

We have attempted to cover a lot of ground in this brief chapter, and we hope that we have shed some light on areas of concern and perhaps asked questions that you will contemplate in your journey through the plagiarism maze. As we have previously stated, plagiarism is a relatively new concept, historically speaking. Certainly, the idea that plagiarism is on the rise can be debated; however, the medium (i.e., the Internet) has changed the way students plagiarize and has vastly increased the variety and availability of sources, putting a new spin on an age-old problem. We talked about the idea that concepts of plagiarism vary from culture to culture. We have touched on how plagiarism becomes undoubtedly more complex for ESL students. Vocabulary, syntax, and rhetorical patterns can be a particular problem for ESL students, as is paraphrasing. Internet translation sources can have outcomes ranging from the grammatically incorrect to the outlandishly comic. Patchwriting is a controversial but certainly plausible alternative for modeling syntax for ESL students. Most importantly, however, is the consistent detection and correction of plagiarism infractions. We have to get L2 learners to buy into the philosophical concept that borrowed words and ideas should be attributed to the original authors.

Providing compelling reasons for appropriately documenting sources is not enough, though, for L2 students to improve their writing. Providing resources and the time to practice writing in English for L2 students is paramount. Fortunately, there are excellent online resources that provide ample explanations, tutorials, and exercises that can assist L2 writers attempting to make the transition to more sophisticated academic writing. Of course, teachers must be willing to accommodate their L2 students by providing sufficient time for them to practice with these online resources, both inside and outside of the classroom. Teachers of ESL need to help their students find and create their own voices.

Works Cited

AltaVista. *Babel Fish Translation*. Available: http://world.altavista.com.

Ashworth, Peter, and Phillip Bannister. 1997. "Guilty in Whose Eyes?: University Students' Perceptions of Cheating and Plagiarism in Academic Work and Assessment." *Studies in Higher Education* 22(2): 187–203.

Beare, Kenneth. "English as 2nd Language: About." Available: http://esl.about.com.

Bowden, Darsie. 1996. "Stolen Voices: Plagiarism and Authentic Voice." *Composition Studies/Freshman English News* 24(1–2): 5–18.

Campbell, Cherry. 1987. "Writing with Others' Words: Native and Non-native University Students' Use of Information from a Background Reading Text in Academic Compositions." California University. Los Angeles: Center for Language Education and Research. ERIC, ED 287315.

Deckert, Glenn D. 1993. "Perspectives on Plagiarism from ESL Students in Hong Kong." *Journal of Second Language Writing* 2(2): 131–148.

Education World, Inc. Site review archives. Available: www.education-world.com/awards/past.

Evans, Faun Bernbach, and Madeleine Youmans. 2000. "ESL Writers Discuss Plagiarism: The Social Construction of Ideologies." *Journal of Education* 182(3): 49–65.

Feldman, Dick. 1989. "The International Student and Course-Integrated Instruction: The ESL Instructor's Perspective." *Research Strategies* 7(4): 159–166.

Google. Language Tools. Available: www.google.com/language_tools.

Hansen, Brian. 2003. "Combating Plagiarism." *CQ Researcher* 19 September: 773–796.

Harris, Robert. "Anti-plagiarism Strategies for Research Papers." VirtualSalt. (March 7, 2002) Available: www.virtualsalt.com/antiplag.htm.

Hu, Jim. 2001. "An Alternative Perspective on Language Re-Use: Insights from Textual and Learning Theories and L2 Academic Writing." *English Quarterly* 33(1–2): 52–62.

Hyland, Fiona. 2001. "Dealing with Plagiarism when Giving Feedback." *ELT Journal* 55(4): 375–381.

Internet TESL Journal. Available: http://iteslj.org/.

Leki, Ilona, and Joan Carson. 1997. "Completely Different Worlds: EAP and the Writing Experiences of ESL Students in University Courses." *TESOL Quarterly* 31(1): 39–69.

Lexico Publishing Group. Dictionary.com Translator. Available: http://dictionary.reference.com /translate/text.html.

Li, Rongchang. "English as a Second Language." Available: http://www.rong-chang.com.

Librarians Index to the Internet. Available: http://lii.org/.

Moder, Carol Lynn, and Gene B. Halleck. 1995. "Solving the Plagiary Puzzle with Role Plays." *TESOL Journal* 4(3): 16–19.

Morgan, Peter W., and Glenn H. Reynolds. 1997. *The Appearance of Impropriety: How the Ethics Wars Have Undermined American Government, Business, and Society*. New York: Free Press.

Myers, Sharon. 1998. "Questioning Author(ity): ESL/EFL, Science and Teaching about Plagiarism." *TESL-EJ* 3(2): 1–20.

Online Writing Lab. "English as a Second Language (ESL) Resources, Handouts and Exercises." Purdue University. Available: http://owl.english.purdue.edu/handouts/esl/index.html.

Pennycook, Alastair. 1996. "Borrowing Others' Words: Text, Ownership, Memory, and Plagiarism." *TESOL Quarterly* 30(2): 201–230.

Recksieck, Charlie. "Automated Translations: Fun with Automatic Translation." Shtick! Available: http://shtick.org/Translation/.

SBC Knowledge Network Explorer. Blue Web'n. Available: www.blueWebn.com/ wired/blueWebn/.

SDL International. FreeTranslation. Available: www.freetranslation.com.

Silva, Tony. 1993. "Toward an Understanding of the Distinct Nature of L2 Writing: The ESL Research and Its Implications." *TESOL Quarterly* 27(4): 657–677.

Smart Link Corporation. PROMPT-Online Translation. Available: http://translation2 .paralink.com.

Sperling, Dave. Dave's ESL Café. Available: www.eslcafe.com/.

SYSTRAN S.A. SYSTRAN 4.0. Available: www.systransoft.com/.

WorldLingo. Online Translator. Available: www.worldlingo.com/products_services/ worldlingo_translator.html.

Yamada, Kyoko. 2003. "What Prevents ESL/EFL Writers from Avoiding Plagiarism?: Analyses of 10 North-American College Websites." *System* 31(2): 247–258.

Finding Remedies: Proven Faculty, Departmental, and Institutional Strategies

The goal of Part II of *The Plagiarism Plague* is to give you, the reader, hope. Part I outlined many of the problems regarding plagiarism; Part II will empower you with some solutions.

This second section of the book begins with two chapters that build on each other. Chapter 5 discusses how to design a tutorial on the topic of plagiarism. Chapter 6 takes that theoretical framework and supplies an example of just such a tutorial, created for undergraduates at a large, urban, academic library.

Chapters 7, 8, and 9 are included in this section to emphasize that learning intellectual honesty is a process that must be nurtured throughout a student's academic life. The chapters in this section were written (respectively) by a former high-school teacher (who now trains student teachers); a faculty member who teaches undergraduate English; and a department chair. Each of these authors brings a unique perspective to the topic, but all discuss the importance of good pedagogy combating the problem of plagiarism at all levels of the educational experience.

Chapter 10 concludes this section of the book with a survey of current policies regarding intellectual honesty at American universities. This chapter is useful for providing a snapshot of what institutions of higher education are doing at the macro level in addressing the topic of plagiarism. This chapter contains links to the policies discussed. You might find it useful to use the CD that accompanies this book with this chapter to follow along with the author's discussion and get an in-depth feel for the different approaches that these institutions take.

CHAPTER 5

Intellectual Honesty: Selling It!

Vibiana Bowman

Introduction

First a Brief Word from Our Sponsor

Good teaching practices are hard to define. The impact of a well-taught class hits us viscerally. It can be difficult to describe what *exactly* it was that made it effective; as Supreme Court Justice Potter Stewart wrote regarding a definition of pornography, "...I know it when I see it" (*Jacobellis* v. *Ohio*). So, when writing about pedagogy, authors tend to rely on analogies and draw on strategies from outside the discipline of education—such as sports, military science, or the world of theater. The strategies that I will draw upon for this discussion are from marketing and advertising. I chose this approach for the following reason: good advertising works.

Imaginative and well-researched marketing campaigns, promulgated through mass media, Internet, and viral marketing (i.e., the creation of a "buzz" through person-to-person contact), get the message out about what to buy. The youth market, the teens and twenty-somethings, the same group that high school and college educators are trying to reach, is a primary target for many advertisers. A debate on the ethics of targeting teens with the intent of selling them consumer goods is beyond the scope of this discussion. I believe, however, that as educators, it behooves us to take a closer look at some of the marketing tools and strategies used by businesses in order to sell *our* message—the value of intellectual honesty.

In the sections that follow, I will present some suggestions on how to plan, execute, and present a tutorial on the topic of plagiarism. In this particular context, I am using the term "tutorial" is its broadest sense—a prepared lesson to teach a particular topic. The final product could be a lesson plan for an in-person instruction class, a worksheet, or a Web-based product. The projects on which I have worked and will use to illustrate my points are Web-based. However, the underlying principles can be used in designing for any format. A word of caution: The excerpts from my own work are not offered as models to emulate, but rather offer a starting point from which you can build and improve.

This framework for designing a tutorial on plagiarism is based on the standard structure of a lesson plan combined with basic marketing and advertising principles. These advertising techniques have been used for decades and are the underpinning of campaigns such as Speedy Alka-Selzter, "Where's the Beef?" and "Just Say No." The United States Small Business Administration offers an excellent resource guide regarding marketing and advertising basics and is available online at www.sba.gov/starting_business/marketing/basics.html. Information about standards for writing lesson plans can be found at the United States Department of Education's Web page for teachers (U.S.DOE, "Teachers"). A chart summarizing principles found in R.F. Mager's *Preparing Instructional Objectives* is available on the Web at www.coe.ecu.edu/ltdi/colaric/KB/Mager.html ("Mager's Instructional Objectives"). I also draw upon the terminology and pedagogy found in *Information Literacy Competency Standards for High Education* from the Association of College and Research Libraries, available at www.ala.org/ala/acrl/acrlstandards/standards.pdf.

Creating a Tutorial Step-by-Step

Step One: Establish Your Mission and Your Message

For your own planning purposes, before you begin writing your tutorial on plagiarism, write a clear mission statement. A mission statement defines the underlying philosophy of what you intend your project to achieve. It should reflect the values and aspirations of the stakeholders involved with the project—the administration, the faculty, and the creative team. Keep the mission statement short and positive in tone. It may be necessary and appropriate in the statement to reference school policy and disciplinary measures. Wherever possible, keep the emphasis on the fact that part of the mission is to teach the students the importance of writing in a clear and scholarly manner—a skill that will serve them well throughout their professional lives. An example of a mission statement for a series of tutorials on plagiarism for students would be:

> The faculty of the Paul Robeson Library is committed to educating our students about information literacy. Our mission is to create independent, lifelong learners who can gather, assess, and use information. As part of this mission, this project addresses the topic of plagiarism and is intended to provide students with a clear understanding of: appropriate and fair use of materials from other sources; what plagiarism is versus good scholarly practices; and what the consequences of plagiarism are.

The value of a positive tone throughout the project, starting with the mission statement, cannot be emphasized enough. People are more receptive to a positive message than a negative one. When planning a tutorial on how to avoid plagiarism, plan in terms of an active message—the value of intellectual honesty. Focus on a list of "thou shall" rather than the "thou shall not." Intellectual honesty implies that a writer is playing by the rules of good scholarship—defined as gathering, assessing, using, and documenting the information that she has gathered, processed, and presented in a written or oral format. Scholars-in-training need to understand the importance of documenting their work so that the results can be independently verified and reproduced for the advancement of the discipline in which they are working. This is part and parcel of the "scientific process" and a cornerstone in every discipline that they might choose to pursue from culinary arts to genetic engineering. Part of a broader mission for a tutorial in plagiarism is to give students specific skills for producing the formal, nonfiction style of writing required at an academic level. Students learning these skills need a clear understanding of what is required for this kind of prose.

Step Two: Identify Goals, Incorporate Standards, and Target Instructional Outcomes

A goal differs from a mission statement by the degree of specificity and intent. A mission statement is a general description of broad purpose—the philosophical underpinnings. Goals are derived from the mission statement but are intended to describe specific, measurable outcomes. A sample goal of a plagiarism tutorial based on the above mission statement would be:

> The educational goal of this tutorial is that upon its completion, the student will be able to write a short research paper that includes correctly cited source material.

Depending on the setting that the instructor is in, secondary or higher education, the incorporation of educational standards may be an important, if not mandatory, part of creating the lesson plan. For example, in higher education, the Association of College and Research Libraries (ACRL) *Information Literacy*

Competency Standards is a set of standards that is often used in articulating goals relating to producing information-literate students. Each of these standards defines specific performance indicators and educational outcomes. These "indicators" and "outcomes" are related to the concept of "educational objectives" as defined by Mager. Outcomes or objectives should both be written as a set of clearly defined, observable, measurable skills or actions that the student will be able to perform (Lignugaris-Kraft et al., 2001: 53). Standards, performance indicators, and instructional outcomes are usually defined by an agency outside the classroom teacher. Educational objectives are statements typically written by a teacher for a specific lesson and based on the specific institution's mission statement and educational goals. For the purpose of this discussion, the term "outcomes" will be used to cover both "objectives" and standards-based "outcomes." This discussion will also use the term "goals" with the understanding that many instructors and librarians will also be incorporating specific sets of standards into their lesson plans.

Clearly, stated instructional outcomes aid with assessment of both what the student has learned and how effective the tutorial is. A sample statement for a plagiarism tutorial based on the above goal would be:

Students will be able to identify the components of a citation
(author, article name, journal name, volume, issue page number)
written according to the *Chicago Manual of Style*, 15th edition.

This would adhere to "Standard Five" of the ACRL *Information Literacy Competency Standards* (ACRL, 2000: 13.) It is based on the performance indicator: "The information literate student acknowledges the use of information sources..." (ACRL, 2000: 14) and the outcome "selects the appropriate documentation style and uses it consistently..." (ACRL, 2000: 14).

Plagiarism is a complex issue with many components. For the purpose of clarity and effectiveness, it is advisable to keep tutorials short and simple. To this end, a packet of modules on the topic of plagiarism might serve to make the project more manageable. The modules will all share the same mission; each module will have its own goal; each module may have several instructional outcomes. As you plan for the instructional outcomes, keep the characteristics of a well-written statement in mind. It should describe a positive action that your students will be able to perform and that you will be able to assess.

When writing your missions statement, goals, and outcomes, keep in mind that the process is more art than science. Though each step of the process is important and each segment should be written as clearly as possible, it is inevitable that there will be overlap and a bit of blurring of lines between the categories. Remember that the very act of engaging in the process will help you to clarify what you intend to teach and what you expect your outcomes to be.

Step Three: Identify Your Target Audience

Market research is used to customize advertising campaigns for all kinds of goods and services, from pharmaceuticals to television shows. The better that you know your intended audience, the better you can pitch your product. You will need to identify who your target audience is before you plan the details of your educational campaign. You have already detailed why you are teaching, what you are teaching, and what you expect the results to be. The next step is to customize your module for your audience so that they will be receptive to your message. You have made your message clear, now you want them to hear it and pay attention to it.

According to the United States Small Business Administration's "Marketing Basics":

> Successful marketing requires timely and relevant market information. An inexpensive research program, based on questionnaires given to current or prospective customers, can often uncover dissatisfaction or possible new products or services (U.S. SBA, "Marketing Basics").

Assuming that you have some lead time for research before your project is due and some access to your potential user group, standard survey tools like interviews, focus groups, and questionnaires are fairly inexpensive and can provide you with the written documentation that is useful for planning your goals and outcomes. This kind of paper trail will also provide a valuable tool for assessment. It gives you a staring point for establishing whether documented user needs were met. In my own experience, I have found that conversations with students, in both formal and informal settings, have been the best resource for insights about their mindset. Use the opportunities and tools that you have at your disposal; keep your mission, goals, and outcomes in mind; listen to what your students have to say.

Advertising professionals also make use of government statistics and surveys and trade journal literature. Instructors can use scholarly indexes, databases, and table-of-content services in order to stay current with literature regarding their target audience. It is my experience that educators tend to be an empathetic, creative, and curious group of people. That in mind, I would also suggest that you expose yourself to your students' pop-culture environment. Listen to some of their music; catch a few of their television shows and movies; visit some of the Web sites that are popular. This will clue you in to some of their frames of reference. As a starting point, I would suggest the cartoon Web site Homestar Runner at http://homestarrunner.com. (Note: Go to "Toons," then "Features." Search in the "E-mail" section for the cartoon called "The English Paper." It is especially well-done and provides a humorous insight into the student's point of view.)

The size and constituency of the intended audience will vary greatly according to the specific educational setting in which you are situated. An instructional librarian designing an online tutorial for all freshmen taking English composition at a 4-year college will have a different set of challenges than an English professor teaching about plagiarism as part of the curriculum of an honors seminar in Victorian women writers. However, no matter how large the class or how little face-to-face contact you have, use some strategy to gather information about your target audience. Remember that the perceived user need, what you think they should be taught, does not always coincide with the users' articulated need, what they are saying they want. Through research, you can close that gap and customize your message for optimum educational impact.

As mentioned previously, the plagiarism module that our team created was Web-based. Our target audience was all the undergraduate students at a large, urban university—a very large and very diverse group. Much of our understanding of our user group was drawn from our work with students in bibliographic instruction class. In addition, we used questionnaires and interviews with students. As we finished portions of the module, we would have students preview and critique them. We found the student input invaluable, and we incorporated most of their suggestions into our final product.

Step Four: Identifying an Appropriate Format for Promoting the Concept

A decision of appropriate format for presentation builds on the discussion of identifying the target audience. Again, what is feasible varies greatly according to individual circumstance. The choices for presentation format are constrained by the resources that you have at your disposal with regard to hardware, software, graphics capability, the talent pool available to you, and financial resources. Again, the discipline of marketing offers an interesting context in which to frame these choices. The United States Small Business Administration offers this advice to beginning entrepreneurs:

> Your next step is to select the advertising vehicles you will use
> to carry your message, and establish an advertising schedule.
> In most cases, knowing your audience will help you choose
> the media that will deliver your sales message most effectively.
> Use as many...tools as are appropriate and affordable (U.S.
> SBA, "Ads and PR").

If you substitute "educational vehicles" for "advertising vehicles" and "content" for "sales message," the advice seems particularly apt.

To aid you in a decision-making process that involves a variety of choices and alternatives, it is often useful to create a decision-making chart. Enchanted Learning, a Web resource for teachers, has printable decision charts for three and four alternatives, available online at www.enchant-edlearning.com/graphicorganizers/decision/. Just as with the interviews and surveys in assessing user needs, these decision charts will provide documentation on how your decision was reached, how it supports your mission statement, goals, and instructional outcomes, and how it relates to the financial and creative resources that you have on-hand. The creation of these alternate scenarios will also help you to plan for future purchases of instructional technology tools, if funds become available, as you can tie their acquisition to specific educational goals and instructional outcomes.

You have identified your audience; you have made an assessment of the tools and resources available to you; the next step is to identify what kind of instructional format you are going to use to construct the tutorial. As you consider the various presentation formats, consider planning for learning diversity. Everyone learns new skills and concepts differently. There are a variety of learning modalities but, for the sake of simplicity, we will use three major divisions: auditory, visual, and kinetic (learning by doing) (PBS Teacher Source, "The Issue: Learning Modalities").

Most students use a combination of strategies, but most learners are stronger in one modality than in others. An effective learning tool incorporates an awareness of different learning modalities into its design. This helps to ensure that all students have an opportunity to use their strengths. Incorporating different kinds of presentation strategies also makes the lesson more engaging. Talking heads, written materials, lectures, and graphics can become easy to tune out when overused. It is more attention grabbing when different skills or bits of information are imparted in a variety of ways.

Some examples of some different strategies and the learning modalities that they address include:

- Text passages are effective for short, important pieces of information such as definitions (for visual learners).
- Web-based movies such as those done with Camtasia or Macromedia Flash. This could be done using a cartoon format, live actors, or stills for pieces of information that require a lengthier explanation or are a little "dry" in content (for visual and auditory learners).
- Interactive quizzes that can be used to reinforce a concept or to assess where the student is with regard to the information already presented (all learners—visual, auditory and tactile learners).
- Role-playing especially involves the tactile/kinetic-based learner.
- Peer editing again engages all three kinds of learners especially if material is read aloud and the students are given the opportunity to move about the room.

Step Five: Assess Effectiveness of Message Promotion

Assessment is an essential component of any lesson plan. Specific skills such as the ability to identify correctly a definition of "plagiarism," demonstrate the use of quotation marks around an exact quote, or locating the link to the school's intellectual honesty policy on a Web page are easily measurable through assessment tools such as written or online quizzes and student presentations. Some outcomes, those related to changes in attitude, are more difficult to assess because they are more personal in nature. Tools such as exit interviews, essays, and other more open-ended measures can give some insight. In addition to assessing the individual student, educators are also concerned with the effectiveness of the tool that they have devised.

The ability of the student who uses the tools to perform the stated instructional outcome is one measure of the tutorial's effectiveness. The effectiveness of changing or influencing patterns of behavior during long periods of time is a more difficult outcome to assess. This is a topic that has been researched in relation to the effectiveness of public service announcements (PSAs), particularly those ads aimed at preventing illegal drug use by teenagers. In one recent study, researchers interviewed students, grades 5 through 12, after viewing a series of drug-related PSAs. The students rated the ads that were specific with their message (e.g., possible consequences of heroin use) as effective and general message ads, like the "Just Say No" campaign, as ineffective (Fishbein et al., 2002: 245). The researchers cautioned that further evaluation of the topic is needed because of the difficulty of determining whether any behavioral changes actually came about as a result of viewing the PSAs. All they could claim to measure was the students' perceived effectiveness of the ad (Fishbein et al., 2002).

Conclusion

With the increased awareness in public schools, colleges, and universities about plagiarism and increased resources being used to address the problem, new research will undoubtedly be forthcoming regarding outcomes of educational initiatives regarding intellectual honesty and their effectiveness. As educators, we can start by instilling our students with the values shared by the academic community and teaching them the skills that they need to demonstrate those values.

One last thought regarding your tutorial: After you create your product, if at all possible, put it out there—on the Web or in the classroom—use it with your students. View it as a work in progress, and do not be afraid of failure. Innovative projects sometimes get shelved because people get frozen in fear. Teaching is a creative process, and teaching tools should be fluid, mutable, and constantly changing.

Works Cited

Association of College and Research Libraries (ACRL). 2000. *Information Literacy Competency Standards for Higher Education*. Chicago: The Association of College and Research Libraries.

Fishbein, Martin, Kathleen Hall-Jamieson, Eric Zimmer, Ina von Haeften, and Robin Nabi. 2002. "Avoiding the Boomerang: Testing the Relative Effectiveness of Antidrug Public Service Announcements before a National Campaign." *American Journal of Public Health* 92, no. 2 (February): 238–245.

Jacobellis v. Ohio, 378 U.S. 184 (1964).

Lignugaris-Kraft, Benjamin, Nancy Marchand-Martella, and Ronald C. Martella. 2001. "Writing Better Goals and Short-Term Objectives or Benchmarks." *Teaching Exceptional Children* 34, no.1 (September/October): 52–58.

"Mager's Instructional Objectives." Available: www.coe.ecu.edu/ltdi/colaric/KB/Mager.html.

PBS Teacher Source. "The Issue: Learning Modalities." Available: www.pbs.org/teachersource/prek2/issues/1101issue.shtm#overview.

United States Department of Education (U.S. DOE). "Teachers." Available: www.ed.gov/teachers/landing.jhtml?src=fp.

United States Small Business Administration (U.S. SBA). "Ads and PR." Available: http://www.sba.gov/starting_business/marketing/adspr.html.

United States Small Business Administration (U.S. SBA). "Marketing Basics." Available: www.sba.gov/starting_business/marketing/basics.html.

CHAPTER 6
_____

Cite It Right: A Tutorial

Vibiana Bowman

and

John B. Gibson

Introduction

Gentle Reader...

In the previous chapter, a step-by-step process was outlined as a guideline for creating instructional materials by combining basic marketing principles with a lesson plan. Using that process as an outline, we are going to walk you through a real-life example of how we created a Web-based plagiarism tutorial, "Cite It Right." We repeat the caveat found in the previous chapter, in that we do not offer our own work as an example of excellence, but rather as a conversation starting point. Please also refer to Chapter 5 for a discussion of the terminology used. We will analyze our module to illustrate the educational underpinnings and the instructional technology used to create a product that, in focus groups, students like, will engage with, and which seems to be effective in getting across some basic ideas about plagiarism.

What Was Our Mission and Our Message?

As part of a university-wide initiative to curb the rise of plagiarism and to teach good research and writing skills to our students, the Paul Robeson library decided to create a packet of Web-based teaching modules as part of its bibliographic instruction program. They are specifically geared to the undergraduate student and are intended to teach the student about the research process in general and about plagiarism specifically, especially with regard to what plagiarism is and how to avoid it. The modules use Web-based movies, cartoons, and games. The rationale is that if we can make the learning process entertaining through animated characters, humor, and interesting story-lines, we will be able to engage undergraduates and inform them through an online learning process.

"Cite It Right" is part of this set of modules. It is a Macromedia Flash cartoon that can be viewed on the Web using any Windows-supported media device such as Real Player or Windows Media Player. The specific mission of this product is to raise the student's awareness of when citations need to be used in writing papers. The message is that even if the student gets just one example wrong, that lack of a citation could get them involved in an accusation of plagiarism.

That message was established for the tutorial for a very specific reason. During the information-gathering stage of this project, we had dozens of conversations with a variety of undergraduates. These conversations were both in formal settings, like bibliographic class sessions, as well as informal, "on-the-fly," settings (e.g., with students at the reference desk.) We became aware of the fact that students were unclear about what information was considered "intellectual property." Many students were under the impression that content from books, articles, and the Web did not need to be cited so long as they paraphrased the material (i.e. "put it in their own words"). The message of this quiz is that all content (except for common knowledge) that comes from a source other than the student's own head needs to be cited. Otherwise, the student has engaged in some degree of plagiarism.

Goals and Targeted Instructional Outcomes

In designing this tutorial, we were using a macro and micro set of goals and instructional outcomes. At the macro level were the goals and outcomes that we set for the entire project. We also had micro-level goals and outcomes for each specific tutorial, including "Cite It Right." The overall educational goals of the plagiarism project for our students were the following:

- Promote the values of intellectual honesty.
- Teach good scholarly writing skills especially with regard to the importance of documentation.
- Promote information literacy skills specifically with regard to what constitutes intellectual property.

The instructional outcomes that we established for the plagiarism project were that, upon completion of the modules, the student would be able to do the following:

- Accurately define plagiarism.
- Recognize what kind of source materials needed to be cited in a research paper.
- Demonstrate an understanding of the Rutgers University policies, procedures, and guidelines regarding academic integrity.

Goals and instructional outcomes for students are predicated on the understanding that there must be some means to determine if they have been met. Assessment determines two different kinds of success: (1) Was the student successful? Did she do the task that was required of her? (2) Was the educational tool successful? Was it an effective means of imparting the skill or concept it was designed to teach? Assessment will be discussed more completely in the section that follows, but it should be noted that "Cite It Right" has assessment tools built into the interactive quiz as part of the teaching process.

"Cite It Right," as an educational tool, had its own specific goals and outcomes. The goal of this tutorial was to teach students that different kinds of materials, in addition to exact quotes, need citations. The stated instructional outcomes were that the student would identify the need to cite sources for statistics; and the need to cite arguments, opinions, and conclusions that she got from her research. The activity used was a quiz with specific examples that the student had to use. The assessment was in the form of immediate feedback whether the answer was right or wrong and an explanation of why (Figure 6-1).

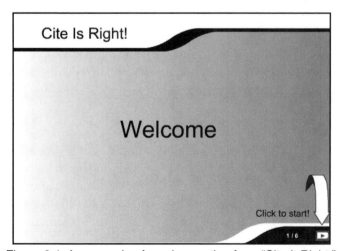

Figure 6-1. An example of a quiz question from "Cite It Right."

Identifying the Target Audience

Our target audience, as defined by our mission statement, was primarily our undergraduate students—our largest potential user group. We set about doing our marketing research by using a variety of tools. First, we wanted to establish an understanding about the attitudes and concerns, for this age group, regarding the topic of plagiarism. As previously mentioned, we gathered information- a lot of information—about student attitudes and skills from Q&A sessions during bibliographic instruction classes as well as during individual reference interviews. We interviewed faculty members, especially the English composition instructors, to establish their insights regarding needs and others areas of concern of students. Finally, we did research regarding the demographic group in the professional literature, especially with regard to attitudes regarding use of the Internet, file sharing, cheating, and other intellectual property and academic honesty issues.

Next, we wanted to establish what kind of format the students might find engaging or appealing with regard to a Web-based product. Again, we did student interviews and research in popular literature. Based on leads from students, we watched a lot of online cartoons that are popular with the age group to gather some insights into what the students are watching for entertainment online and what kind of games they are playing. The intent was to tap into the preexisting mindset and use a format that the student already recognizes as engaging in order to engage them in learning. As we came up with ideas, we tried them out on student workers, student library visitors, and friends of students who were not regular library users. We found that students visit many Web sites that use Macromedia flash movies. Students are willing to watch cartoons of several minutes in length as long as they are somewhat witty and visually interesting, even if the visuals are fairly simple. A fast pace and humor, especially with a good dose of irreverence, irony, and satire, are common elements in the Web 'toons that this age group enjoys (Figure 6-2).

Selecting the Format

One major advantage to beginning the process with a clear educational/marketing plan is that it helps you to narrow your decisions as you move through each step of the process. If you know what you want to accomplish (what is your ideal-your mission statement), then you know what you need to accomplish (what is your charge-your educational goals and instructional outcomes), you know who you have to reach (you have identified your target audience), and you have some idea of the best way to reach them (through background research on your target audience). Now, you reach the point in your decision tree where you must answer

Figure 6-2. Self-deprecating humor helps to deliver educational content.

the following questions: How are you going to package the product? What instructional technology tool are you going to use?

For us, much of the hardware, software, and training that we needed to create Web tutorials were already in place. A robust Web presence has been one of the goals of our library's strategic marketing plan for several years. Consequently, as funds became available, our director was able to justify the purchase of educational technology tools because they had been identified as necessary for meeting the goals established in our strategic plan.

For this specific project, we knew that we wanted to create a Web cartoon modeled after some of the more popular sites that the students watched (being very, very careful not to steal any ideas or step on any intellectual property rights). We already had purchased a site license for Macromedia Flash software and we had a high-end PC specifically configured for video creation. Our instructional technology specialist had the skill-set required to create the video, and our outreach librarian had the skill-set for creating the educational content. The information regarding viewing habits and preferences supplied by the

Figure 6-3. From the Introduction to "Cite It Right": Earnest
Student gets ready to play the game with host Shabby Scholar.

students themselves and research about the demographic group supplied the basis for what we wanted-a cartoon with educational content (Figure 6-3).

When developing this software, the first thing we had to do was decide the most attractive way to relay our content to our target audience. This being the case, we took the information we gathered earlier from students and decided to have our medium broadcast over the Internet. We then choose Macromedia Flash and Real One's video player as hosts to our final output. To create content suitable for these mediums, we created our objects using either Macromedia Freehand or Adobe Photoshop. After creating objects, we then put those items into animation using Macromedia Flash. After this we choose, for rendering reasons and animation simplicity, to capture our creation from a Flash player using Camtasia Studio's Recorder program. This allowed us to output a raw AVI file to Adobe Premiere for editing. After editing, we then used Premiere to export Real One content that could pseudostream from our server, which in this case means a video file that can download to a user's computer while allowing them to watch the video. Though it was possible for us to develop this entire tutorial in Macromedia Flash, having these other external programs available made it easier for us to harness the power of several quality tools to tweak further and maximize our final project for use on the World Wide Web. This part of the creation process was made easier by following an initial storyboard we developed for following the flow process.

Shabby: OK, for the viewers at home let's review how to play the game.
- Ernest will type out the paper that he is working on.
- You, the home viewer, will decide if the sentence that he typed is "right"—that is it doesn't need a citation—or if it should be "cite"—it needs a citation.
- By playing along at home you can win up to 5,000,000 guacamoles if the answers are all correct. (Audience—YAAAAAAH!)
- You and Ernest of course split the guacamoles. (Audience—AWWWWWW!)
Shabby: Let's try a practice run, Ernest.

Figure 6-4. A rudimentary stick drawing (with script)...

The outline for the educational goals and outcomes had already been established. When planning out a tutorial, especially a graphics-based one, a storyboard, such as the ones animators and cartoon-strip artists use, are very useful for plotting out ideas in a systematic fashion. Storyboards also serve as a good communication tool, especially if a team is working on a project. Storyboards also serve as a way of documenting your project and for reviewing changes, additions, and deletions. Drawings with the script accompanying also make it easier for your talent if you are doing voiceovers, music, and sound to accompany your project (Figures 6-4 and 6-5).

Assessment

As mentioned above, with any education tools there are two areas of assessment that need to be addressed. When creating a lesson, the teacher always

Figure 6-5. ...morphs into a more sophisticated visual.

includes a mechanism to assess if the student has achieved the established goals and outcomes. In "Cite It Right," because it is an interactive quiz, the student gets immediate feedback. She will win or loose "guacamoles" as part of the game depending on whether she answered correctly or not. This immediate feedback is also intended to help reinforce the concept that many different types of information require citations, not just direct quotes. One of the instructional outcomes of the tutorial is that the student will recognize that various kinds of information need to be cited and that one needs to be careful in scholarly research. Scholarly writing is a very specific and disciplined form of writing for which the student needs specific skills. For "Cite It Right," it is our intent that the assessment part of the tutorial is also an integral part of the teaching process. It is also our intent to make the student aware that they need to be careful, but that scholarly writing is not an impossible task and that it can be rewarding and even entertaining (Figure 6-6).

The tool itself also needs to be assessed to see if the students respond to it and if it is actually teaching them a skill that they can translate to a practical application. Educators know that the long-term effects of instruction are notoriously difficult to assess-but we also know that it is crucial to try. Tools need to be refined and re-done to respond to actual user need and effectiveness. It is our

Figure 6-6. Earnest Student wins the game, wins the guacamoles, and is cheered by an adoring crowd in the cartoon's soundtrack.

long-range plan to continue to asses the tutorials through student and faculty surveys, questionnaires, and interviews. These evaluations will be used to refine and enhance the module packet in order to support the curriculum goals of our faculty and the information literacy needs of our students. For this project, student and faculty engagement and feedback were essential in its development. To date, some very preliminary assessment of the project has been done with students and faculty. The response we have received has been very positive. We hope to learn from the feedback: listening to the stated needs and concerns of our user group and continually tweaking our product.

CHAPTER 7

Teach Your Children Well: The High School Research Experience

Michele D'Angelo-Long

Introduction

As a teacher for 15 years in middle school, high school, and college, I have spent my professional life observing the evolution of young writers. I am familiar with the writing curriculum of elementary schools, have taught in middle schools and high schools, and am now an instructor of undergraduates. I also supervise student teachers. I know first-hand that plagiarism is an important issue in the high school classroom. From my experience, I would theorize that the main problem regarding intellectual dishonesty is not so much an increase in frequency as the fact that it is more difficult to detect because of sophisticated technology and a shift in attitude, on the part of students, as to its acceptability. Students have always cheated. Some hand-copied the bulk of their papers out of the encyclopedia. Others made crib notes-written formulas and test answers on the rims of baseball caps, on hands, or on rubber bands. Now, students text-message answers on cell phones or PDAs. What is perhaps the most disturbing trend for educators is that students, from all levels, are indicating an attitude that plagiarizing papers and cheating in school are not major, ethical transgressions.

According to Professor Donald McCabe, a study of students revealed that 74% have cheated on an exam at least once, 15% have downloaded papers or bought them, and 51% omit their sources in bibliographic entries (Straw, 2002). This problem of cheating is not just a problem in the United States. According to Sadie Williams (2001) from Lancaster University, United Kingdom, of the students in Great Britain, males admit to cheating more than females; weaker students plagiarize more than able ones; and cheating/plagiarism is rarely detected, and when it is, little or no action is taken.

In addition to the trends cited above, high school teachers frequently encounter habits/traits in their students that work against the values of intellectual honesty: lack of motivation or incentive, novice writing skills, faulty research skills, and tendency toward procrastination. Furthermore, it is my experience with young adults that many of them do not understand the significance of plagiarism; they tend to view it as a victimless crime. Finally, I have found that though many high schools have policies on plagiarism, they are frequently not enforced. In the sections that follow, I will attempt to address the culture of high school with regard to plagiarism: student attitudes, the establishment and enforcement of intellectual honesty codes, and attitudes of teachers and administrators. I will also provide some suggestions for teaching strategies that are designed to help eliminate plagiarism.

Attitudes of High School Students Toward Plagiarism

Is it a lack of understanding, indifference, or deliberate dishonesty on the part of students that contributes to incidences of plagiarism? According to Scanlon and Neumann (2002), students tend to understand what plagiarism is, but they do not care. In addition, some students believe that teachers do not actually read their papers. Savvy students are skeptical of papers that come back with grades but no comments. There seems to be a disconnect between the student and teacher in expectation and communication of those expectations. Certainly, then, it would seem that whereas some incidences of plagiarism are inadvertent, some are deliberate. There is a distinct difference between those who honestly do not understand the principles of scholarly writing and those who attempt to play the odds and see if they can cut corners.

According to Ashworth and Bannister (1997), an educational system of mass participation, with broad ranges of students included as well as the introduction of technology into the classroom, allows for less direct student contact with the teacher and a heavier reliance on fellow students through collaborative and group learning and writing. Ashworth and Bannister interviewed a number of students and asked them questions essentially of a moral and ethical nature and found some interesting results regarding attitudes of students toward plagiarism. For example:

Student no. 11 stated: "You can plagiarize someone who's written a book, because they're not on the same level as you. If you copied your friend's work, when you get marked for it you'd be getting her mark, but you're not getting someone else's who's way above you" (Ashworth and Bannister, 1997: 192).

This last notion, that plagiarism is an issue of a *personal* code of conduct based on *situational* ethics, is a curious insight. Students designate types and degrees of cheating. Furthermore, Ashworth and Bannister (1997) claim that students take their cues from teachers and administrators. For instance, if desks are not separated and a no-talking policy is not strictly enforced during an examination, students are more likely to believe that teachers are ignoring-if not permitting-potential cheating. Although as teachers we assume that we have adequately addressed the policy, students often need more emphatic gestures in order to internalize and accept these policies. In addition, these same authors found that students find a contradiction between individually assessing group work and penalizing copying from the group in a collaborative learning exercise (Ashworth and Bannister, 1997: 199). Ashworth and Bannister conclude, "...plagiarism is a far less meaningful concept for students than it is for academic staff, and it ranks relatively low in the student system of values" (Ashworth and Bannister, 1997: 200).

Many of my colleagues who are high school teachers are becoming more alarmed about incidences of student cheating on their class assignments and homework rather than incidences of plagiarism in their papers. They feel that though cheating on assignments (e.g., copying a friend's work or downloading answers from a Web site) is ethically wrong, such actions do a further disservice to the student. He deprives himself the opportunity to practice a skill or learn the new information that the assignment was designed to teach. Conversely, in my work with high school students, I have found the opinion often expressed that teachers do not care and that most of class work and homework is busywork. In response to these assumptions, students use short-cuts-like downloading summaries, outlines, papers from the Internet-and submit it as their own work. If the work is not valued as an expression of an individual or critiqued very carefully, why, a student might wonder, bother with much effort? This brings me to my next point: As high school teachers, those charged with teaching student research and writing skills, we must fully engage in mentoring and guiding the writing process. The next section will outline some strategies for incorporating concepts of intellectual honesty into the curriculum.

Strategies for Teaching Intellectual Honesty

High school teachers know that their students are emerging writers and are likely to make inadvertent plagiarism errors with regard to paraphrasing and summary issues. These students are guilty of lack of skill, not dishonesty. Unfortunately, this is not true for all students. Some attempt to play the odds and see if they can "get something over" their teachers. When asked about tips or strategies to help students avoid plagiarism, Steve Garwood (personal communication), noted New Jersey librarian and lecturer on plagiarism prevention, responded in a December 12, 2003, e-mail interview, offering a three-pronged approach: "1. Have a universal understanding of what plagiarism is and why it is wrong; 2. Have an academic honesty/integrity policy that all follow and are constantly and consistently reminded of; 3. Have that academic honesty policy enforced."

It would seem then that teaching about plagiarism and a systematic enforcement of the school's plagiarism policy should certainly be part of the pedagogy portfolio of a high school teacher. How to deal effectively with a student who is caught plagiarizing is a hot topic in teacher lounges all across America. Boards of education and governing bodies of private schools have differing criteria regarding what constitutes an act of plagiarism. As stated previously, many schools have well-developed policies-but problems can arise with their enforcement. One reason is that it is sometimes difficult for a teacher to navigate the circuitous path of the disciplinary review process schools require in cases of alleged plagiarism. These administrative procedures are often complicated because they contain measures for privacy protection for the student and the teacher. My own experiences as a high school teacher have led me to run through many administrative gauntlets when trying to enforce the ethic of intellectual honesty with my own students. I have, on occasion, been personally frustrated by a lack of the enforcement of policies on plagiarism, especially in instances where parental pressure for leniency or dismissal of charges had been applied. Based on conversations with other high school instructors, I would hazard to say that such instances occur regularly-mine is not an isolated experience.

But it is also important to make sure that the research and writing process is one in which the student is fully engaged. One strategy for making the experience more participatory is to require our students to create a paper trail. Something as simple as changing assignments and suggested topics every semester can serve to prevent paper sharing among students. Requiring students to document a paper trail of the entire process, though time-consuming for both teacher and student, serves to engage actively students in a step-by-step guided research procedure. This would include submission on the part of the student of a working bibliography, potential thesis statement, abstract, outline, note cards, rough draft, and so forth. Perhaps most crucial at this level are scheduling face-to-face conferences with students on their research papers and give them written feedback on their submissions. This personal interaction serves to prevent the student forming the perception that the work they submit is neither properly read nor properly respected by the teacher. Having the students photocopy or print-out all of their research articles serves to organize them and their research material and provides explanatory information should any question of improper referencing of materials arise. Perhaps most importantly for high school students is a clear classroom discussion of what exactly plagiarism is, how it violates all established codes of information ethics, and what the school policy is regarding acts of intellectual dishonesty.

Even with all these safeguards in place, plagiarism may creep into a student paper. However, it would seem to preclude the outright purchasing of papers from paper mills, downloading free papers from the Web, or borrowing papers from other students. The anonymity of the author is gone because the student and teacher are engaged in negotiations throughout the research process. Many high school teachers require research logs to accompany student papers. Some require students to do an oral report to the class along with a written paper. The student is then required to submit to a sort of peer review, as she is expected to defend her paper to her fellow students in a question and answer session. All of these techniques emphasize the importance of proper citation of material and help to teach good scholarship.

Finally, cross-disciplinary initiatives are imperative in teaching the importance of intellectual honesty to our high school students. Good writing is good writing across the curriculum.

With regard to the enforcement of codes, as high school educators, we need to make sure that all students receive stringent sanctions when called for. If punishment seems arbitrary and capricious, or at times nonexistent, students will be more likely to gamble. In our increasingly litigious society, many teachers are concerned about potential litigation resulting from charges of plagiarism. Attorney Ronald B. Standler reviewed cases of alleged plagiarism in 1999 and determined that the court held in all cases against the students accused (Standler, 1999). It would seem then that the courts give weight to the opinion of the educators in these instances.

Of course, we should lead by example and follow the guidelines with regard to fair use and copyright restriction. Public figures as well as historians and journalists have been in the news recently about their lax attribution practices. Plagiarism in high schools can be managed by educating students and imposing consistent consequences. Improved assignment design by faculty as well as collaboration with librarians can help mitigate some of the transgressions. Respect for intellectual property can be promoted through, for example, music examination and concepts of artistic ownership, something students may care much more about than somebody's opinion on Dickens. (Note: See Garwood's Web site Steve Garwood: Classes and Presentations for Libraries, available at www.stevegarwood.com/classes. It is a free Web site and suggests a comparison of oldies as they are used in hip-hop music and makes a comparison to plagiarism.)

Final Thoughts and Conclusion

Clearly, we need to be active educators if we expect to teach our students to meet the challenges and temptations of plagiarism in the twenty-first century, which brings me to another point that has been raised by students: What are they expected to know that they can write about with any kind of certainty and authority? In other words, when we assign complex readings of literature, for example, how do we expect them to write papers honestly with real and interesting voices on subjects that we ourselves have worked long and hard to understand? We need to look at the complexity of the assignments and determine if a student would be able to discuss them in writing using his or her own words.

There are games for students to play to determine what plagiarism is and is not on Purdue University's Online Writing Lab (OWL) site (http://owl.english.purdue.edu/handouts/research/r_plagiar.html). That might make an interesting lesson, and the class could end with students developing their own academic integrity policies for use in your classroom as Garwood suggests. It is important for us to remember that academic honesty is a lesson that must be repeated and emphasized throughout the school year. Garwood suggests exhibiting the integrity policies that the students devise, as well as the official school policy, on the school and classroom Web sites in addition to posting around photocopiers and printers, on bulletin boards, and sending the policies home via newsletters.

Scanlon and Neumann (2002) suggest that high school plagiarism is roughly double that of college plagiarism. Their research results from students self-reporting plagiarism infractions. Clearly, all of the research points to at least 80% of all high school students admitting to at least one instance of plagiarism, and that number seems to be consistent from studies conducted in the 1960s (Hansen, 2003). According to Scanlon and Neumann (2002), students know that plagiarism is wrong but continue to do it. Ashworth and Bannister (1997) found in Great Britain that students felt stealing from someone they knew was far worse than stealing from a book or a university professor.

It is important for educators to acknowledge that deliberate cheating and incidences of plagiarism occur among students. These students should be held accountable according to the policies established by the schools that they attend. According to McCabe, cheating is actually much higher than reported because when students self-report their plagiarism, they still seem to misunderstand the nuances of plagiarism, and many have varying views on what plagiarism is. McCabe believes that college cheating is higher than in the past, due mostly to cut-and-paste technology options and massive increases in exam cheating (Hansen, 2003). In a keynote address on December 3, 2003, at the College of St. Elizabeth, New Jersey, Donald McCabe reported the results of a 2001 survey of 4,500 high school students, which indicated that widespread cheating occurs and that the students find it easy to rationalize that cheating (McCabe, 2003). He also stated that students feel that many teachers ignore cheating and that 30% of those students admitted to repetitive serious cheating-and this is just what the students self-reported!

So where does that leave us in our quest to prepare our high school students to be information-literate citizens who value the idea of intellectual honesty? I think that our approach must be on several fronts. First, we must make sure that we are clearly explaining what intellectual honesty is and what constitutes plagiarism. Second, we must establish clear policies and consequences for violations to the policies that protect intellectual integrity. Third, we must incorporate cross-disciplinary, guided research assignments that engage students and give them ownership of their finished product. Last, we must have the courage of conviction to follow the process through if a student is caught deliberately cheating.

Cheating will always occur. The determined student will try to outsmart any safeguards a teacher may build into the research process. However, through good pedagogy, personal involvement, and a clear articulation of expectations, we will be better prepared to navigate an age-old problem in a high-tech age.

Works Cited

Ashworth, Peter, and Phillip Bannister. 1997. "Guilty in Whose Eyes?: University Students' Perceptions of Cheating and Plagiarism in Academic Work and Assessment." *Studies in Higher Education* 22(2): 187–203.

Hansen, Brian. 2003. "Combating Plagiarism." *CQ Researcher* September 19: 773–796.

McCabe, Donald. 2003. "Promoting Academic Integrity in the Internet Age." Keynote address at the Ethics and Legal Issues Symposium 2003, New Jersey.

Scanlon, Patrick, and David Neumann. 2002. "Internet Plagiarism among College Students." *Journal of College Student Development* 43(3): 374–385.

Standler, Ronald B. "Plagiarism in Colleges in USA." Dr. Ronald B. Standler's Professional Homepage. (December 1999) Available: www.rbs2.com/plag.htm.

Straw, Deborah. "The Plagiarism of Generation 'Why Not?' " *Community College Week* 14(24): 4–6.

Williams, Sadie. "How do I Know if They're Cheating? Teacher Strategies in an

Information Age." *Curriculum Journal* 12(2): 225–239.

CHAPTER 8

Communicating Honesty: Building on the Student-Teacher Relationship

Dr. Mallika Henry

Introduction

Consider this encounter. At a political rally, I mention to the woman next to me that I teach writing at Rutgers University. She replies, "Oh yes. It's a good program. I used to work as a contract writer for a company that also sold parts of dissertations to Rutgers students. Some of these students actually rewrote the parts of their dissertations that they bought from the company." Nothing is sacrosanct. Apparently, it is commonplace for students to purchase or repackage their essays or dissertations, so much so that it comes up in casual conversation as a "given" of academic life. Equally troublesome is that there is no "magic bullet" for plagiarism detection. Software packages available for plagiarism detection are only useful for online resources. No software program can detect work copied from hard-copy sources, work that other students have written and shared offline, material that is online but a few layers within a database, or the student papers that fraternities may keep on file.

But why *is* it so important to detect and prevent plagiarism? Is this only to enforce "the rules" of academia? No, I believe preventing plagiarisms contributes crucially to the unfolding of a student's education. I have helped a wide range of individuals learn to write English—from United Nations officials and research scientists to homeless mothers and, most recently, college undergraduates. I believe that writing is an important and personal process of communicating one's ideas in increasingly sophisticated symbolic terms. The frontline against plagiarism should be in nurturing the pride and interest students take in their own work. Faculty cannot ignore incidences of plagiarism. To do so prevents students from taking those conceptual and rhetorical steps needed to develop their own ideas and language. By ignoring plagiarism, we have given them tacit permission to appropriate the language and ideas of others. However, if our students find an assignment compelling, find their own progress compelling, or see the scholarly writing process as an important achievement, they are unlikely to plagiarize. I maintain that the main focus of educators should be on the ideas of their students, their efforts to develop new concepts through language, and their ability to convey them. The other crucial component in plagiarism prevention is for faculty to make the expectations of the assignment clear and for the process to be as transparent as possible.

In the chapter that follows, I will discuss the underlying principles of a pedagogy based on my experiences with teaching undergraduate research and writing courses in very different educational institutions—York College of the City University of New York and Rutgers University. It focuses on the process of developing clear communication through good writing skills-in combination with close faculty attention, guidance, and input for each stage of the student's writing process. An additional benefit to this pedagogical strategy is that the student learns to think analytically, read carefully, make connections among ideas, develop theses logically, and present ideas clearly. Intellectual dishonesty is circumvented.

Trust and Pedagogy: The Student-Teacher Relationship

And if it should be asked to what the writer is appealing, the answer is simple. The writer appeals to the reader's freedom to collaborate in the production of his work
  —Jean Paul Sartre (1965: 41)

In any scholarly endeavor, the act of writing is an exercise in learning to communicate. Sartre puts it more elegantly: This communication frees the writer, and the reader, to affirm their respective existences through a new possibility of action and thought. In my freshman writing classes, I teach students who are at a new threshold—one of new standards of academic scholarship and a new level of independence. They are on their own in the college classroom where learning is their own responsibility. They are making a transition from living at home, with the parental relationships this entails, to managing their time and energy on their own with much less supervision. Freshmen often seem confused about expectations inherent in the relationships with adults around them. Perhaps they are not so much confused as testing assumptions and approaches that they can use in their lives as independent adults. Important relationships in this calculation are those with their teachers.

Students need to trust their instructors in order to take the risks that can lead them to excellent work. Writing is, in fact, a particularly intimate activity that reveals personal perceptions more than other kinds of schoolwork. The first-day writing samples that we have students produce implicitly narrate the many kinds of adventures students are having as their first year away from home begins. The attitudes of students toward the process of scholarly writing (i.e., whether students will learn to accept the challenges of their academic adventure and its newly available freedom by struggling with difficult learning processes or whether they will take short-cuts, including plagiarism) cannot be decoded from the first few initial assignments. An in-class writing assignment, however, can show whether a student has a basic ease with her own words or whether she is lost without extra help. I always keep the in-class writing samples on hand as a first indication of what to expect from my students, a kind of baseline study for reference. But I also try to understand each student from this initial sample in order to follow her trajectory through the semester. No matter what the discipline, an initial in-class writing assignment, no matter how short, can serve as a snapshot of each student's writing ability and stage of development in the scholarly writing process. It also communicates to the student: I am interested in what you have to say.

Attention to a student's initial writing sample is crucial. With this first exchange, the student begins to form a perception of the teacher as well as a perception of how the teacher views *him*. Students watch to see if the teacher is paying attention: Is she really reading what I write? Is she interested enough that it is worth my while to try, or is she going through the motions? Is she attentive to my work as an individual, or will she just settle for any assignment turned in on time? Within any class, students register a range of attitudes toward their instructor. Some students expect to be overlooked. They hide in the back of the class and recoil from group activities. Some of these students may have very interesting things to say if given a free rein in in-class writing exercises but approach group assignments with dread, because they are not enjoying the task and not expecting to succeed. Most students look for the teacher's political agendas, prejudices, or other ways to label the teacher. What does she want me to say-what kinds of ideas will she reward, and what kinds will she punish? I also find it important at this stage to comment on whether the student is using her own words. Even at this stage, an instructor can easily point out, "If you want to quote your source, you must use quotes, or it is considered plagiarism." A nonconfrontational comment can set up expectations that "proper use of sources" is being monitored.

The task of grading and assigning writing projects is a time-consuming one for faculty members but one that presents an opportunity for communicating individually with each student. It can be an important part of forming a student/teacher relationship. Within this relationship, the process of grading papers (or even just commenting on them) and judging each student on the merits of his scholarly writing skills, including intellectual honesty, is perhaps one of the most difficult tasks for an instructor. Smothering a student with comments leaves him no room to see his own way forward. Sparse comments leave a student clueless or overconfident. Every faculty member develops a method of getting through the stacks of assignments by determining what is important to the conversation with students in the grades and comments given. In my experience, one of the first expectations that a teacher needs to communicate to the student is that, in accordance with all established codes of intellectual honesty, all work turned-in should be his own and plagiarism will not be tolerated. Second, the student needs to know that the teacher *is* paying attention; is in fact trying to understand what the student is trying to say. Finally, faculty should communicate to the student that each task assigned is designed to help that student further and develop his own research and writing through work on his project. Faculty should clarify the reason for each assignment in terms of the student's needs. For example, in research courses, I align each assignment with the student's ultimate research project. Faculty should also let a student know, in a constructive way, when a chosen project is unacceptable for intellectual or logical reasons and emphasize that any critiques are to further the student's skills and help him toward academic success.

One tactic I use with students in research courses is to request that they bring their own discussion in to every use of quotes or source material. I request that students demonstrate a logical analysis of the sources they are using and not use the sources as substitutes for their own words. If language looks unusually polished, seamless, or overly sophisticated to me, I ask the student to discuss, in her own words, the meaning of the information. I also request that she include discussion and analysis in all future use of sources, because I am asking her to write, not just summarize, information. I let them know that writing means stretching your verbal muscles to make sense of, discuss, analyze, and critique the readings and sources they use. In any discipline, the teacher or professor can require that students "unpack" or analyze the information they are using as a regular exercise in using sources.

Another approach is to use the public forum of the class for explaining comments on papers, engaging students in a critical discussion of what may be wrong with individual student's theses or development. By extending this discussion to the whole class, it becomes possible to treat the student's work as containing intellectual challenges and not personal mistakes. By asking the rest of the class to participate, we invite students to understand that they can enter the public discourse themselves, much as a graduate seminar provokes discussion, critique, and brainstorming about papers that enter the public domain of the group. Their ideas and their critiques become instruments of learning for the entire class. Using the public domain is a check on plagiarism that keeps the writing process transparent.

It is my experience that this kind of close attention to the student's work is actually becoming the exception in college classrooms. Many students attend lecture courses with hundreds of people in an auditorium. The experience of students may be such that they do not expect a teacher to become too closely involved with their personal expression. Furthermore, it is my observation, having worked in the multicultural environment of the United Nations, that Americans, more so than other world citizens, find it difficult to debate ideas on their purely intellectual merit. We tend to take intellectual stances personally. Of course, college freshmen, in particular, need to adjust to the notion that their teacher will critique their writing closely, to help them develop intellectually responsible ways of reasoning and writing. In this, students need to learn to trust their instructor to guide them through the process of thinking, reasoning, and critiquing as part of intellectual development.

In the writing courses I teach, students read, discuss, and build on ideas of readings. Readings in a freshman writing course may be various cross-disciplinary essays; in some research courses they may focus on a particular discipline. In either case, I normally use readings of a political nature, because I consider my students as citizens-in-training. Many students react with suspicion (Is this professor trying to push a leftist agenda?). Some react emotionally and can cling dogmatically to political positions. For precisely these reasons, I try to get students to use critical reasoning to explicate their ideas and logical reasoning about political issues. In keeping with the current political climate, my students often initially assume that their political views are inviolate, off limits as far as my comments go. It has been my experience recently that due to current events, political attitudes in the United States are becoming increasingly polarized and solidified. Our in-class ideological debates have become highly charged. Each person is encouraged to develop her own ideas, and all ideas are respected. As the instructor, however, it is my responsibility to point out any flaws in a student's critical thinking: faulty logic, superficial reading habits, deliberate misreading to further her own agenda, use of emotional arguments over logic, or a tendency to harangue the reader rather than logically develop a point. Once students can see the elegance and power of clearly articulated ideas over dogma, they often learn to enjoy the exercise of logic and thematic development. This is the greatest insurance against plagiarism: the actual enjoyment and ownership of ideas.

Finally, in their relationship with their instructor, students must realize that this process of scholarly research and writing is entirely about the development of their skills and their work. In my writing classes, the emphasis is on student performance, peer and self-review, with me overseeing the process. We spend the first day of class doing in-class writing: students respond to a reading and essay question with an in-class writing sample. The first day of class they immediately begin to do their own work. It is their work that we discuss, their response to readings, their successes and failures. When students realize that the work of the semester is their own, they can rise to the challenge or try to avoid it, but they must know that attention is focused on each step of their writing process. That is a first step to engaging in an agreement between us-that they will work hard and I will be attentive to it, helping them as best I can.

Relationships among Students

The imagination of the spectator has not only a regulating function, but a constitutive one. It…is called upon to recompose the beautiful object beyond the traces left by the artist.
—Jean Paul Sartre (1965: 41)

Through peer evaluation, students collaborate in the process of research and writing. This is only possible when students learn that this process is one that requires constant assessment and revision until a project's completion. I try to teach my students to be self-critical and self-conscious about their work. Otherwise the writing process seems like a kind of black box. Take a topic, riff on it, and out comes one's precious, inviolate personal expression. Instead, I try to instill the notion that writing is a process that can be tweaked (in essay writing, almost endlessly) for a higher academic standard of achievement, otherwise students tend to identify closely with their writing without quite understanding the skills and critical process involved. A lack of understanding of the scholarly writing process also renders a student more vulnerable to the temptation of simply using another person's black box. With my students, I attempt to expose the process of expository writing and lay bare the mechanics of the essay.

In my opinion, students in all disciplines should know the anatomy of the research and writing process for the discipline they are engaged in studying. This demystification establishes teacher expectations for writing projects and encourages intellectual honesty and good work habits. It is the sad perception among many writing instructors that they are responsible for correcting long-neglected problems for students, language issues that have been passed over by their other instructors. Writing professors, especially in institutions where student populations demonstrate significant skill gaps, face their seemingly

Sisyphean tasks with a sense of stoicism, feeling they just cannot resolve all the issues within a semester or a year. In fact, the National Commission on Writing in America's Schools and Colleges reported last year that whereas writing is the most important of learning skills and "the mechanism through which they learn to connect the dots in their knowledge," it is generally ignored in most American schools. "Writing, always time-consuming for student and teacher, is today hard-pressed in the American classroom," the report said. "Of the three R's, writing is clearly the most neglected" (Lewin, 2003). Fortunately, this is not true everywhere—my 12-year-old nephew studies in a private school in Oregon. Each course involves extensive writing, to the extent that in American history class he is writing a Civil War novella. Though this may seem an unaffordable luxury in public schools throughout the country, it is not necessarily a luxury at all. Writing, reading and thinking—we all know they are the essential tools for learning.

The importance of a hands-on approach can be illustrated with an experience that I had with a foreign-born student whose first language was not English. Her family placed great value on grades. She confided that she felt under tremendous pressure to achieve good grades in her writing courses, although she did not have a personal aptitude in language arts. She had started her college language courses at the most remedial level and worked her way up, with pretty good grades, to the level at which I taught her, a writing and research course that requires manipulating conceptual frameworks to analyze research cases. Though she had a good record, her work in my class was opaque and made little sense. Working with her tutor, I finally understood how she wrote. She had mastered a kind of cut-and-paste method of rearranging the words of her sources to sound fluent and sensible. But she herself could not explain what the words really meant. She could not discuss her work at all. She was using the verbal skills of others to get through her writing courses. Her tutor told me he had spent an hour and half in one session trying to help her form three sentences of her own. Her method had gotten her past many instructors and had gone undetected as a form of plagiarism. She was not engaged in deliberate dishonesty but rather needed instructional intervention and guidance. She had a lack of understanding of the process and the procedures of scholarly writing.

Unless instructors insist on having a dialogue with students about their work, students can find successful strategies for avoiding learning to write at all. Rather, instructors must be alert to the efforts students make to express new ideas and encourage them. They must also pay close attention to redrafting and editing. Making demands on students to clarify and take control of their own risky ideas may be a struggle, but it can finally empower the student to really learn to write.

Peer review is one way to teach the editing process. Having students share their work and pose questions to each other reinforces skills and can be very effective. Furthermore, it teaches students to lay their work on the table, without personal embarrassment, and discuss it as a process. I use two main methods of peer work: peer reviews of one another's drafts, and student sample work in which the class works on copies made of samples of certain student work. In the peer review process, students pass their papers back to one another for comment on initial drafts, using a set of guidelines the instructor prepares. Often, student comments show a level of sophistication that the writing itself does not show. Students learn from scrutinizing another's work more easily than scrutinizing their own. They also learn by instructing one another through their comments.

In my use of the student sample process, I have groups of students work on copies of selected student papers. They address specific technical problems with the papers based on the writing skills that have been discussed in class. Through this collaborative process, the class eventually knows who is writing what and what needs work. This reinforces for students the purely technical aspects of writing—rhetorical, grammatical and logical—helps them to more easily accept criticism, and encourages them to constantly improve their own efforts.

I have found that students are more demanding and less diplomatic with one another than faculty tend to be. They also tend to recognize writing trouble-spots more in someone else's work than in their own. I have also observed with my students that criticism of their work seems less stress-inducing when it comes from a fellow student rather than the instructor. Research shows that students can learn more from their own peers, who are a few steps ahead of them, than from someone of an entirely different status like a teacher. This finding, called the Blatt effect, refers to studies of moral education through peer education, in which it has been found that students tend to learn from peers who are one step ahead of them. In this educational method, the teacher plays a Socratic role, probing the students and confronting their assumptions (Scharf, 1978: 3). For these reasons, it is important to foster good working relationships among students. At the same time, this peer-evaluation process serves as a safeguard against plagiarism, as it fosters a notion of interest, pride, and ownership in one's own work.

Relationship to Ideas: Learning to Fly

I feel that the student's relationship to learning may be the crucial piece determining her likelihood of plagiarizing. Learning does not just depend on the student's comfort level in the classroom, with the instructor, or with the curriculum. Learning occurs, needless to say, throughout daily life and depends on the student's enthusiasm about new ideas, taking conceptual risks, and actualizing her own potential. It depends on the student's willingness to actively construct her own world while respecting the constructions of others.

One problem I encounter with students in this increasingly nonverbal age is that they often think of ideas as limited in quantity, in a parsimonious universe that doles units of thought out to the elite. This is understandable, given the many ways our world is shaped by mercantilist metaphors. Paulo Freire describes the "banking" concept of education, "in which the students are the depositories and the teacher is the depositor" (Freire, 1994). This makes knowledge a limited quantity, resistant to wide distribution. Students are often afraid they cannot have any ideas, because someone's taken them, someone more privileged than they. Students who are not avid readers sometimes do not trust that ideas are infinite. This pedagogy asks students to construct new ideas by making connections between readings. When first challenged to do this, students often feel as if it will simply be impossible to find a new idea and be completely out of the question to fill five pages with their own writing unless they pad the margins or use extensive quotes. It sometimes takes the entire semester for a student to understand that he can have an infinite number of his own ideas without resorting to summarizing the ideas of others.

Obviously, this issue involves the individual's self-concept as well, as does any issue of confidence. The student who is intimidated by the English language for some reason, and who fears failure or who fears success, will struggle before he even gets to the starting line. Such a student cannot easily fly with new ideas. Faculty guidance and mentoring is especially crucial for such a student.

Another root of the problem is the age of the "24/7 media." Interesting discussions of the effect of our nonverbal media on our psyches began with Daniel Boorstin's seminal work *The Image,* published in 1962. More recent treatments include Todd Gitlin's (2002) *Media Unlimited: How the Torrent of Images and Sounds Overwhelms Our Lives*, which describes the ways in which we are shielded from reality by a kind of plasma of artificial emotions, and an essay by Mitchell Stephens on the difference between the logic of print and the flow of the visual, printed in *The New Humanities Reader* used by the Rutgers Writing Program (Stephens, 2001). Because of the bombardment of advertising and spin, not only do students struggle with realizing there are an infinite number of ideas available in the intellectual ether, they also struggle with realizing that they can have power over these ideas. Though many students are sophisticated about decoding the messages advertising uses to manipulate them, they often remain in a passive relationship to these messages. Though their cynicism and worldly wisdom render them critical about received ideas, they often have little experience with actively formulating messages of their own. Often, their first attempts are crude and confrontational. It is only through working with the skills involved in understanding their own promising moments, learning to develop them, and mastering the conceptual elements of their own writing that students can learn to fly. If students can fly with their own ideas, plagiarism comes to seem merely a crutch for those unable to get off the ground.

Furthermore, many students today seem to have absorbed the notion that everyone in the world is divided into partisan camps, and that once they understand what "side" someone is on, they can predict everything that person will say (Leo, 2003: 66). This incredibly unfortunate climate means that students are all the quicker to look for labels and ideologies and less likely to listen carefully to someone's potentially new point of view. All of this imposes the task on the instructor of discussing the ideas of students in the classroom, pointing out their value and potential and giving logical explanations for strengths and weaknesses. My work with undergraduate students has convinced me that students today need to learn that ideas really do matter. Ideology shapes world events, and critical thinking skills are needed to analyze the ideology behind the events. I often wonder why so many of my students seem unwilling to use real examples, rather than vague generalities, to make their points. Is it because they are afraid of a possible confrontation with political stances, or are they somewhat afraid of starting to think about the powerful implications of confronting real events?

Are students afraid to test their critical powers against this world, or do they feel they are being discouraged to do so? Many of my older students, who are experienced in the working world as business people, military personnel, or police officers, feel intimidated about writing about any controversy. Or have they simply lost faith in the power of ideas? There is probably some mixture of all of these possibilities in the minds of my students. Naturally, I have found that the more these students actually make an effort to use their own critical capacity on current events, the more discerning and humane their personal politics become and the clearer their writing becomes.

Here is an example. A recent student of mine was a nontraditional undergraduate—a middle-aged, African-American woman, obviously intelligent and well informed, but not well organized in her written self-expression. Initially, her class work was sketchy, grammatically incorrect, colloquial, and imprecise. During one session, the class analyzed a *New York Review of Books* essay on the problems of social safety nets. We were researching material to respond to the topic question: What are the differences, in America, between the perceptions and the realities regarding the recipients of social welfare programs? This student was clearly disturbed by the content of the article and missed the next class. When she returned on the following class, she handed in her first articulate, clear, precise piece of writing: a research proposal to study the strategies African-American women use to combat poverty in their lives. When this student gave herself permission to tackle a real problem she faced in her writing, she suddenly found a reason to write well.

Trust and Writing: The Mechanics of Teaching Writing across the Curriculum

It has often been observed that an object in a story does not derive its density of existence from the number and length of the descriptions devoted to it, but from the complexity of its connections with the different characters. The more often the characters handle it, take it up, and put it down, in short, go beyond it towards their own ends, the more real will it appear.
—*Jean Paul Sartre (1965: 55)*

Constructing Knowledge Through Connections

Scholarly writing is about making connections between ideas, a process fundamental to the pedagogy I use. In the section that follows, I will outline, step-by-step, the process that I use in my courses with undergraduate students. Although this approach is specifically designed for the teaching of writing, the methodology aims to teach students scholarly writing in any discipline and could definitely be used in any curriculum. The approach described here is based on the synthetic knowledge constructed on making connections among works of existing scholarship. These connections can give students the opportunity to create knowledge, which is the work of scholarship.

(1) Students are assigned readings, one at a time, but usually two or more are required for each of the student's own written essay. In some courses, the readings cohere around a particular research area. For example, I have developed a curriculum for teaching human rights, and a packet of readings that all pertain to human rights. I introduce readings with discussion or with a worksheet I call "Introducing (the author)." The worksheet lists different excerpts from the reading, with some general study questions. (Sometimes I simply require students to type-up answers to study questions, to monitor how well they understand the readings.) I ask individual students to read these excerpts out loud to introduce the students to the style, rhythm, and content of the essay. None of these essays is simple—most give the students a fair degree of difficulty. I spend some time on these selected excerpts, assisting the students just so far with exploring the possibilities of their new assignment, as they themselves will have the further task of finding connections among the readings. The assignment is then to read the text carefully, underlining and making marginal notes to assist in making further use of the text.

(2) Having read the essay(s), students are given a written assignment to write their own essay. This assignment asks them to make connections among the assigned texts in an essay that responds to a fairly general question. The essay question is nonspecific enough to challenge the students to formulate their own theses for their essays. They are told to resist summarizing the readings-that will ensure failure. With the assignment in hand, students are divided into groups, each group tasked to look for specific connections among the assigned texts. Each group presents its findings with relevant quotes from the texts to support their points.

(3) Students are expected to produce a first draft by the next class. The first draft is three to five pages long, substantive enough that we can use it for class work, but clearly an initial attempt that will require revision. One of the educational outcomes for the "Research in the Disciplines" course at Rutgers University is that the student will identify different types of scholarly articles—those that use a theoretical/conceptual framework versus those that are based on case studies. The students are expected to articulate what conceptual framework the author of the article uses. The students are then *required* to use the theoretical frameworks from the readings in their own research essays. Students are required to show analysis using a frame and a case and are graded accordingly. This can be a useful tool for focusing students on analytic writing, though it may have less relevance in certain topic areas.

(4) Students peer review each other's drafts, using guidelines the instructor provides to direct their critical comments. Students are asked to be encouraging with one another and to find promising moments in each other's papers. Students should learn to rely on one another and to read each other's papers constructively to help them to self-correct their own work.

(5) The next classroom session is for student sample work. The instructor selects excerpts from various drafts for Xeroxing so the whole class can participate in commenting, critiquing, correcting, and understanding some student work in common.

(6) The next assignment is to complete the final draft of at least five pages. This will be graded according to precise grading criteria that measure the quality of the thesis, the use of texts in supporting points, the development of the thesis, and overall presentation.

(7) Students hand in the final draft with the first draft and peer review comments stapled behind it. The instructor then has a clear view of the progression of the individual's writing and a solid record of the process, making plagiarism difficult to conceal. I require students to hand-in first drafts if they expect their final drafts to be graded.

(8) The second assigned essay should include a reading the student has found, through library and database research, on his own research interest. Students are still required to use a conceptual frame to analyze a specific case, but this time that case is one of their own choosing. The same process of peer review and student samples can be followed, but it may not always be possible to find student samples that can help the entire class, as each student has selected a different case study. However, it may be relevant to use excellent student papers from previous semesters to demonstrate specific technical issues.

(9) Further essay assignments are drafts of the final research project. They specifically focus on the student's chosen research topic, with increasing source requirements, page requirements, and criteria of analysis and complexity. Each can be subjected to peer review and student sample work. As the students intensify their research, the temptations to plagiarize may increase, and it may become more difficult for the instructor to monitor. At this point, I require that students begin to structure their paragraphs according to the following criteria: each paragraph should have more than one source, quoted or cited, and must discuss the synthesis and analysis of these somewhat divergent views from their sources on the given issue. The student's own analysis must be clear in the paragraph and must be reflected in the topic sentence. Paragraphs that simply report or summarize information taken from readings must be revised to show discussion and analysis. As students develop topic sentences that reflect their own analysis, they find their emerging projects and their clear positions through close reading and writing from the textual sources. An excellent paper will have a clearly developed project that is based on transparent analysis of the given sources. It will carry its own weight in terms of evidence and have a well-controlled development. Through successive drafts, the instructor can monitor and guide the student in making the best use of sources, analyzing them clearly, deriving a succinct and developed conceptual structure, and refining its expression.

Other steps may take place at the discretion of the instructor. The instructor can ask the student questions about various stages of her work. Concepts, connections, and analysis of points of view can be discussed in class. Students can be asked to present their work verbally. Thus, it should be clear that the student's writing is exposed at various steps of the process, even publicly reviewed, and discussed for further development. This makes it difficult to pass off a fully formed essay that has not gone through stages of development—a plagiarized essay. The instructor sees many different moments of the student's work, making it clear if it suddenly changes quality or style. Another tool for the teacher is an actual set of grading criteria that assesses the critical abilities of the student's own thinking.

Students should be given clear grading criteria that also enable the instructor to look for new and original ideas, high-quality connections, and well-digested reading comprehension and writing ability. The first category of criteria I use corresponds to the development of a thesis; the second category to the use of quotes in developing and extending ideas and in supporting them. The third category corresponds to the mechanics of developing ideas, logically, paragraph by paragraph. The last category corresponds to presentation. Each essay must conform very closely to the readings of the specific class, discussions and essay questions, as well as establish the trajectory of the student's original thinking. These qualities make it rather difficult to find a made-to-order essay for sale that matches all of these conditions.

Conclusion

Finally, I would like to focus on some key issues in the teaching of writing across the curriculum and discuss the needs of students in various learning environments. Scholarly writing entails the use of a special skill-set and involves special strategies in reading, researching, and analyzing material. Undergraduate students come to us from a wide variety of backgrounds and educational experiences. We should be careful about the assumptions of the skill sets that they bring to their college classrooms—what can be regarded as "givens." The guided research process described above serves to highlight any trouble-spot gaps in knowledge of the procedure that a student has. It is difficult for students who have not learned how to use scholarly sources to appreciate the balance they need to strike between close reading and understanding and developing their own analyses.

Actually, for some of my students, the most difficult barrier to scholarly writing lies in a lack of reading skills. Many of these students have not been previously exposed to material written at a scholarly level—material that they will be expected to read, analyze, and synthesize throughout their college careers. To help these students build their comprehension levels, faculty can give assignments (with feedback mechanisms built in) that require annotating, summarizing, paraphrasing, and discussing scholarly sources. Most plagiarism that I have encountered stems from students' frustrations that they cannot understand, or are too intimidated to try to understand, the readings they are expected to use.

In using scholarly sources, students may also benefit from seeing the exercise as one of simultaneously reading and writing. Each use of a quote is an opportunity for a student to expand upon and develop his own critical thinking skills. As a student writes about a scholarly idea, he often finds it easier to understand the reading itself in more depth. The interplay of reading and writing helps students hone their reading skills and take mastery over their written work. I have found that once students begin to use precise logic to examine a scholarly work and maintain a critical analysis of it, it expands their repertoire and they enjoy these new skills as well.

Students must continually learn to exercise their skills of analysis in order to understand what the writer is saying and to better judge the effect of their own written words. I frequently tell students to analyze their own work to understand the critical points they can develop much further to expand and deepen their essays. Faculty can help improve students' skills of critical analysis through this process of student self-assessment with feedback from the instructor. As with other steps of the guided research process, this monitoring also alerts instructor to any difficulties that a student is experiencing.

The method of frame/case analysis can be very useful for helping students discipline their own analytic skills as well as for preventing plagiarism. The following example illustrates the procedure. In my human rights course, I begin with assigning the class common readings that supply some conceptual frameworks (frames) for the students to use in their initial essays—frameworks for processes of truth and reconciliation, for example, or for relating cultural relativism to human rights. The students then use these frames to analyze cases such as the child amputees of Sierra Leone. But as the students develop their own research, it becomes necessary for them to find their own frameworks. In human rights this is not so difficult, as various human rights conventions are conveniently applicable to specific topics: the Convention on the Rights of the Child covers child labor and other child issues; the Convention for the Elimination of Discrimination Against Women covers women's rights; and so forth. For example, several students have written about the silk industry in India, pinpointing the specific conventions and constitutional laws that are being violated and developing their own discussion around the nature, causes, or impact of such child labor violations. Some very interesting papers have come from my Islamic students who have written about human rights issues for Muslim women, who wish to maintain their own religious context. Some of these students have used passages from the Koran to analyze how interpretations and misinterpretations are used to justify these human rights violations. These students have used as their frames, for example, a synthesis of strictures from the Koran and international law, to analyze issues such as honor killings or the situation of women in Afghanistan. It is clear that this kind of exercise can evoke the student's own ideas and development if pursued carefully. The use of frames requires students to switch perspectives and use a coherent viewpoint to analyze a case. A good essay will maintain a critical distance even from the frame it uses, so it can critique the frame as well. Because conceptual frameworks exist in every scholarly pursuit, this is a widely useful exercise in analytic writing.

In conclusion, when we teach writing skills, we teach the art of self-expression, individuality, scholarly communication, and action. Using this paradigm, plagiarism could be interpreted as the last resort of those who do not yet understand the procedures or of those who feel unequal to these tasks. Thus, one way to head-off the act of plagiarism is to help students understand how important scholarly writing is, how seriously their instructors take it as an indication of a student's understanding and synthesis of the materials presented in class, and how enriching it can be for students as a means of expressing their own beliefs and opinions in a sophisticated and compelling manner.

To write is thus both to disclose the world and to offer it as a task to the generosity of the reader. It is to have recourse to the consciousness of others in order to make one's self be recognized as essential to the totality of being...as the real world is revealed only by action.
         (Sartre, 1965: 54).

Works Cited

Boorstin, Daniel. 1962. *The Image: A Guide to Pseudo Events in America.* New York: Atheneum.

Freire, Paulo. 1994. *Pedagogy of the Oppressed.* New York: Continuum.

Gitlin, Todd. 2002. *Media Unlimited: How the Torrent of Images and Sounds Overwhelms Our Lives.* New York: Henry Holt & Co.

Leo, John. 2003. "Splitting Society, Not Hairs." *US News & World Report* 135, no. 21 (December 15): 66.

Lewin, Tamar. 2003. "Writing in Schools Is Found Both Dismal and Neglected." *New York Times* April 26: Section A, col. 5, p. 15.

Stephens, Mitchell. 2001."Thinking Above the Stream: New Philosophies. In *The New Humanities Reader,* ed. Richard Miller and Kurt Spellmeyer, 541–563. New York: Houghton.

Sartre, Jean Paul. 1965. *What is Literature?* New York: Harper & Row.

Scharf, Peter, Ed. 1978. *Studies in Moral Education.* Minneapolis: Winston Press.

CHAPTER 9

Encouraging Excellence: A Departmental Approach

Dr. Robert E. Wood

Introduction

"It does not identify or credit any sources, but nor does it claim any exclusivity of authorship."

Is the above quote a statement by a student trying to weasel out of an act of blatant plagiarism? No, these were the words of Prime Minister Tony Blair's spokesman in 2003, trying to account for a much-ballyhooed U.K. intelligence document claiming Iraqi possession of weapons of mass destruction that was not only mostly lifted—spelling, grammatical errors and all—from unacknowledged Internet sources but that also failed to mention that much of the data on which it was based was 12 years old (BBC, 2003). Hailed practically as the smoking gun in making his case to the United Nations by U.S. Secretary of State Colin Powell, the episode was an abject reminder of how students hardly have a monopoly on plagiarism and other forms of intellectual dishonesty.

Any teacher trying to fashion a way to deal with plagiarism has to begin with the recognition that a myriad array of forms of intellectual dishonesty not only surround us in the wider world but are often celebrated and rewarded. If the moral compass of students seems shaky at times, we cannot be overly surprised. As a sociologist, I have the good fortune and indeed obligation to address and analyze this societal context in some of my courses. But for most teachers,

95

the societal context is simply an unfortunate fact of life, and the question of what can be done about plagiarism is properly focused at the individual, departmental, or, occasionally, the institutional level.

The fairly extensive literature on academic plagiarism, discussed more fully elsewhere in this volume, reveals clearly that it is a problem with multiple sources that requires multiple strategies to combat. Rutgers-Newark Professor Donald McCabe and his associates (2001a) have been both leading researchers in this field and activists in the Center for Academic Integrity, whose Web site provides access both to research reports and to information on institutional strategies and policies around the country. This chapter provides an account of how the Department of Sociology, Anthropology and Criminal Justice at the Camden campus of Rutgers University has sought to combat plagiarism through a three-pronged strategy designed to address several of the factors that McCabe and others have identified. These consist of:

- Devising assignments and other testing instruments that make plagiarism difficult and self-defeating.
- Using online syllabi and resources to educate students about the seriousness of plagiarism and about how to avoid it.
- Using our "Web-enhanced curriculum" to enhance the knowledge and skills of students in ways that reduce the temptation to plagiarize.

The importance of properly constructed assignments and of educating students about plagiarism is widely recognized in the literature, and the discussion of these two issues below will be relatively brief, mainly emphasizing those factors that have been somewhat innovative in my department's approach. The third strategy of developing a "Web-enhanced curriculum" to reduce the incentive for plagiarism is to my knowledge unique and will elicit more detailed attention in the discussion below.

Making Plagiarism Difficult and Self-Defeating

Amidst the plethora of alarmist headlines and magazine article titles about the "epidemic" of plagiarism, the casual researcher might be startled to come across the following paper titles:

- "Plagiarism: Is It Really So Bad?" (Bates, 2003)
- "Four Reasons to be Happy about Internet Plagiarism" (Hunt, 2003)
- "Forget About Policing Plagiarism. Just Teach" (Howard, 2001)

What these and similar articles collectively argue is that the silver lining of the current plagiarism problem is that it represents—properly interpreted—a wake-up call for overdue reform in our pedagogical strategies. Bates (2003) suggests that the threat of plagiarism can inspire us to get to know our students better, communicate more openly, create truly unique and interesting assignments that vary from semester to semester, to emphasize process by incorporating in-class work, and to require public presentation of the student's work. All these, Bates suggests, will enhance both our teaching and student learning.

Hunt (2003) argues that the advent of downloadable term papers represents "a salutary challenge to practices which ought to be challenged." He asserts that it is "a good thing" that traditional assignments (including the traditional "term paper" itself), the over-focus on grades, and non-interactive rhetorical context of paper-writing are all put into question by the new ease of plagiarism. "By facing this challenge," he suggests, "we will be forced to help our students learn what I believe to be the most important thing they can learn at the university: just how the intellectual enterprise of scholarship and research really works."

Howard (2001) makes a compelling case for the dangers of what she calls the "gotcha" response to plagiarism. Echoing Bates and Hunt, she argues that concern with catching students (ironically made simpler by the very medium that makes plagiarism so easy) should not distract us from addressing shortcomings in our own pedagogy that are to some degree reflected in student plagiarism and that may stem from the failure to adjust our teaching to the changes in our students and in their lives. These shortcomings do not excuse student plagiarism, but "they do demand that we recognize and reform pedagogy that encourages plagiarism because it discourages learning."

Though the vision of Bates, Hunt, and Howard goes beyond merely avoiding plagiarism, the view that teachers often have only themselves to blame for plagiarized assignments has broad currency. In their article on "Internet Plagiarism: Developing Strategies to Curb Student Academic Dishonesty" in *The Internet and Higher Education*, Austin and Brown (1999) provide a useful list of learning approaches that minimize academic dishonesty, culled both from the literature and their own experience. One set involves identifying a type of assignment that will make plagiarism difficult. A second set, closely related, involves specific assignment requirements that minimize the viability of plagiarism: for example, requiring students to turn-in consecutive sections of their assignment over time, including notes and rough drafts; requiring early annotated bibliographies of sources to be used; requiring use of course texts and other materials in the assignment; requiring oral reports and/or in-class written summaries after the paper has been turned in; and so forth. In such a context, a plagiarized paper is likely to stand out like a sore thumb and be quite self-defeating for the student. But in addition, simply getting students working on their papers early by requiring step-by-step assignments greatly reduces the potential for plagiarism, both because plagiarized work would not be tailored to this process and because it helps avoid what is probably the most important immediate source of term paper plagiarism: the combination of delay and panic. In McCabe's and others' research, perceived "laziness" and failure to study or prepare constitute collectively the single most common factor cited by students in explaining why they cheat.

In my department, we have discussed these strategies, and I believe I can say that practically all assignments in our courses incorporate one or more of these techniques, with the partial exception of workbook-based data analysis exercises (usually dealt with mainly by making them a limited part of the student grade). One faculty member has devised a way of submitting these exercises online through WebCT, which at least eliminates the possibility of copying someone else's assignment just before class and which provides an electronic record for easy comparison. In addition, the fact that most of us put our syllabi and assignments online enables us to be familiar with the requirements of other courses, so that "recycling" of work can be more easily identified.

Using Course and Department Materials to Educate Students about Plagiarism

The recent plagiarism literature strongly stresses the importance of "contextual factors"—most notably institutional academic integrity policies and programs, along with student culture—in determining the amount of plagiarism that actually occurs at a given school. Indeed, summarizing their own and others' research, McCabe et al. (2001a: 228) conclude: "The primary implication of this work is that cheating can be most effectively addressed at the institutional level." Well-designed institutional policies and effective educational campaigns are an important ingredient of any good strategy for combating plagiarism (see also Whitley, Jr. and Keith-Spiegel, 2001). Jordan's (2001: 243) study of several predictive variables found "knowledge of institutional policy was the best predictor of cheating rates, followed by mastery motivation and attitudes about cheating."

As with those sources of plagiarism that reside in the larger society, the institutional policy and education program are likely to be outside the immediate purview of most teachers, however. Typically the discussion shifts to the teacher and the classroom at this point, but there is much to recommend a departmentally based strategy as well. For one thing, it helps ensure consistency in standards and expectations among the faculty within the department, as all will be directing students to the same resource.

We have sought as a department to educate students about plagiarism in the following ways:

• Provide online resources both about the university's academic integrity pol-

icy and about what plagiarism is and how to avoid it.
- Link online syllabi directly to the plagiarism and citation Web pages of the department.
- Experiment with required interactive tools, such as online orientation quizzes and online videos.

Though our plagiarism Web page has links to a variety of informational resources, it seeks to be simple, direct, and hard-hitting in its impact. Three key points are bolded and briefly elaborated at the outset. The first seeks to dispel any illusion the student may have that plagiarism is purely an issue between the student and the professor. Most students do not realize that not only are teachers expected to report instances of plagiarism, but that once that is done, a university process kicks in that operates quite independently of the instructor. I often tell my classes about a student who engaged in blatant Internet plagiarism and was easily caught. She was remorseful, and I was prepared to give her a zero on the assignment (which would make it difficult, but not entirely impossible for her to pass the course). The university, however, went ahead and expelled her on its own. Students are often unaware of these broader ramifications of plagiarism.

The second point we emphasize is that most plagiarism is easily detected and proven, thanks in part to the same technological tools that make it easy. Though I believe it is important not to go too far in this direction, having a few "gotcha" professors who help establish a department's reputation for effective sleuthing does not hurt. The point for students is that plagiarism is as stupid as it is dishonest, given the high likelihood of being caught.

The third point is a policy one: that all parties to plagiarism are considered equally guilty. Students providing other students with written assignments are probably the second-largest source of plagiarism that we see (after the Internet). Sometimes the student doing so has little idea that the other student will be stupid enough to hand in the same assignment, but we use our Web site to get the word out that both will be considered equally responsible, and hence no written work should circulate prior to an assignment without explicit instructor approval.

In a fairly typical way, our department Web page on plagiarism also provides links to more detailed resources about what plagiarism is and how to avoid it. A brief section at the end also reminds students that one source of plagiarism is lack of mastery of basic skills and encourages the student to use the resources at our Web-enhanced curriculum, a point that I will return to in the next section.

Many Web pages are forlorn and unvisited, but our plagiarism page receives steady traffic, as documented by server logs. We have devised several ways to encourage this. The most common is to link our online syllabi—which most of us maintain for all our courses—to the department's plagiarism Web page and to require that students familiarize themselves with it as part of the first assignment in the course. It is hard to say how effective this is, but it at least puts the students on notice that knowledge of the policy is their responsibility, and its reiteration in numerous courses and syllabi hopefully reinforces the message. In addition, several of us are experimenting with course-based requirements for online reviews of a variety of basic skills and knowledge (including library research skills as well as understanding of the plagiarism policy) that might become the basis of a departmental-level requirement that, once completed, would apply for all courses.

Increasing Disciplinary Knowledge and Skills via a Web-Enhanced Curriculum

"If teachers taught better we wouldn't have to cheat."
      —12th grade student, cited by McCabe (2001b)

McCabe (2001a) and other researchers have documented with concern the increasing ease with which many students justify plagiarism, including the tendency to blame others—society, teachers, parents—but not themselves. Nonetheless, as noted earlier, it is still worth asking the question whether more effective teaching might serve to reduce plagiarism. As Taylor (2003) explains in his open letter to his students at Oakton Community College in Illinois, real academic integrity requires a great deal from both professors and students alike.

Probably the most important innovation in higher education courses in the past decade has been the Web-enhancement of courses by instructors who have seen in the Web an exciting new tool for teaching. The World Lecture Hall attests to the explosion of increasingly sophisticated experimentation with Web-enhancement, albeit also to its unevenness. Today in my department, almost all full-time members, as well as a number of part-timers, maintain course Web sites that run the gamut from syllabi with hyperlinks to extensive sites with streaming audio and video, the use of WebCT for online quizzes, bulletin boards, online grade access, and more. (Those that use WebCT, however, maintain as much of their course Web sites as possible in nonproprietary Internet space so to retain transparency and maximum public access.)

The pedagogical success of these innovations led several of us in the department to wonder whether the benefits of Web-enhancement at the course level could be scaled up to the department level. This was the beginning of an ongoing project that continues today and that received several years of funding from university grants. The outcome is what we call our "Web-enhanced curriculum." Though plagiarism concerns were not a major factor in its origins, the anticipated increase in student competency in terms of knowledge and basic sociological skills has held the potential to reduce one of the key sources of plagiarism—lack of competence and confidence. It is in terms of this promise that our Web-enhanced curriculum is described below as a departmental strategy for combating plagiarism.

Our goal has been to provide resources for our students that support a broad array of courses across the departmental curriculum and that will help increase student skill and preparedness for upper-level courses. Specifically:

- Clearly stated expectations and guidelines about plagiarism, citation, table and graph format, and disciplinary writing.
- Expanded mechanisms of communication, including an open electronic list, a regular newsletter, photos of department events, advising FAQs, and a Web page on student research opportunities, alongside the standard informational resources found at most departmental Web sites.
- Substantive resources of mastering skills and basic disciplinary knowledge, including online guides and streaming tutorials, a Web page on accessing and using library databases, resources for MicroCase and data analysis, annotated selected Web links for student research, virtual tours of online resources for a variety of subfields, and so forth.

Students sometimes complain about lack of consistency in terms of faculty expectations, and so one function of our Web-enhanced curriculum is to lay out common standards at the departmental level. This allows a variety of different faculty to link to specific pages (e.g., the Web page on proper placement of variables in tables) to define common expectations for their specific assignments. Disciplinary loyalties in our three-discipline department held up agreement on a common citation style for several years, but the department finally agreed in 2004 to standardize on a single (APA) format.

The expanded communications mechanisms are intended not simply to convey information but to build a sense of community among majors and an identification with the department. It is certainly our goal that one part of this will be a student culture of academic integrity. An annual undergraduate research poster session serves both to recognize and to increase the public visibility of the work students do.

Probably the most innovative part of our Web-enhanced curriculum has been the resources that have been developed to facilitate knowledge and master skills not for individual courses but rather for the departmental curriculum as a whole. Some of these resources involve the use of streaming audio and video and are available as streaming slideshows, videos, and "screen movies." Substantively, these resources seek to develop and enhance basic skills and competencies in online library research; quantitative data analysis skills, including the logic of causal arguments and the use of the department's chosen data analysis software

(MicroCase); qualitative data collection and analysis, including ethnographic research; and disciplinary writing. The regularly expanding list of these resources is maintained at the department's Online Research Tutorials and Videos Web page. Specific examples include:

- A video by a department member that uses film footage from her research in West Africa to teach basic ethnographic field techniques.
- A narrated video slideshow of the criteria that have to be met to make a causal argument, including a detailed discussion of the problem of spurious correlations.
- A narrated slideshow on the different types of variables used in multivariate analysis.
- Narrated "screen movies" that demonstrate the steps involved in using MicroCase to test a hypothesis and to introduce a control variable.

Indeed, the Web site even offers a "screen movie" to give students a virtual tour of what is available at the Web site (including guidance on plagiarism) and how it can be useful to them.

Based on surveys and grades, we have quite strong data on the positive effects of the Web-enhancement of courses, something consistent with published reports (e.g., Sanders and Morrison-Shetlar, 2001; Stith, 2000). It is much more difficult to measure the impact of our Web-enhanced curriculum, although server logs show it to be by far the most used department site at Rutgers-Camden, and we have good anecdotal evidence from students about its usefulness for them. Extending the linkage to the level of plagiarism is even more difficult and probably impossible to measure given the tools that we have. Nonetheless, the literature on plagiarism gives us confidence that increasing student skills and competencies should reduce the temptation to plagiarize, and my impressionistic sense is that serious plagiarism, though still with us, has probably declined at a time when national surveys indicate that it is on the rise. And for what it's worth, our Web-enhanced curriculum was a major factor in our winning the Rutgers university-wide "Programmatic Excellence Award in Undergraduate Education" in 2003.

Conclusion

Plagiarism has to be dealt with at many levels, but our department's experience suggests that a department-level response—intermediate to the overall institution and individual instructors—may have some special virtues. The department, being closer to students, may be more effective in spreading the word about institutional policies and expectations. At the same time, the department is more in a position to offer a coherent set of expectations and generally useful resources than individual faculty members can through specific courses.

As discussed above, our department's efforts have focused on three areas: (1) encouraging faculty members to embrace teaching and learning strategies that make plagiarism difficult and very likely counterproductive; (2) using a combination of course and departmental online materials and devices to educate students about plagiarism; and (3) facilitating disciplinary knowledge and skill-building through the development of an extensive Web-enhanced curriculum, thereby reducing the temptation to resort to plagiarism born of ignorance and desperation. We offer our experience and Web site as a potential model for others and encourage readers to explore and make use of the resources there.

Web Sites Referenced

Center for Academic Integrity: www.academicintegrity.org/index.asp.

Rutgers Department of Sociology, Anthropology and Criminal Justice

Homepage: http://sociology.camden.rutgers.edu/.

Web-enhanced Curriculum Homepage: http://sociology.camden.rutgers.edu/curriculum/.

Plagiarism Policy Web Page: http://sociology.camden.rutgers.edu/curriculum/plagiarism.htm.

Online Research Tutorials and Videos Web page: http://sociology.camden.rutgers.edu/curriculum/tutorials.htm.

World Lecture Hall: www.utexas.edu/world/lecture.

Works Cited

Austin, M. Jill and Linda D. Brown. 1999. "Internet Plagiarism: Developing Strategies to Curb Student Academic Dishonesty." *The Internet and Higher Education* 2(1): 21–33.

Bates, Laura. 2003. "Plagiarism: Is It Really So Bad?" Indiana State University, Center for Teaching and Learning, Terre Haute, Indiana. Available: www.indstate.edu/ctl/tips/tip4_12.html.

British Broadcasting Corporation (BBC). 2003. "Iraq Dossier 'Solid'—Downing Street." *BBC News World Edition* 7 February. Available: http://news.bbc.co.uk/2/hi/uk_news/politics/2735031.stm.

Hunt, Russell. 2003. "Four Reasons to be Happy about Internet Plagiarism." Russell Hunt, Homepage. St. Thomas University, Fredericton, New Brunswick, Canada. Available: www.stu.ca/~hunt/4reasons.htm.

Howard, Rebecca Moore. 2001. "Forget About Policing Plagiarism. Just Teach." *Chronicle of Higher Education* 16 November: B24. Available: http://chronicle.com/weekly/v48/i12/12b02401.htm.

McCabe, Donald L., Linda Klebe Trevino, and Kenneth D. Butterfield. 2001a. "Cheating in Academic Institutions: A Decade of Research." *Ethics and Behavior* 11(3): 219–232.

McCabe, Donald L. 2000b. "Academic Integrity-A Research Update." PowerPoint Presentation to Center for Academic Integrity, Texas A & M, October 20, 2001. Available: http://ethics.acusd.edu/video/cai/2001/McCabe/index_files/v3_document.html.

Sanders, Diane W. 2001. "Student Attitudes toward Web-Enhanced Instruction in an Introductory Biology Course." *Journal of Research on Computing in Education* 33(3): 251–262.

Stith, Brad. 2000. "Web-Enhanced Lecture Course Scores Big with Students and Faculty." *THE Journal* 27(8): 20. Available online through subscription: http://ebscohost.com.

Taylor, Bill. "Integrity: Academic and Political. A Letter to My Students." (cited 14 December, 2003) Available: www.academicintegrity.org/pdf/Letter_To_My_Students.pdf.

Whitley, Bernard E., Jr., and Patricia Keith-Spiegel, 2001. "Academic Integrity as an Institutional Issue." *Ethics and Behavior* 11(3): 325–342.

CHAPTER 10

Academic Remedies: A Survey of University Policies on Intellectual Honesty

Dolores Pfeuffer-Scherer

Introduction

To curtail student plagiarism, the academic community has historically had in place a number of measures designed to maintain intellectual honesty. These have included strict sanctions for the student ranging in severity from reprimands, to failing grades, to expulsion. Armed with the knowledge that more students have access to sources via the Internet, and thus engage in the act of plagiarism more easily, colleges and universities have had to reexamine their policies and punishments on the subject. Training for both students and instructors involving comprehensive information on the subject has become part of student and faculty orientations. The role of each, student and professor, have expanded to involve them as active participants in the process of avoiding plagiarism. Whereas heretofore, these matters were traditionally been handled between student and teacher, times have changed.

In high schools, colleges, and universities, the process of addressing a suspected incidence of plagiarism can involve a number of administrative levels. This process can entail a variety of rules and sanctions defined by the academic institution and can include such actions as transcript notations of academic dishonesty, suspension from school for one or more terms, even official hearings

105

presided over by students and faculty. Normally, the school is the first and last link in the entire process-from describing what constituted the violation to prescribing the sanction. Instructors are frequently required to incorporate antiplagiarism measures into their teaching and curriculum. For example, departments may require instructors to subscribe to plagiarism-detection Web sites and to include materials about plagiarism on the class syllabus or Web site. Students are instructed to learn what specifically constitutes plagiarism and to recognize the institution's rules and punishments. This process, from administrative level to faculty to student, then back to the administration, is a multifaceted, continually evolving entity that rests on the principles of academic honesty, truth, and the constantly evolving society in which we live.

This chapter examines university policies that deal with plagiarism. A wide sampling of schools will be used, including universities that are geographically, economically, and racially diverse. The differences and similarities between policies and process will be analyzed with the purpose of offering a comprehensive overview of how students and faculty have become an integral part of the entire procedure. The plague of plagiarism has created a new culture within the academic community. This comparison and analysis is intended to help understand some of the structures of this new culture and its impact on the community.

Common Ground: Normative Policy and Procedures

As a sign that the issue of plagiarism has crept into the daily academic life, it is interesting to note that each school examined for this chapter posts established policies on their Web sites that prescribe specific ramifications for those suspected of plagiarism. However, there was no commonality among the universities examined regarding where such information is found. Some schools house their policy within the code of academic conduct; others have theirs available through the Web sites for student affairs offices. Regardless of its placement, the information carefully outlines the specific procedures that the university will follow when investigating a suspected charge of plagiarism. What is interesting is the variation not only of the prescribed chain of action, but how some universities offer students specific examples of what constitutes plagiarism and how to avoid it. There seems to be a distinct line between viewing the offense in terms of an occasion to teach the student what their precise error was, working with them so they learn from the mistake, versus a focus primarily on punishment for failure to adhere to university standards. Many schools strongly suggest that in by engaging in academic dishonesty, intentionally or not, the student sullies the reputation of the school and must come under harsh sanction to maintain its integrity.

For example, issues of honesty in California state-sponsored universities are defined under Title 5, California Administrative Code, Section 41301, which states "the code of conduct for which students may be sanctioned" (Sonoma State University, "Cheating and Plagiarism Policy"). This regulation also outlines possible outcomes for those who break the discipline code: "Any student of a campus may be expelled, suspended, placed on probation or given a lesser sanction for one or more of the following causes which must be campus related: Cheating or plagiarism in connection with an academic program at a campus" (California State University, "Code Governing Student Conduct in the California State University"). The specific policies for disciplinary measures, however, are given to the university's chancellor, to be followed by all campuses. In establishing a state code that outlines what offenses are punishable, California appears to have taken the lead away from the universities in creating the parameters of what constitutes misconduct. A state policy establishing a code of conduct leaves less opportunity for the universities to face charges of favoritism or unfairness.

The establishment of this state code, however, does not mean that California state schools are the most stringent in their policies toward plagiarism. This is not to say that they do not take the offense seriously; they do. The guidelines at Sonoma State University give the faculty discretion to determine if the accusation should be dealt with formally or informally. The policy instructs:

> The University recognizes the importance of informal communication between faculty and students and encourages informal communication as a means of resolving concerns over cheating or plagiarism. In many instances, when a faculty member suspects cheating or plagiarism, informal discussion between the faculty member and the student may resolve the concern. The faculty member should be mindful that a suspicion of cheating or plagiarism need not be an accusation, and that an accusation is a serious matter. Every effort should be made to respect the rights of the student (Sonoma State University, "Cheating and Plagiarism Policy").

If a resolution is reached between student and professor, the faculty member can opt to complete a "Cheating and Plagiarism Record of Informal Resolution" that will remain with the faculty member, with the student receiving a copy (Sonoma State University, "Cheating and Plagiarism Policy"). The instructor and student may also opt to include a third party such as the department chair to help facilitate the process.

At Sonoma State University, the option to initiate formal proceedings also lies in the hands of the instructor. If a faculty member feels the situation demands it, they can file a formal complaint that will ask that the case come up for consideration of academic and administrative sanctions (Sonoma State University, "Cheating and Plagiarism Policy"). Options of formal punishments include redoing the assignment; the assignment of a failing grade on the paper or project; a reduction of the course grade, or a failing grade in the course; and the possibility of multiple sanctions that incorporate more than one of the above. Serious violations fall under the purview of the coordinator of university student discipline, and they can result in probation or suspension or expulsion from the university. The hearing process is meticulously outlined, with the jury consisting of both faculty and students. Time specifications are also included, with the hearing jury being mandated to convene within five days after the instructor files the complaint. Pending the outcome, the jury's report must be filed within ten days. Members of the panel serve for one year, and participation is restricted to tenured faculty and students selected by the president of the Associated Students.

Even in a formal proceeding, faculty and student participation extends to the hearing process, with both being afforded the chance to "each reject one voting member of the Cheating and Plagiarism Jury; the Cheating and Plagiarism Jury Chair shall fill any such vacancies" (Sonoma State University, "Cheating and Plagiarism Policy"). Both may also request the hearing be closed, and each is entitled to receive a copy of the audio transcript of the proceedings at their own expense. Perhaps recognizing the antagonism that can arise from such accusations, it appears that Sonoma State University includes the student and instructor as part of the whole process, rather than leaving the matter entirely in the hands of an administrative body. Though the formal complaint is judged by a jury, the fact that the student and professor can participate in jury selection and dictate the openness of the proceedings indicates that the university is trying to incorporate them as active participants in the process from beginning to end.

The University of North Carolina-Chapel Hill follows a somewhat similar format, offering the faculty member the opportunity to meet informally with the student, although instructors are mandated to file a report. The informal meeting allows "the instructor [to] share his concerns and the student will have the opportunity to provide additional information" (University of North Carolina, "Honors System: Honor System Procedures"). Students may only participate in this meeting only if they have been apprised of their rights under the institution's honor code. Despite this informal meeting, instructors are not entitled to sanction the student themselves-they instead recommend to the student attorney general whether or not the student should face charges. Faculty can also suggest particular punishment, or they can ask assistance in pursuing an investigation based on lack of evidence or information.

The University of North Carolina-Chapel Hill student attorney general determines if charges will be filed, and if sufficient grounds exist, the student is instructed to inspect the Preliminary Conference Information on the Web site, or they can request to hold a preliminary conference in person with a member of the student attorney general's staff (University of North Carolina, "Honors System: Honor System Procedures"). The office appears intent on ensuring that students are thoroughly apprised of their rights and that they fully understand the entire process. Once it is determined that a hearing is warranted, the student attorney general appoints defense counsel and an investigator to examine the evidence and prepare for the hearing. The appointment of a defense counsel to work on behalf of the student is again a means to ensure the student is aware of her rights and a way to ensure the student receives a fair trial. It is the defense counsel's job to work with the student to "gather information that reflects the version of events put forward by the student and help the student organize and present it in an orderly and coherent fashion" (University of North Carolina, "Honors System: Honor System Procedures"). All defense counsels are trained and certified by the vice chancellor for student affairs. The hearing process at the University of North Carolina mandates a closed hearing. Students must receive five days' notice of the intended hearing, and sanctions include failing grades in the course or on the assignment; probation that allows the student to attend school, but bars them from participation in any activity where they would officially serve as a university representative; suspension for a specific or nonspecific time period; indefinite suspension; expulsion. Other penalties can include, "Written warnings, community service, completion of an educational sanction, restitution where applicable, loss of automobile privileges, and other sanctions" (University of North Carolina, "Honors System: Honor System Procedures"). The inclusion of community service as a sanction is extremely interesting as an alternative to simple punitive measures.

Rutgers, The State University of New Jersey, offers only formal means to investigate accusations of plagiarism. Unlike Sonoma State University and the University of North Carolina, Rutgers' policy states that once an instructor suspects a student of committing plagiarism, that instructor is not to meet in an informal manner with the student, but instead must submit the complaint to the dean of students of the student's school, or the Office of Compliance, Student Policy, and Judicial Affairs (Rutgers—The State University, "Policy on Academic Integrity"). These offices individually review the material submitted by the instructor, and the dean of students determines the severity of the offence and whether the matter is grievous enough to warrant a university hearing. The university classifies offenses into four separate levels, offering students punishments based on the level of violation, with levels one and two being least severe and normally adjudicated in the school where the incident occurred. The dean of students or equivalent member of the staff notifies the student of the charges and then meets with the student, without the instructor present. The sanctions can include failure of the assignment, a failing grade in the course, or suspension with a notation on the student's transcript for the duration of the suspension and expulsion.

If a university hearing is warranted, the student is advised to select an on-campus advisor and is given a list of trained advisors who can aid in their defense. Students can select any member of the university community, however, even if they have not been trained. The advisor attends the closed hearing with the student, which is presided over by a hearing officer with a board composed of two professors and three students. Students may elect to consult with an attorney; however, they cannot speak on behalf of the student during the proceedings. The hearing board then makes a recommendation to the vice president of student affairs regarding the sanction, but does not determine or impose the actual punishment.

The Role of Faculty

Though sanctions appear consistent at most state schools, the one issue where we see the greatest variation is in terms of faculty involvement. Many schools like Sonoma State University encourage faculty-student interaction throughout the process, trying to foster a resolution to the charge that relies on the instructor and the student meeting in an attempt settling the dispute in some fashion. Instead of employing intermediary offices in the adjudication process like at Chapel Hill Office or Rutgers, some schools instruct professors to play the pivotal role in the outcome of the suspected plagiarism incident. Examples include The University of Albany, Florida State University, Montana State University, and the University of Illinois, which all allow instructors, not only to informally meet with the student, but they instruct faculty in ways to personally resolve the problem. The University at Albany policy states that:

> When a faculty member has information that a student has
> violated academic integrity in a course or program for which
> he or she is responsible and determines that a violation has
> occurred, he or she will inform the student and impose and
> appropriate sanction (University at Albany, "Policy on
> Violations of Academic Integrity: Penalties and Procedures
> for Violations of Academic Integrity").

Instructors must then file a written report to the Offices of Graduate or Undergraduate Studies, describing the violation, and what penalties they imposed. Professors may also refer a case to the University Judicial System if they cannot reach an agreement with the student, and a hearing will be held to determine how the case will be adjudicated. Like Albany's policy, Florida State University specifies that the professor must attempt to resolve the issue with the student directly:

> When an instructor believes that a student has violated the Academic Honor Code in one of the instructor's classes, the instructor should discuss the matter with the student. The instructor and student may resolve the problem in a manner acceptable to both. The instructor may consult with or invite the participation of the instructor's department chair or dean in the effort to reach acceptable agreement with the student. The student may discuss the appropriateness of any academic response with the instructor's department chair or dean. Any agreement involving an academic penalty shall be put in writing, signed by both parties concerned, and reported by the instructor to the chair or dean and, for information only, to the University Judicial Officer. The student shall not be further penalized based on this report alone (Florida State University, "Student Handbook Codes and Policies").

If the professor and student cannot agree, the case is sent to a hearing with a panel of five members, including two students. The decision of the panel is the final, and they determine the appropriate sanction.

Montana State University also requires professors to address personally the matter with the student. Much like the other schools mentioned above, Montana's policy states:

> The instructor should personally and privately advise the stu-dent that there is reason to believe that the student has com-mitted an act that constitutes academic misconduct. The student should be allowed a reasonable opportunity to respond or explain. If, after hearing the student's response (if any is provided), the instructor continues to believe the stu-dent engaged in academic misconduct, he or she will inform the student of his or her determination and of any intended sanction(s) (Montana State University, "Policies and Procedures—Academic Misconduct Procedures").

Montana's policy, however, offers faculty members five specific sanctions that they are allowed to use, none of which involve suspension or expulsion:

An instructor is limited to imposing sanctions within the scope of the academic activity; [these include] A. oral reprimand; B. written reprimand; C. an assignment to repeat the work or an alternate assignment; D. a lower or failing grade on the particular assignment or test; E. a lower grade or failing grade in the course. The instructor will prepare the Academic Misconduct Notification (forms available at department office) and submit a copy to the student, the Department Head, Graduate Dean (if a graduate student) and the Dean of Students. The instructor has the right to refuse to sign a drop form for the class in question (Montana State University, "Policies and Procedures—Academic Misconduct Procedures").

Any severe offenses must be referred to a hearing board, which can invoke a combination of sanctions, including suspension or expulsion. The ability of the faculty to participate in the process, however, is key to the implementation of the code of conduct and ensures that the process is governed from the start from its origin.

The University of Illinois at Urbana-Champagne takes the idea of faculty involvement in determining the validity of an accusation further, dubbing faculty as:

...having the dual role of fact-finder and determiner of penalty. In the role of finder of fact, the instructor has broad powers to determine whether an infraction has occurred (through collecting relevant evidence, questioning other students, etc....) As the determiner of penalty, the faculty member should feel certain that an infraction has been committed by the student. This decision may be based not only on the facts revealed by the investigation, but other factors that are relevant in the best judgment of the faculty member (University of Illinois at Urbana-Champagne, "Code of Policies and Regulations Applying to All Students: Rule 33—Academic Integrity").

What is striking about this particular policy is the ability of the faculty member to question other students regarding a pending accusation. How far are they allowed to delve, and does such investigation by an instructor trespass on the rights of the student? Or, does this allow for a more fair process for the student, as the professor investigating the matter is the one directly involved with the situation, and perhaps best familiar with the work of the student?

Other universities maintain some faculty involvement, but like the University of North Carolina-Chapel Hill, they require a formal report to be filed. The University of Maryland College Park policy states that:

> Any member of the University community who has witnessed
> an apparent act of academic dishonesty, or has information
> that reasonably leads to the conclusion that such an act has
> occurred or has been attempted, has the responsibility to
> inform the Honor Council promptly in writing (Code of
> Academic Integrity, part 2.) Give us a complete written
> description of the incident, including all relevant details and
> information (University of Maryland College Park, "Student
> Honors Council: Academic Integrity Referral").

The university offers instructors an online form to complete to simplify the process. Instructors can participate in a preliminary meeting, but the Honors Council maintains control over the process, including gathering all pertinent information. Like Maryland, The University of Washington also requires charges be submitted to an administrative office, and students facing an accusation meet with the dean's representative for academic conduct. The instructor is required to submit an "X" grade until the case is resolved. Once resolution has occurred, the grade is changed accordingly.

Policy Statements at Private Universities

Private universities, much like state schools, have had to include policies regarding academic integrity as part of their handbooks. Like public institutions, they vary in their approach to determining the validity of a case and in terms of faculty involvement in the development and adjudication of the incident. A random sampling of private colleges and universities indicate varying degrees of explanation and codification of policies regarding plagiarism. At Southern Methodist University in Texas, the honor code is in the form of a signed pledge made by students enrolled in the college and upheld by a council composed of five faculty members and twenty-six students who are appointed by the faculty and student senates respectively (Southern Methodist University, 2003–2004.) Of all the schools examined for this chapter, this is the largest student contingent within an honor council. Faculty members are reminded that they "serve as the gatekeepers of academic integrity in a university setting," and that any "instructor who is unwilling to act upon offenses assumes the role of accessory to the student offender in facilitating the corrosion of integrity of the University and the individual's character" (Southern Methodist University, 2003–2004). The faculty member who elects not to pursue the matter with vigilance is thereby guilty of violating the honors code himself. The faculty handbook further states: "The faculty must be aware that permitting dishonesty is not open to personal choice" (Southern Methodist University, "Code of Academic

Honesty," 2002). As such, faculty are not permitted to handle the matter at their discretion, but instead must refer the matter to the Honors Council, which will then assemble a hearing board composed of four students and one faculty member (Southern Methodist University, "Faculty Senate Advisory on 'Academic Dishonesty and Plaigarism'," 2002). As with the Honors Council, most of the members are students, not faculty. Student participation appears to be a vital component of the academic integrity policy versus reliance on administration and faculty. The hearing board then determines the validity of the charges as well as the appropriate sanctions.

Unlike Southern Methodist University, the University of Denver does not mandate faculty members to report the incident to their office of Office of Citizenship and Community Standards, although the practice is highly encouraged as a means to resolve a charge of plagiarism. Faculty members may consult unofficially with the office to seek assistance on how to pursue a violation of academic integrity. According to the honors code:

> Before initiating a formal inquiry or filing an Academic
> Dishonesty Allegations Form (ADAF see Appendix A), any
> member of the University community who becomes aware of
> an actual or possible violation of the Honor Code may consult
> with the Office of Citizenship & Community Standards to
> request anonymous advice as to the nature of the procedures,
> information about available options, as a sounding board, or
> on any other relevant matter. No records are kept of such con-
> sultations (University of Denver, "Academic Integrity Honor
> Code Statement").

Instructors may also meet with the student for "gathering additional information and clarifying perceptions of student behaviors" amongst other purposes, and she has the right to handle the matter if this is the student's first offense (University of Denver, "Academic Integrity Honor Code Statement"). If the professor elects to administrate the matter, they can do so with or without filing an Academic Dishonesty Allegations Form. She must then notify the Office of Citizenship & Community Standards as to the resolution in the matter. However, instructors are:

> ...strongly urged to refer the case directly to the Academic
> Conduct Review Board in order to maintain consistency
> across cases and to support the principle of student ownership
> of the Honor Code process. Honor Code violations are a mat-
> ter of community concern, not merely a private issue between
> instructor and student (University of Denver, "Academic
> Integrity Honor Code Statement").

As with state universities, the student has the right to an advisory conference, an advisor, and a right to present witnesses in his defense. Students may also request a member of the Academic Conduct Review Board be replaced if they can demonstrate the person in question may exhibit a personal bias against the student.

Despite the variations in requirements regarding the role of faculty in handling the case, at University of Denver students are an integral part of the judiciary process. Much like Southern Methodist University, students, not administrators, deliberate and judge the validity of the complaints and assign sanctions. The presence of students on the Academic Conduct Review Board (ACRB) is quite striking, as noted in the honor code:

> Composition: The ACRB shall be composed of four students and one non-voting faculty advisor. The chair of this board will be a student. For undergraduate students, 3 of the 4 undergraduates will be from the accused's school (AHUM/SOCS, NSME, DCB). For graduate students, all 4 of the graduate student members will be from the accused's school. If representation as described in 1 and 2 is not available, students may be randomly chosen from the pool (University of Denver, "Academic Integrity Honor Code Statement").

Eligibility for participation in the board is also clearly defined:

> Students—Must be registered as a full or part time student in good academic standing after completing at least 3 quarters of continuous enrollment academic quarters at the University. Students on academic or disciplinary probation are not eligible. Faculty—Any faculty member who has been employed by, and has taught courses at the University for a minimum of three (3) academic quarters. [They also] must be recommended by the Faculty Senate or the Provost (University of Denver, "Academic Integrity Honor Code Statement").

Students may serve on the board until they graduate or no longer wish to participate; faculty terms are restricted to two years of service. Hearings are closed, and an audio recording of the proceeding is taken. Sanctions can take on the traditional forms of punishment such as suspension, probation, expulsion, and so forth, but they can also include workshops offered through the Office of Citizenship & Community Standards as well as Community service (University of Denver, "Academic Integrity Honor Code Statement"). The inclusion of mandatory workshops for students indicates the university's interesting in using the incident as an opportunity not only for punitive measures, but also as time to re-educate students on scholarly procedures.

Bowdoin College in Maine takes a more traditional approach that is similar to the policies at other institutions where administration of punitive and judiciary measures rest in the hands of an administrative body rather than with a faculty member's discretion. "Individuals who suspect violation of the Academic Honors Code and/or Social Code should not attempt to resolve the issues independently, but are encouraged to refer their concerns to the Office of the Dean of Student Affairs" (Bowdoin College, "Student Handbook 2003–2004"). The office then reviews the allegations and decides if the offense warrants a hearing or can be resolved without a trial. If the case goes to trial, the student is notified in a timely fashion and the judiciary board is composed of "three students including the chair two faculty members" (Bowdoin College, "Student Handbook 2003–2004"). The accused are afforded an active role in the trial: "at the hearing, Respondents may, in an orderly fashion, present evidence, make opening and closing statements, respond to questions from the Board, offer witnesses and a character reference, and hear and question evidence against them" (Bowdoin College, "Student Handbook 2003–2004"). The faculty handbook only instructs that "violations of the honor system are to be reported to the Dean of Student Affairs"; it does not allow professors to speak or meet directly with the student, nor does the instructor play a role in assigning the sanction (Bowdoin College, "Faculty Handbook 2003–2004"). Though students are involved as part of the judiciary board, they do not serve as the dispensers of justice. That falls under the purview of the Dean of Student Affairs, without the professor determining what sanction would be appropriate.

Ivy League schools also have carefully outlined their policies on academic integrity. Plagiarism, as would be expected, is treated as a serious offense that requires

The University of Pennsylvania's Charter of Student Disciplinary System oversees the process on the campus, from the initial complaint through to the imposition of a sanction. The handbook states:

> The Office of Student Conduct is the central office responsible for resolving alleged violations of University policies by students. The duties of the OSC include determining whether complaints warrant action by the OSC, referring complaints for mediation or resolution by other University offices, investigating complaints, determining whether to charge a student with violations of University policies, resolving complaints by voluntary agreements to sanctions, bringing charges of violations to a disciplinary hearing, presenting evidence at hearings, monitoring and enforcing the fulfillment of sanctions

imposed pursuant to voluntary agreements or after disciplinary hearings, maintaining records of all disciplinary matters, providing administrative support for all aspects of the disciplinary process (including hearings), and preparing reports and compiling statistics (University of Pennsylvania, "Charter of the University of Pennsylvania Student Disciplinary System").

There is a University Mediation Program that is staffed by volunteers, which includes students, faculty, and staff who have received training in conflict resolution, and who try to work with the student and professor to come up with an appropriate sanction. The University Honor Council oversees the disciplinary hearing process. What is interesting about this group is the student participation. Though not on the same level as Southern Methodist University's student-run panel, Penn incorporates a large number of students into the process, perhaps viewing them as an integral link in the process of enforcing the university's policy:

> The UHC consists of a minimum of 20 undergraduate students, recommended by the Nominations and Elections Committee (NEC) in cooperation with the current members of the UHC, and appointed by the Provost for renewable terms of one year. The NEC and UHC are encouraged to ensure that nominees represent a broad cross section of the undergraduate student body (University of Pennsylvania, "Charter of the University of Pennsylvania Student Disciplinary System").

The UHC is also active in trying to prevent plagiarism. Throughout the academic year, "The UHC also initiates and participates in educational programs in the areas of academic integrity and of student conduct (University of Pennsylvania, "Charter of the University of Pennsylvania Student Disciplinary System"). Though many faculty members include a discussion or handout on plagiarism in the syllabi or course, Penn's use of a separate administrative body that includes a large population of diverse students speaks to the university's attempt to reach students by another, independent means. As such, the administrative moves away from punitive duties to prevention.

Yale University uses a mixture of tenured and nontenured professors and students to adjudicate cases of academic dishonesty in the classroom. Of the universities examined for this paper, this is the first instance where faculty members without tenure are included as part of the committee. Dubbed the "Executive Committee," this group is appointed by the dean of the college. The structure of the committee is as follows:

> The committee shall have ten regular voting members: three
> tenured members of the Yale College faculty, three untenured
> members of the Yale College faculty, three undergraduates,
> and the dean of Yale College or the dean's designated repre-
> sentative. The presence of seven of these members shall con-
> stitute a quorum. A majority vote of those present shall be
> required for any decision.... In addition to the regular voting
> members there shall be three officers of the Executive
> Committee who are also members: chairman, secretary, and
> fact-finder. They shall be appointed annually by the dean of
> Yale College and shall be charged with particular responsibili-
> ties (Yale University, "2003–2004 Undergraduate
> Regulations").

As with other universities, Yale allows the accused to enlist the assistance of an advisor, and if the student finds difficulties in procuring such assistance, the college dean will provide a list from which the student can select an advisor.

> Normally, the adviser will be the student's residential college
> dean, but the adviser may also be the residential college mas-
> ter, a freshman or sophomore academic adviser, a Yale College
> faculty member, a Yale College administrator, a coach, or any
> other member of the University community who is not a
> member of the Executive Committee or the Office of the
> University General Counsel. Should a student find himself or
> herself unable to locate an adviser, the dean of Yale College
> shall furnish the student with a list of persons willing to aid
> students in these situations (Yale University, "2003–2004
> Undergraduate Regulations").

Much like Rutgers, there are a number of campus advisors who have been trained in the process that are willing to assist students and help guide them through the process of questioning witnesses, presenting their case, and preparing the student for the format of the hearing. Though students at Yale are a part of the Executive Council, they form a minority of the judiciary, with the majority being composed of tenured and nontenured professors. Unlike the University of Pennsylvania, there is not a student body that reaches out to help instruct students on academic integrity.

Conclusion

Plagiarism has become an important part of the academic landscape. Regardless of the type of university or college, academic institutions are enlisting faculty, staff, administrators, and students alike to help investigate and pass sanctions regarding intellectual honesty. Though penalties such as dismissal, suspension, probation, and warnings are standard across the majority of schools, some offer alternative sanctions such as community service to help foster the learning aspect of the incident. The greatest variations appear to be in the involvement of faculty and students. Whereas some faculty members are entitled to handle the complaint between them and the student, others are mandated to remove themselves from the process by turning the complaint in to an administrative unit designed to investigate the accusation. There are some schools that urge faculty to find an informal resolution, whereas others insist on a formal process, even if the end result is derived not by a hearing, but my mediation. Some universities insist on student-run hearings, with governance by faculty and/or staff, whereas others rely on the role of faculty in conjunction with administration and staff. Regardless, all appear to have some formal policy that governs such cases; with an increasing number of students being caught in the web of plagiarism, such policies are necessary to protect faculty as well as the students themselves.

The question is whether or not the policies are affecting students by serving as a deterrent, or are they simply serving as a stopgap measure after the fact? Do universities do enough to publicize their policies, or does the majority of students learn of the rules once they have engaged in plagiarism and been caught? Aside from faculty including the relevant information on syllabi, are students truly aware of what constitutes plagiarism and how to avoid it? Though much is written regarding punishment and sanctions, what are universities and high schools doing to ameliorate plagiarism at ground level-that is to say within the classroom? Are students given enough of an opportunity to learn and experience what constitutes plagiarism, or are they simply given handouts, lectures, and a book containing vast descriptions of punitive measures that will befall them should they engage in such an act? The key question that kept popping up during this research is whether or not the academy has moved forward to incorporate units and teaching on plagiarism in a pedagogical fashion to elucidate the lesson for its pupils, or has it been so focused on the establishment of sanctions that it has not given enough time to prevention? Do secondary schools, or even elementary schools, incorporate this into their English courses? From the increasing number of cases in colleges, it appears that answer is "no"; but is that necessarily fair to pin the blame on the school systems when universities themselves are lagging in their own efforts to educate its students? What is amazing is how many schools have not focused on prevention but instead on the end result, which involves punishment. Though policies and procedures to deal with plagiarism are necessary, what is being done to stop it and to assist students in grappling with the concept of what specifically is plagiarism? When does it become about educating versus punishment?

Working closely with students, it is impossible not to realize that whereas many do understand the concept of plagiarism, others remain uncertain. They certainly know what constitutes cheating and recognize the need for sanctions for those who do so, but the issue becomes far more murky when dealing with plagiarism. One issue that crops up continually is that many pupils do not comprehend how severe the punishments can be, and that once they are charged with such an offense, their whole academic career can be put in jeopardy. Sometimes it revolves around intent; students who willfully plagiarize may have done so before and not have gotten caught; as such, they are willing to roll the dice again, figuring they will go undetected. Others genuinely do not fully grasp that they are engaging in academic dishonesty and as such are completely bewildered when facing such charges. Some see bibliographic citations of Web sites or books in their bibliography as all encompassing, not realizing each copied sentence must be cited. For a student who is either unaware or careless, the path from average student one day to suspended student with a notation of "Violation of Academic Integrity" attached to his transcript a few months later can be an angst-ridden path filled with confusion and resentment. It is far too easy for schools to mete out punishments; the more difficult task is to create a comprehensive lesson on plagiarism that continually keeps up with technology while being basic enough for students to assimilate into their body of knowledge to the point where it become second nature to a student as they prepare to write. Though some schools are creating online tutorials, offering handouts, and holding sessions in English courses on the basics of plagiarism, many are still lagging behind. Web sites dedicated to the subject matter are blooming, but on an individual per school level, is enough being done to explain not only what plagiarism is, but what will occur if a student engages in such an offense?

Looking at all the schools studied for this chapter, several trends stand out and deserve further analysis. One aspect that appears to be missing from most places is direct action and involvement from students at educating other students about what specifically constitutes plagiarism. Student government associations, student groups, college newspapers, even academic councils with students are lacking in terms of spreading information on their schools' formal procedures governing plagiarism charges or even of working to facilitate an understanding of what plagiarism actually entails. It could be argued that this falls under the aegis of academic departments, if not student services, or even the school's tutorial center; however, by involving students in the process, it would certainly aid students in comprehending what constitutes plagiarism. If student groups actively promote an understanding of the subject, it certainly could only help others as they are coping with understanding their academic environment. How many students read the campus newspaper versus the number who may read the school catalogue where academic policy is normally outlined? If all student groups held one meeting dedicated to a comprehensive explanation of what entails plagiarism and how it can be avoided, it could only help other students, particularly freshmen, to avoid the pitfalls of academic dishonesty. Presentations should be technologically savvy, however, if the presenter is simply one person droning on for hours, students will not listen; multimedia presentations would be best, particularly those that would actively engage the students by soliciting their participation. What appears to be missing from most places, however, is direct action and involvement from students at educating other students about what specifically constitutes plagiarism. Some academic departments within universities have begun to include examples and definitions of academic integrity on their Web pages as a means to reach out to students and clarify academic integrity. If departments, student services, and even tutorial centers partnered with student clubs and organizations, the information would be disseminated more quickly and probably be better understood by all pupils. The excuse of "I did not know" or "I did not understand" would fall by the wayside if the information is part of a campus effort that includes and engages students.

Academic departments also need to take an active role, and schools should have some policy that helps assist them in disseminating the information to the students. Many academic departments within universities have begun to include examples and definitions of academic integrity on their Web pages as a means to reach out to students and clarify academic integrity. Several have done an admirable job of detailing the above, and it would appear that this trend is on the rise as more professors realize that the information must be disseminated to students on multiple levels; however, there are great variations even on the same campus, so that a sociology major may find a plethora of information on their department's Web site, whereas a biology major may face a dearth of information on his discipline's Web site. If there is to be a campus-wide or school-wide effort aimed at eliminating plagiarism, then each academic department needs to join the effort to ensure all students are aware of what plagiarism is and how it can be avoided; professors, department chairpersons, and even academic deans should consider implementing a policy where each department would include a section relating to academic integrity on their Web pages and include the university policy as well. This up-front posting of information will make it easier for students, professors, and even interested potential students to access and incorporate into their body of knowledge. To have marked variations between departments only ensures greater confusion for the students and misinformation versus information. Simply including the information on syllabi is not enough; students are Web savvy and should be able to access policies at their leisure. To do so, the information needs to be available, up to date, and presented in a manner that engages the student and promotes a thorough understanding of the subject.

Finally, the third suggestion would be to get student services involved in presenting plagiarism as a major part of freshmen and transfer orientation. There was a time when orientation meant meeting the school pep squad, seeing the dorms, and meeting the administrators. Today, the orientation can include alcohol awareness, sexual harassment, and should include a significant session on plagiarism. Students should again be incorporated into a multimedia presentation that illustrates what plagiarism is, how to avoid it, and what the penalties are should a student still engage in academic dishonesty. To return to the first suggestion, by using student groups, student services could engage greater numbers of students on the subject and potentially avoid the increasing number of cases. Without including a comprehensive component on plagiarism, schools are negligent by not supplying the students with the information from the beginning of their time at the school. Secondary schools should hold orientations, much like colleges, and include the information as part of student introduction to the school. If not caught on the high school level, then universities need to really bring the point home to the freshmen and transfers before they find themselves enforcing stopgap measures that do not ameliorate the problem.

Though the Internet has caused plagiarism cases to grow in terms of formal charges handled by school administrators, it is interesting to see how markedly policies to prevent and punish academic dishonesty vary. There is no comprehensive interschool plan, and teachings on the subject vary from instructor to instructor. Within the same academic setting, policies can vary, and instructors can either incorporate it as a lesson into their course, or they can just ignore the subject and not deal directly with it unless confronted with such a case. However, there seems to be a gap within universities between student-powered information and activism in regard to academic integrity. As more departments react, as more institutions of higher education codify their policies, it will be interesting to note the role of students in assisting other students, particularly freshmen. The involvement of students to assist the school in preventing plagiarism may prove to be the pivotal issue in terms of success. Without enlisting their assistance, it appears to be more difficult to reach other students, and the information comes across simply as administrative chatter that is often tuned out. In addition, departments need to unify to present the information in a cohesive, interesting, and informative manner on their Web sites, so to promote understanding for all students in all majors. Without student involvement, direct Web information that is easily accessed, and lack of information at student orientations, plagiarism will remain a murky issue, fraught with uncertainty and misinformation. To reach the goal of lowering disciplinary cases involving plagiarism, schools need to become much more active in the delivery of the information that will help students avoid the pitfalls of plagiarism.

Works Cited

Bowdoin College. "Faculty Handbook 2003–2004". Available: http://academic.bowdoin.edu/academics/for_faculty/forms_policies/dissemination/03–04FacultyHandbook.pdf.

Bowdoin College. "Student Handbook 2003–2004." Available: www.bowdoin.edu/communications/publications/pdf/studentHandbook.pdf.

California State University, Fresno. "Code Governing Student Conduct in the California State University." Available: http://studentaffairs.csufresno.edu/discipline/code.html.

Florida State University. "Student Handbook Codes and Policies." Available: www.fsu.edu/Books/Student-Handbook/2003codes/honor.html.

Montana State University. "Policies and Procedures—Academic Misconduct Procedures." Available: www2.montana.edu/policy/student_conduct/cg400.html.

Rutgers—The State University, Campus at Camden. "Policy on Academic Integrity." Undergraduate Catalog. Available: http://ruWeb.rutgers.edu/catalogs/camden-ug/03–05/general.pdf.

Sonoma State University. "Cheating and Plagiarism Policy." Available: www.sonoma.edu/uaffairs/policies/cheatingpolicy.htm.

Southern Methodist University. "Academic Integrity—The Honor Code of Southern Methodist University." 2003–04 Undergraduate Catalog Student Affairs. Available: www.smu.edu/catalogs/undergrad/studentaffairs.asp.

Southern Methodist University. "Code of Academic Honesty." March 11, 2002. Faculty Handbook. Available: www.smu.edu/ir/provost/handbook%202002.pdf.

Southern Methodist University. "Faculty Senate Advisory on 'Academic Dishonesty and Plaigarism'." March 11, 2002. Faculty Handbook. Available: www.smu.edu/ir/provost/handbook%202002.pdf.

The University of Illinois at Urbana-Champagne. "Code of Policies and Regulations Applying to All Students: Rule 33—Academic Integrity." Available: www2.uiuc.edu/admin_manual/code/rule_33.html.

The University of Maryland, College Park. "Student Honors Council: Academic Integrity Referral." Available: www.studenthonorcouncil.umd.edu/referral.html.

The University of North Carolina at Chapel Hill. "Honors System: Honor System Procedures." Available: http://honor.unc.edu/procedures/index.html.

University at Albany. "Policy on Violations of Academic Integrity: Penalties and Procedures for Violations of Academic Integrity." Available: www.albany.edu/tree-tops/docs.eas/104/penalty.htm.

University of Denver. "Academic Integrity Honor Code Statement." Available: www.du.edu/honorcode/studentprocedure.htm.

The University of Pennsylvania. "Charter of the University of Pennsylvania Student Disciplinary System." Available: www.upenn.edu/osc/Charter.htm#label4.

Yale University. "2003–2004 Undergraduate Regulations." Available: www.yale.edu/ycpo/undregs/pages/appendB.html#A.

PART III
A Practitioner's Toolkit: Resources and Guides

Part III is the "toolkit" part of this book; that is, a practical, hands-on listing of resources. The CD for *The Plagiarism Plague* is intended, particularly, to be used with this section. As you, the reader, refer to chapters as you use this book, you will be able to access the online resources discussed through the links provided on the CD. We hope that this will make the resource lists easier to use and provide a "just-in-time" access to resources that you need in dealing with different aspects of the topic of plagiarism.

Part I outlined the problem; Part II provided some theory and suggestions for solutions. In Part III, my collaborators and I hope to give educators tools that they can use in their pursuit of teaching their students about academic integrity. When planning this project, we envisioned this book being used by a variety of educators: high school teachers, librarians, instructors, and administrators. Each of these types of users will have different charges and different needs for information regarding plagiarism. Part III is intended to point the way to resources that would be useful for designing lesson plans for information literacy, aiding in the teaching of research and writing skills, detecting plagiarism in student papers, and obtaining information and insights for writing policies and guidelines about intellectual honesty.

Topics covered in this section include legal issues, recommendations from professional organizations, Web resources for plagiarism detection, online style sheets and citation guides, and examples of Web-based plagiarism tutorials. This section concludes with an annotated bibliography of resources for additional reading, research, as well as audiovisual materials that can be used in instruction about plagiarism.

125

CHAPTER 11

Read the Fine Print: Legal Issues Related to Student Plagiarism

Luis F. Rodriguez

Introduction

This chapter examines some of the legal and administrative issues involved in student plagiarism, with a focus on student plagiarism at American institutions of higher education. It begins first with a discussion of the relationship between copyright law in the United States and plagiarism. In many discussions, copyright infringement and plagiarism are treated as one and the same. However, there are some significant differences between the two. Next, some of the legal and administrative issues involved in dealing with issues of student plagiarism at institutions of higher education will be addressed. Though much of the conversation on plagiarism focuses on the student, there are also institutional and legal considerations of which faculty members and librarians should be aware.

The efforts of some states to minimize student plagiarism go beyond the walls of the university. A brief overview of the way in which some states have tried to stop student plagiarism-not by prohibiting certain forms of student behavior, but by attempting to restrict businesses who supply term papers to students-will be presented. Finally, this chapter closes with a discussion of another way in which institutions have tried to diminish student plagiarism-through the use of plagiarism detection services. The questions that have been raised over legal issues regarding the manner in which some services detect papers will be examined. These questions involve the intersection of copyright and plagiarism. This time, however, the copyright infringer may not be the student, but the plagiarism detection services.

Copyright and Plagiarism: Two Sides of the Same Coin?

Some Basics on United States Copyright Law

Article I, Section 8 of the United States Constitution gave Congress the power to "promote the Progress of Science and useful arts, by securing for limited times to Authors and Inventors the exclusive right to their respective Writings and Discoveries." Copyright law gives the author of an original work, or those authorized by the author, the exclusive right:

- To reproduce the work;
- To make derivative copies based upon the work;
- To distribute the work by selling, renting, lending or leasing it or by transferring ownership of the work; and
- In the case of literary, musical, dramatic, and choreographic works, pantomimes, and motion pictures and other audiovisual works, to perform the work publicly;
- In the case of literary, musical, dramatic, and choreographic works, pantomimes, and pictorial, graphic, or sculptural works, including the individual images of a motion picture or other audiovisual work, to display the work publicly; and
- In the case of sound recordings, to perform the work publicly by means of a digital audio transmission (U.S. Copyright Office, "Copyright Basics, Circular 1").

The Digital Millennium Copyright Act added another wrinkle to these rights by making illegal most reverse engineering of technology that prevents the copying of a digital work (Ogden, 2003).

However, not all things and not all works are copyrightable. Facts are not copyrightable, but the language used to describe facts, if original enough, may be copyrighted (Ogden, 2003). Ideas are not copyrightable, although according to some interpretations, the unattributed use of an idea would be plagiarism (Gibaldi, 2003). Though an idea would not be copyrightable, an original manner of expressing an idea would be, even though the plagiarism policies of many colleges and universities would require a student to cite the source of the idea, no matter how original the student's manner of expressing that idea. In addition to ideas, procedures, methods, systems, processes, concepts, principles, discoveries, or devices are not copyrightable. Descriptions, explanations, and illustrations of these-if original enough-would be. Originality and creativity are the key to copyright. Thus, a typical phone book is not copyrightable because it uses a commonplace and traditional method of arranging raw data (subscribers' names, towns, and telephone numbers), and the raw data are arranged in a way that "lacks the modicum of creativity necessary to transform mere selection into copyrightable expression" (*Feist* v. *Rural Telephone*, 1991: 362). Works of the United States government are not copyrightable, but those of foreign, state, and local government are.

To be copyrighted, a work must be fixed in a tangible form. Thus, improvisational speeches and performances are not copyrightable, but recordings and written transcripts of those performances are. You could, however, plagiarize improvisational speeches and performances. To promote the Progress of Science and the Useful Arts, the Constitution did not make copyright perpetually; it is granted for a limited time. Thus, copyrighted works eventually pass into the public domain. Once in the public domain, you need not ask permission to make copies of those works. You could even designate yourself as the creator of such a work. Neither the act of copying a work in the public domain or of making oneself the author of such a work would be an infringement of copyright. Most would agree that stating that you wrote a book in the public domain would be plagiarism.

United States copyright law allows for certain exceptions and limitations on the rights of copyright holders. The most well-known exception, at least among those employed at institutions of higher education, is the exception for "fair use" of copyrighted works. A "fair use" of a copyrighted work (i.e., a use that does not infringe the rights of a copyrighter holder) is made by weighing four factors:

- The purpose of the use: Is the use of a copyrighted work for nonprofit educational purposes or is its use of a commercial nature? Use of a work for educational purposes weighs toward fair use. Use of a copyrighted work in criticism, commentary, news reporting, parody, or other transformative uses, such as use in a research paper, are also favorable factors toward a determination of fair use.
- The nature of the copyrighted work: This factor focuses on the characteristics of the work being used (Crews, 2002). The courts have typically found it fairer to use nonfiction and published works than to use works of fiction. Use of published works is generally found to be more within fair use than use of unpublished works.
- The amount copied: This is both a quantitative and qualitative assessment. Generally, copying a small part of a work and no more than is needed for the purpose at hand is considered within fair use. However, courts have

found that copying the "heart of a work," no matter how small, weighs against fair use (Crews, 2002).

- Effect on the value of the original work: This is not always easy to determine. Effect often relates to the purpose of a use (i.e., whether the use is of a commercial nature or for use in a nonprofit setting). According to Kenneth Crews, "this factor means fundamentally that if you make a use for which a purchase of an original theoretically should have occurred-regardless of your personal willingness or ability to pay for such purchase-then this factor may weigh against fair use (Crews, 2002).

This final factor is sometimes called the "tipping" factor. This means that courts will consider the first three factors to determine if fair use of a copyrighted work applies. If the use of a work is fair, based on an examination of the first three factors, then courts will usually not consider the effect of copying on the market for the work. However, if an examination of the first three factors indicates that the use of a copyrighted work is not fair, then the effect on the market for a work will be considered (University of Texas, "Fair Use of Copyrighted Materials"). Though there are exceptions to copyright, with "fair use" being one of them, there are no exceptions for plagiarism (Green, 2002: 167).

United States copyright law allows for other exceptions and limitations on the rights of copyright holders. Among the other exceptions and limitations to the rights of copyright holders are exceptions for libraries (see the United States Code, Title 17, Section 108) and for the performance or display of copyrighted works in face-to-face and digital classroom settings (see the United States Code, Title 17, Section 110). A discussion of these exceptions and limitations is outside the scope of this chapter.

Guidelines, often assumed to be part of the copyright law, have been developed that some use in place of conducting a fair use analysis:

The so-called "Classroom Guidelines" presents the most conservative safe harbor, short of only using copies for which permission has been received. Although the Guidelines are reported by Congress as, " '...a reasonable interpretation of the minimum standards of fair use,' they are not the legal standards of fair use" (Washington State University, "Fair Use").

Where Plagiarism and Copyright Differ

By now, it should be clear that whereas copyright and plagiarism are often treated as equivalent, in many important aspects, they diverge. Understanding the ways in which copyright and plagiarism diverge will help our understanding of both.

- As Stuart Green notes, plagiarism can occur "when a writer fails to acknowledge the source of facts, ideas, and specific language, copyright infringement occurs only when specific language is copied or used in a derivative work" (Green, 2002: 200–201).

- Copyright does not extend to ideas, only to expressions of those ideas, a distinction that is not always easy to make (Stearns, 1992: 513). One cannot copyright an idea, but one can plagiarize an idea.
- Copyright does not extend to works in the public domain; you cannot be charged with a copyright infringement if a work is in the public domain. You can plagiarize a work in the public domain. However, with appropriate attribution, you cannot be accused of plagiarizing a work-whether it is the public domain or not.
- Copyright does not extend to facts, only to the way in which those facts are expressed. In one case, a court found that the author of a work of historical fiction did not infringe the copyright of an author of a nonfiction work "because the material copied was not a 'sequence of creative expression,'" consisting of an insubstantial quantity of the nonfiction work and not the "heart" of the nonfiction work (Stearns, 1992: 567).
- Paraphrasing "which remains sufficiently close that, in spite of changes, it appropriates the craft of authorship of the original" can be considered as copyright infringement (*Craft* v. *Kobler*, 1987). Unless it is done poorly or without attribution, paraphrasing is not considered plagiarism.
- The heart of plagiarism is failing to attribute authorship for an expression or idea. Proper attribution is not a defense against copyright infringement.
- Intent to deceive is often an issue in plagiarism cases. Intent is not an issue in copyright (Stearns, 1992).

Legal and Administrative Issues in Dealing with Student Plagiarism

Given the alarming statistics on plagiarism, it is quite likely that you will encounter a case of plagiarism. Though there are many good strategies for designing assignments to minimize plagiarism, to paraphrase the poet, the best laid plans of a faculty member can often go awry. Therefore, you should be prepared to deal with cases of student plagiarism. This section discusses legal and administrative issues involved in taking action against a student that involves suspected or proven plagiarism.

First Things First

There are several things you should take into consideration before you take any action against a student who has plagiarized. One important question to ask is: What kind of student plagiarism have you found? Was it the fraud of submitting a paper written by another student or purchased from a term paper mill, the failure to cite when a student fails to acknowledge the source of an idea or words, the failure to quote by not providing quotation marks for a direct quotation, or what some have called "patchwriting," that is, the patching together of words and phrases from several sources, acknowledged or not, to form new sentences (Howard, 2001b)? Making these distinctions allows you to determine if you have the case of a student who has intentionally committed plagiarism or one of a student who has accidentally done so, or if you cannot reasonably determine the student's intentions. Not only should you consider the nature of the plagiarism, but also the amount of material plagiarized. Determining a student's intentions when plagiarizing often cannot be made without considering the amount of material the student has plagiarized. Finally, you should determine if the student is a one-time offender or if he or she is a serial plagiarizer. You can do usually do this by talking to the person charged with keeping records of student misconduct, usually someone in your dean of students office.

Determining the "intent" of the student, the amount of material plagiarized, and whether or not the student has been found to have plagiarized previously, are important because many campus policies on plagiarism and other forms of academic dishonesty revolve around questions of intent, faculty discretion and leniency, and serial misconduct. Processes and penalties are often quite different for deliberate forms of academic dishonesty as opposed to plagiarism of the accidental kind and for students who have been found to have plagiarized in the past. Considerations of the amount of material plagiarized can help determine if leniency is warranted. The repeat offender may be well aware of how to cite properly but may decide not to do so.

Thinking about issues related to intention and amount are also useful in helping faculty members avoid the tendency to treat all students who plagiarize as criminal. It may well be that after thinking about the kind of plagiarism you find and/or the amount of material plagiarized, you may decide that the most appropriate action to take is to treat this as an opportunity for a teachable moment: you may decide that given the situation, the best action to take is not to impose any penalty or sanction, but to treat the interaction with a student who plagiarizes as that of an interaction between a teacher and a student rather than as an interaction between a police officer and criminal (Howard, 2001a).

Reporting Allegations of Plagiarism: Faculty Reluctance and Myths

You are not alone if you find that a student has plagiarized and you decide not to take any action against student plagiarism. In 1999, one third of the 1,000 faculty at 21 campuses who were aware of student cheating in their classes within the last 2 years did nothing about it (Center for Academic Integrity, "CAI Research"). There are many reasons and rationales for this inaction. Gerdeman's summary of research on why faculty at 2-year colleges are reluctant to report instances of academic dishonesty most likely applies to faculty at all levels of higher education: "Time constraints, due process protocol, fear of backlash, lack of administrative support, and misunderstanding of policies may all contribute to faculty reluctance to act on suspicions of cheating" (Gerdeman, "Academic Dishonesty and the Community College").

Fears associated with pursuing charges of plagiarism against a student may stop some faculty from doing anything about a case of a student suspected or proven of having plagiarized material. However, some of these fears turn out to be, on further examination, based more on myth than on the ways in which courts have decided issues of academic dishonesty-the form of misconduct under which student plagiarism is associated. One such myth is that a faculty member will always lose a case if it is his or her word against that of a student. Gehring notes that hearing boards will often find for the faculty member (Gehring, 1998). Faculty members also fear being sued for defamation by students cleared of charges of academic dishonesty. This, too, is more myth than fact. A review of more than 30 years of pertinent case law reveals not "even one case in which administrators, faculty, or students have been assessed damages for reporting alleged acts of academic dishonesty (Gehring, 1998).

Furthermore, as Gehring and Pavela (Gehring, 1998: 88) argue, in cases of academic misconduct, faculty have at least a "qualified privilege," if not, as some courts have found an "absolute privilege" against defamation suits. A person or a group of persons with absolute privilege have "complete freedom of expression, without any inquiries as to…motives" (Pavela, 1988: 54). It is more likely that a court would hold that a member of the faculty would have a "qualified privilege." This means that the faculty member would be free from a defamation suit in inaccurately referring or reporting a case of student plagiarism unless he or she did so in bad faith.

Ronald Sandler has reviewed cases of student and faculty plagiarism as of December 1999. He finds that "in *every* plagiarism case that I have found involving a student or professor, the court upheld the punishment imposed by the college. Further, the court often make [sic] gratuitous, pejorative comments about the bad character of the plagiarist, which show that it is *unwise* for a plagiarist to complain about he/she was treated" (italics in the original) (Sandler, "Plagiarism in Colleges in USA").

Should You Handle a Case of Plagiarism on Your Own?

As mentioned earlier, faculty are often reluctant to use institutional processes to deal with cases of plagiarism. Those who do deal with such cases often want to handle the case on their own-by confronting the student whom they suspect of plagiarism. Alschuler and Blimling argue that faculty are often reluctant to pursue cases of plagiarism and other forms of academic dishonesty through institutional processes because they bear the burden of proving that plagiarism occurred in such processes, and they find that faculty think that constitutionally guaranteed due process procedures built into institutional procedures are often time-consuming and usually adversarial (Alshculer and Blimling, 1995).

Though acting alone may appear to be the best way to deal with student plagiarism, it is not necessarily the most prudent. Courts have consistently found that students in public institutions of higher education are guaranteed due process protections when faced with potential loss of property or liberty rights, that at a minimum this right includes that students be informed of the specific charges against them, the evidence for those charges, and that students be given the ability to challenges these charges (Silvergate and Gewolb, 2003). Though students in private institutions are not guaranteed a due process right, courts have viewed the relationship between a student and a private institution as a contract. Not following policies and procedures outlined in student handbooks and other official institutional publications would be seen as a breach of this contract. Courts would also hold public universities to this standard; they, too, must abide by published policies and procedures (Silvergate and Gewold, 2003). A faculty member acting on his or her own could personally be liable for violating a student's due process right or the implicit contract between a private institution and a student. Also, an institution may not be obliged to provide legal representation to a faculty member who has not followed procedures outlined in official publications (Gehring, 1998).

Not only may acting alone not be the most legally prudent course of action, from an educational perspective, it also may not be the best course of action. It does nothing to stop the repeat offender. It does little to send a message to students that academic dishonesty is not tolerated institutionally. Giving a student an "F" for an assignment or course without interacting with the student fails to serve as a deterrent to that student, can mislead other schools to which the student applies, and "most important, the practice deprives the student of an adequate opportunity to confront the ethical implications of the behavior" (Kibler, 1998: 30–31).

Interacting with a Student Who May or May Not Have Plagiarized

Your campus policy may require, or you may decide that before you take any action, you first want to meet with the student whom you suspect of plagiarism. This certainly seems warranted in cases in which you think the plagiarism accidental or in which you cannot make a reasonable determination if the plagiarism was accidental or intentional, and it is probably prudent to do so if your campus requires such a meeting before any penalties or sanctions are imposed.

If you have to meet with a student, several sources offer useful advice for faculty members when having such a meeting (Davis, 1993; Harris, 2001; Stevens, 1996). Among some of the things they recommend are the following:

- Review your institutional and departmental policies on plagiarism and academic dishonesty-the academic offense under which student plagiarism is typically classified. Institutional policies can be found in student and/or faculty handbooks. As noted above, the policy may speak to the issue of intent, offer you some ability to be lenient, or require you to report instances of plagiarism-even if you find that the plagiarism was unintentional and/or inconsequential. And, as mentioned earlier, regarding a student in a public or private institution, courts have favored students who bring suit against institutions that do not follow policies and procedures listed in the student handbook or other official publications.
- Talk to your department chair before you meet with a student to determine options that are acceptable and practices that are not mentioned in any policies and procedures but are what Howard calls "local customs." As Howard notes, you can make the problem of a questionable paper worse "by making a decision that the next person up in the food chain is compelled to overturn" (Howard, 2001b).
- Talk to your campus's student conduct or judicial officer for information on due process and student confidentiality issues and procedures to follow in this meeting and afterwards (see below for more on the issue of due process in plagiarism cases). Though some may dispute whether due process is needed in these meetings, as Stevens notes: "A professor or department head who can legitimately claim to have attempted to follow due process principles in her decision making finds herself in a more defensible position in court" (Stevens, 1996: 141).
- Be calm and rational. Avoid feelings of anger, betrayal, or insult.
- Treat the student with respect.
- Treat the student with an attitude of "innocent until proven guilty." Harris argues that this is (1) just and fair, (2) legally smart, (3) psychologically smart in stopping you from falsely accusing someone, and (4) prudent in that you may be wrong (Harris, 2001). Though Harris does not elaborate on why such an attitude is legally smart, assuming that the student is innocent until proven guilty will better insure that your interaction with a student allows the student to present his or her side or to question the evidence you have of plagiarism-in other words, that you will use procedures that follow due process.
- Deal with issues of evidence: Verify evidence from third parties, keep it secure before the meeting, and have it available at the meeting.

- If you think that it is warranted, have a colleague at the meeting. However, having a colleague may make the student more hostile, anxious, or distracted. There are also privacy issues involved. In cases where you have a colleague attend a meeting, the best person is someone in the administrative chain.
- During the meeting:
  - Treat the student with respect. Show concern for the student as an individual, but do not minimize the seriousness of the situation.
  - Read your institution's rules to the student.
  - Avoid using the words "cheating or plagiarism." Objectively explain the problem as you see it, especially in the ways in which it makes it difficult for you to grade or evaluate the student's work.
  - Ask questions rather than make accusations and ask questions that are nonspecific.
  - Listen to the student's explanation. If the student denies plagiarizing, ask questions about specific aspects of the paper, such as definitions of terms, interpretations, or restatements. Be sure to ask questions about sources or about the process the student used to find or obtain these sources.
  - Be prepared for rationalizations, pleas, and excuses. Be prepared to be cited as the cause of the student's misconduct.
  - Be sympathetic to students who are distraught or upset. Suggest a referral of the student to the counseling center if appropriate.
- At or near the end of the meeting, explain what will happen next. Harris advises not to tell the student your decision at this time. However, whatever decision you make, inform the student as soon as you reached a decision. Also inform the student of the processes to appeal the decision.
- Respect the student's confidentiality. Speak to your department chair, dean, or campus conduct officer but avoid "gossiping" to colleagues about the student.

Disciplinary Offense or Academic Judgment

One of the debates over the handling of student plagiarism in colleges and universities revolves around whether the student's plagiarism is to be classified as a disciplinary offense or whether its disposition is a matter of academic judgment (Stevens, 1996). One reason for the importance of this distinction is that the courts have traditionally been reluctant to breach the principle of academic freedom, except when an academic judgment "can be shown to have been influenced by improper factors, such as the student's race or political viewpoint" (Sandler, "Plagiarism in Colleges in USA"). When cases of academic misconduct are categorized as involving academic judgment and evaluation, courts will be reluctant to overturn an academic judgment. Academic judgments typically involve more subjective judgments and evaluations than the factual questions found in nonacademic disciplinary cases (Green, 2002). In nonacademic disciplinary cases, such as theft and vandalism, the courts have given students in public institutions of higher education more due process protections, with the protections reflecting the nature of the potential penalty, but not equal to those for defendants in criminal cases.

Whatever your personal view whether or not plagiarism and other forms of academic misconduct fall within the realm of academic evaluation, your institution's categorization of academic misconduct is what counts. A student will have a strong basis on which to challenge legally a faculty member's decision if the faculty member did not follow institutional policy. Furthermore, due process protections increase as the potential penalty to the student increases. Asking a student to redo a paper would not require the same sorts of procedural protection as would a process that could lead to a student's expulsion from an institution. However, as Stevens notes, due process is important even when a faculty member attempts to resolve informally a case of plagiarism—it creates a situation in which the student is not exposed to an arbitrary exercise of academic discretion. The suggestions on interacting with a potential or actual student plagiarist discussed above are not only legally prudent, they are also designed to deal with students in ways that are fair and just.

Prohibitions against Selling Term Papers

Some states have enacted statutes that make it unlawful to sell a term paper, essay, thesis, report, or dissertation to students. Sandler found 14 states that, as of early 1999, had enacted such legislation, although Sandler does note that he makes no claim that his list is complete or current (Sandler, "Plagiarism in Colleges in USA"). Green, in a footnote, provides references to such statutes and lists statutes to the same set of states as found in Sandler (Green, 2002). They both mention the same set of reported cases against businesses that sell papers to students:

- *United States* v. *Int'l Term Papers, Inc.*, 477 F.2d 1277, 1280 (1st Cir. 1973);
- *Trustees of Boston Univ.* v. *ASM Communications, Inc.*, 33 F. Supp. 2d 66 (D. Mass. 1998);
- *People* v. *Magee*, 423 N.Y.S.2d 343 (N.Y. App. Div. 1979);
- *State* v. *Saksniit*, 332 N.Y.S.2d 343 (N.Y. Sup. Ct. 1972).

Typically, the offense is treated as a misdemeanor, with penalties between 2 to 6 months in jail and fines not to exceed $1,000. Some states, such as Colorado, New Jersey, and Virginia, have given a college or university official the right to request that a "court enjoin a business from selling term papers, etc. to its students." In some other states, the attorney general can apply for an injunction against such businesses (Sandler, "Plagiarism in Colleges in USA").

The difficulty in putting such establishments permanently out of business is illustrated by the Boston University case (Sandler, "Plagiarism in Colleges in USA"). The university unsuccessfully sued several companies that sold term papers for wire fraud, mail fraud, and racketeering under the Racketeer Influenced and Corrupt Organizations Act, also known as the RICO Act. The court's decision was based on the university's misuse of the RICO Act and its inability to prove that its degrees had suffered a loss of value sufficient for a RICO suit (Guernsey, 1998: A23.) That it is difficult to put such companies permanently out of business can be seen from the fact that, in 1981, Boston University had obtained permanent injunctions in state court prohibiting at least one of the defendants-and maybe others that were successors or alter egos to the companies against which the university had obtained the injunction-from selling term papers to Boston University students (Sandler, "Plagiarism in Colleges in USA").

Legal Issues Surrounding Plagiarism Detection Services

In an attempt to deter student plagiarism, some institutions have turned to commercial plagiarism detections services. Some have raised questions about the legality of the use of some of these services. Not all companies that provide plagiarism detection services store student papers in a company-controlled database. However, for those that do store papers, in effect making a copy of them, the concern is that the storage of students' papers, without the students' permission, on these servers constitutes copyright infringement. As Dan Burt argues in a recent Chronicle of Higher Education article on this controversy, such use is undermined by three of the four factors used to determine if use of a copyrighted work falls within the "fair use" exception to U.S. Copyright Law: the entire student paper is copied; the paper is a creative work; and "they are being submitted to a commercial enterprise, not an educational institution (Foster 2002.) In an ironic twist, the argument here is that in an effort to use these services to prevent or minimize student plagiarism leads to copyright infringement.

Turnitin.com, a well-known provider of plagiarism detection systems and a company that stores student papers on its server, argues that:

> ...by submitting the work [the student paper], the student
> implicitly agrees that the teacher may comment on, criticize
> and otherwise evaluate the academic quality of the work, an

138

evaluation that should include consideration of both the work's content and integrity (Foley and Lardner, "Legal Document").

Submitting the student work to Turnitin.com would fall within this "evaluation license." However, Turnitin acknowledges that this implied license may not extend to the archiving of student papers-the practice whose legality has been most questioned. Here, the company argues that such a practice constitutes "fair use" of a student's work and is thus allowable under U.S. copyright law. Turnitin.com acknowledges that its use is commercial in nature-its plagiarism detection system is provided to institutions on a for-profit basis-but that this commercial use of a work still falls under the "fair use" exception of U.S. copyright law (Foley and Lardner, "Legal Document").

In addition to copyright infringement, some have argued that the practice of storing student papers is illegal because it may be a potential invasion of a student's privacy. Sending a student paper to such a service, without that student's written permission, would make available personally identifiable information. This would be violation of the Family Education Rights and Privacy Act (FERPA). Under FERPA, institutions of higher education are not permitted to release personal information about students without their consent. Having such information on a paper written by a student under the age of 13 would be a violation of the Child Online Privacy Protection Act (COPPA). According to LeRoy Rooker, director of the U.S. Department of Education's Family Policy Compliance Office: "You can hire a vendor to check for plagiarism [b]ut once they do that, they can't keep that personally identifiable document and use it for any other purposes (Foster, 2002).

Whether or not it is legal to store student papers without permission in a plagiarism detection service database is a disputed issue. In December 2001, James J. Mingle, the university counsel at Cornell University, found that submitting student papers, without permission, to Turnitin.com violated Cornell's Copyright Policy; doing so would violate the copyright ownership that this policy vested in the student author (Mingle, 2001). The article on plagiarism-detection tools in the *Chronicle of Higher Education* states that the University of California at Berkeley decided not to subscribe to Turnitin.com over those concerns (Foster, 2002). (A search of the U.C. Berkeley Web site, however, shows a good number of links to U.C. Berkeley Web pages with instructions on using Turnitin.com.) In defense of such a practice, Turnitin.com devotes an entire section of its Web site to support its claim that such a practice is legal, including a legal document written for Turnitin by a major law firm (Foley and Lardner, "Legal Document").

There are things faculty can do to reduce the risk from the legal questions arising from the archiving of student papers. If this has not already been done, seeking the opinion of an institution's legal counsel seems a prudent action. Faculty can warn students-preferably in their course syllabus-that a plagiarism detection service will be used, that student papers will become part of the company database, and that students will upload their work to the database. Cornell's policy on the use of antiplagiarism services supports some of these approaches and adds that a student's written permission should be obtained. Finally, a student can be given offline alternatives to using Turnitin.com. In an ironic twist, Turnitin.com's offline alternatives are ones often suggested as ways to minimize student plagiarism without the use of a detection service: submitting a photocopy of the first page of all referenced sources, the use of an annotated bibliography, and a short reflection paper on the research methodology the student used (NJIT, "Plagiarism Prevention"). The use of offline alternatives may also assuage the ethical concerns that conditioning enrollment in a course on the student's acceptance of the use of an antiplagiarism service is coercive.

Conclusion

Student plagiarism, as one can see from this review, is not a simple act of copyright infringement or of academic dishonesty. Legally and pedagogically, it makes sense not to treat plagiarism and copyright infringement as one and the same: there are important differences between the two, and understanding where plagiarism and copyright infringement diverge helps inform our understanding of both. Automatically treating a student who has plagiarized as an academically dishonest person, subject to the worst punishment an institution can give, may not be legally or ethically warranted. Using a process that affords a student some due process considerations-even when using informal means to handle the situation-makes sense ethically, legally, and pedagogically.

The most useful way to think about legal issues related to student plagiarism is that, though it is important to understand the law related to student plagiarism, the legal issues should not be isolated from ethical and pedagogical considerations. In many respects, when dealing with a case of student plagiarism, the best advice an attorney can give is to inform your actions with ethical and pedagogical considerations.

Works Cited

Alshculer, Alfred S., and Gregory S. Blimling. 1995. "Curbing Epidemic Cheating Through Systematic Change." *College Teaching* 43, no. 4 (Fall): 123–125.

Center for Academic Integrity, Duke University, Durham, NC. "CAI Research." Available: www.academicintegrity.org/cai_research.asp.

Craft v. Kobler, 667 F. Supp. 120 (1987), 124.

Crews, Kenneth D. 2002. "Fair-Use: Overview and Meaning for Higher Education." Indiana University—Purdue University Copyright Management Center, Indianapolis. Available: www.copyright.iupui.edu/highered.htm.

Davis, Barbara Gross. 1993. *Preventing Academic Dishonesty: Tools for Teaching.* San Francisco: Jossey-Bass.

Feist Publications, Inc. v. Rural Telephone Service Co., Inc., 499 U.S. 340 (1991), 362.

Foley and Lardner. "Legal Document." Prepared for Turnitin.com. Available: www.turnitin.com /static/legal/legal_document.html.

Foster, Andrea. 2002. "Plagiarism-Detection Tools Creates Legal Quandary: When Professors Send Students' Papers To a Database, Are Copyrights Violated?" *The Chronicle of Higher Education.* Available: http://chronicle.com/free/v48/i36/36a03701.htm.

Gehring, Donald D. 1998. "When Institutions and Their Faculty Address Issues of Academic Dishonesty: Realities and Myths." In *Academic Integrity Matters*, edited by Dana D. Burnett, Lynn Rudolph, and Karen O. Clifford, Washington, D.C.: National Association of Student Personnel.

Gerdeman, R. Dean. "Academic Dishonesty and the Community College." ERIC Clearinghouse for Community Colleges. Available: www.gseis.ucla.edu/ERIC/digests/dig0007.html.

Gibaldi, Joseph. 2003. *MLA Handbook for Writers of Research Paper*, 6th edition. New York: Modern Language Association of America.

Green, Stuart P. 2002. "Plagiarism, Norms, and the Limits of Theft Law: Some Observations on the Use of Criminal Sanctions in Enforcing Intellectual Property Laws." *Hastings Law Journal* 54 (November): 167–242.

Guernsey, Lisa. 1998. "Judge Dismisses Boston U.'s Suit Against Online Term-Paper Companies." *The Chronicle of Higher Education* December 18: A23.

Harris, Robert A. 2001. The Plagiarism Handbook: Strategies for Preventing, Detecting, and Dealing with Plagiarism. Los Angeles: Pyrczak.

Howard, Rebecca Moore. 2001a. "Forget about Policing Plagiarism, Just Teach." *The Chronicle of Higher Education* November 16: B24.

Howard, Rebecca Moore. 2001b. "Plagiarism: What Should a Teacher Do?" Paper presented at the Conference on College Composition and Communication, Denver, CO. Available: http://wrt-howard.syr.edu/Papers/CCCC2001.html.

Kibler, William L. 1998. "The Academic Dishonesty of College Students: The Prevalence and Problem and Effective Educational Prevention Programs." In *Academic Integrity Matters*, edited by Dana D. Burnett, Lynn Rudolph, and Karen O. Clifford. Washington, D.C.: National Association of Student Personnel.

Mingle, James J., University Counsel and Secretary of the Corporation, Cornell University. 2001. "Re: Turnitin.com" Available: www.copyright.cornell.edu/policy/Kramnick.pdf.

Narell v. *Freeman*, 872 F.2d 907 (1989), quoted in Stearns, 1992: 567.

NJIT. "Plagiarism Prevention." Available: www.njit.edu/old/tlt/turnitin/legal.htm.

Ogden, Robert S. 2003. "Copyright Issues for Libraries and Librarians," *Library Collections, Acquisitions and Technical Services* 27, no. 4: 473–481. Available www.sciencedirect.com.

Pavela, Gary. 1998. "The Law and Academic Integrity." In *Academic Integrity and Student Development: Legal and Policy Perspectives*, edited by William L. Kibler, Elizabeth M. Nuss, Brent G. Paterson, and Gary Pavela. Ashville, N.C.: College Adminstration Publications.

Sandler, Ronald. "Plagiarism in Colleges in USA." Available: www.rbs2.com/plag.htm #anchor800000.

Silvergate, Harvey A., and Josh Gewolb. 2003. "FIRE's Guide to Due Process and Fair Procedures on Campus." Foundation for Individual Rights in Education, Philadelphia, PA. Available: www.thefireguides.org/guides/due-process.php.

Stearns, Laurie. 1992. "Copy Wrong: Plagiarism, Process, Property, and the Law." *California Law Review* 80 (March): 513-553.

Stevens, Edward H. 1996. "Informal Resolution of Academic Misconduct Cases: A Due Process Paradigm." *College Teaching* 44, no.4 (Fall): 140–144.

U.S. Copyright Office. "Copyright Basics, Circular 1." Available: www.copyright.gov/circs /circ1.html.

University of Texas Office of Intellectual Property, Austin, TX. "Fair Use of Copyrighted Materials." Available: www.utsystem.edu/ogc/intellectualproperty/copypol2.htm.

Washington State University, Pullman, WA. "Fair Use." Available: http://publishing.wsu.edu /copyright/fairuse/.

CHAPTER 12

Call the Pros: Professional Organizations' Recommendations on Intellectual Honesty

Frances Kaufmann

Introduction

You are faced with 20 freshmen in an expository writing class. To pass time before class begins, they are feverishly multitasking on their laptops-"IM"-ing friends, downloading music, and finishing up an assignment for another class in Blackboard. The computers are provided to every undergraduate student as part of the university's mobile computing program. They have become another extension of these students' bodies as have their cell phones. They cannot live without them. It's time to begin a class session on academic honesty. How do you explain to these students the importance of honesty in education and research, why it is important to keep careful records of information they have found in books and library databases, and why it is NOT OK to copy and paste information from databases and the Internet into their papers without giving proper credit to the creators of the intellectual property they are using? Where do you turn for guidance on communicating the importance of academic integrity and the consequences of plagiarism to these Gen Y'ers who believe that all information on the Internet is free and can be used without restriction?

After mulling over these questions for the past few years, I decided to find out what professional and scholarly organizations recommended to their members;

educators and professionals who are engaged in teaching high school through graduate students and who are the creators of the scholarly writing that these students use for their research. What better resource to tap for guidelines and tools to teach effectively our students about intellectual honesty? I was gratified to find a wealth of useful information that is easily accessible and can be adapted for use in the battle against the plagiarism plague. I hope that by sharing this information with fellow educators and librarians, we can begin to make a significant contribution to launching our students on their way to understanding and respecting the importance of using other peoples' intellectual property honestly.

Numerous professional organizations have faced the issues of plagiarism and academic integrity. In response, they have published style manuals and formulated policy statements, codes of ethics, and standards of professional conduct. This chapter will examine resources from professional organizations in the humanities, social sciences, education, and the sciences. What do their policies have in common and how do they differ? Are there some general guidelines that can be gleaned from among these diverse organizations? How can we use these resources to make our students aware of what constitutes plagiarism and teach them the importance of academic integrity and honesty in their research and writing?

The Humanities

Founded in 1883, the Modern Language Association (MLA) is an organization with more than 30,000 members. The mission of MLA is to promote and "strengthen the study and teaching of language and literature" (MLA, "About the MLA"). The organization's *MLA Handbook for Writers of Research Papers* (Gibaldi, 2003) has long been considered the standard guide for college students writing research papers in the humanities. Now in its sixth edition, the book features an excellent chapter on plagiarism. It is interesting to note that in the fifth edition, published in 1999, plagiarism was covered as a subsection of the chapter titled "Research and Writing." With this new edition, the guide has expanded coverage on the topic of plagiarism by devoting an entire chapter to the subject. With this expansion, MLA has certainly indicated the importance of clearly explaining all aspects of plagiarism to today's generation of students. The introduction acknowledges that students may be very aware of charges of plagiarism in the publishing and recording industries. It discusses the existence of guidelines and honor codes at their schools and discussions in their classrooms on the topic. Separate sections cover the definition of plagiarism, its consequences, and how the Internet has transformed the exchange of information.

Section 2.3, "Information Sharing Today," discusses the ease of finding, modifying, and sending information over the Internet. It stresses that authorship of materials available electronically must be properly acknowledged. Section 2.5, "Forms of Plagiarism," shows exactly what constitutes plagiarism and recommends careful note-keeping during research. The section includes excellent examples of plagiarism, presenting the original source material and then illustrating how plagiarism is committed by paraphrasing, borrowing specific terms, or presenting another's line of thinking without giving credit or documentation. It explains how to avoid plagiarism by inserting parenthetical documentation in the narrative and giving credit by proper credit in the list of works cited. Students ought not to be confused about what constitutes plagiarism once they consider this clearly stated guideline: "If you have any doubt about whether or not you are committing plagiarism, cite your source or sources" (Gibaldi, 2003: 73). The chapter ends with a point-by-point summary of what constitutes plagiarism and how plagiarism can be avoided. The sixth edition of the *MLA Handbook* is an excellent resource guide for anyone teaching students research and writing in the humanities.

Another source of guidance from MLA is their "Statement of Professional Ethics" intended to "embody reasonable norms for ethical conduct" (MLA, "Statement of Professional Ethics"). Premise 7 includes plagiarism in the list of unethical behavior, with reference to this explanatory note:

> In this statement we adopt the definition of plagiarism given in *The MLA Style Manual*: "Plagiarism is the use of another person's ideas or expressions in your writing without acknowledging the source (MLA, "Statement of Professional Ethics").

The MLA statement goes on to define plagiarism from its most "blatant form," representing another person's words as one's own without proper citation to the more subtle forms, such as presenting another person's argument or original thinking as one's own (MLA, "Statement of Professional Ethics").

Another excellent resource for faculty, graduate students, and administrators who direct writing programs, writing centers, or teach freshman composition and writing is the council of Writing Program Administrators (WPA; www.wpacouncil.org). The WPA has produced an outstanding document on plagiarism, "Defining and Avoiding Plagiarism: The WPA Statement on Best Practices," adopted January 2003. It is available on their Web site in PDF format at www.wpacouncil.org/positions/WPAplagiarism.pdf. The statement defines plagiarism and examines its causes. It explains the responsibilities of students, faculty, and administrators. The most practical and helpful section is the list of five best practices that merit integration into teaching and guiding students through the research and writing process. Recommendations include how to explain plagiarism, the need for clear policies, and how to design and sequence assignments that promote inquiry. Concise and well written, the WPA strategies support "students throughout their research process" making "plagiarism both difficult and unnecessary" (Council of Writing Program Administrators, 2003). This document is a must have for any librarian or instructor.

Many scholarly organizations publish codes of ethics and standards of professional conduct that include statements on plagiarism. For example, the American Historical Association's (AHA) Professional Division has responsibility for ethical concerns. The division developed and published the "Statement on Standards of Professional Conduct" in May 2003. The online version is available at http://theaha.org./pubs/standard.htm. A complimentary print copy is also available by contacting the association. The introduction to the online version urges members "to share this document with your students and colleagues, whether by ordering additional copies or photocopying this publication" (AHA, 2003). The document includes a separate section, "Statement on Plagiarism," that clearly explains and defines plagiarism:

> The clearest abuse is the use of another's language without
> quotation marks and citation. More subtle abuses include the
> appropriation of concepts, data, or notes all disguised in newly
> crafted sentences, or reference to a borrowed work in an early
> note and then extensive further use without attribution
> (AHA, 2003).

Careful research habits including detailed note-taking, distinction between exact quotations and paraphrasing, and the importance of checking manuscripts against cited sources are obligations of the ethical historian. The importance of having procedures in place to handle suspected cases of plagiarism is discussed, but the responsibility for investigating and sanctioning such misconduct is placed with the employing agency. Shortly after this policy was published, an article in the *Chronicle of Higher Education* reported on the AHA announcement that it would no longer investigate complaints of suspected plagiarism. William J. Cronon, head of the Professional Division, noted that of 50 to 100 inquires annually, fewer than 10 cases required formal investigation. In addition, the organization has no power to impose sanctions (Bartlett, 2003: A12). This has opened up debate about the effectiveness of statements of professional conduct and ethical codes without the power of enforcement. Even in light of this debate, historians are well served by having these guidelines in place and being able to use them to guide the work of their students and their own research.

Social Sciences

The American Psychological Association (APA) has published style manuals for more than 70 years. The *Publication Manual of the American Psychological Association,* better known as the *APA Style Manual,* is the recognized authority in the field of psychology. It has also been adopted as the publication guide for most of the social sciences including sociology, business, economics, nursing, social work, and criminology (APA, "About the Manual"). The fifth edition released in 2001 includes improved and revised guidelines for avoiding plagiarism. A section on ethics explains when to use quotation marks, gives examples of how to appropriately paraphrase sources, and refers to exact section locations that include detailed information on quotations, paraphrasing, and referencing the work of others. The Association also maintains a Web page (www.apasytle.org) to provide information on changes between editions.

The APA, like other professional organizations, is governed by a code of ethics. Their newest code, the 2002 APA Code of Ethics, went into effect on June 1, 2003. Its formal title is "Ethical Principles of Psychologists and Code of Conduct." Section 8 of the code, titled "Research and Publication," clearly defines the organization's stand on plagiarism: "Psychologists do not present portions of another's work or data as their own, even if the other work or data source is cited occasionally"(APA, "Ethical Principles"). This information is also included in the *APA Manual's* "Appendix C, 6.22 Ethical Standards for the Reporting and Publishing of Scientific Information" (APA, 2001). Social scientists, who use APA's varied sources to keep informed about ethical standards in the profession, will be well prepared to teach their students about properly acknowledging sources and avoiding plagiarism.

Anthropologists follow the "Code of Ethics of the American Anthropological Association" (American Anthropological Association, 1998). In the extensive section addressing research, plagiarism is addressed in "Section III. Research, Subsection B. Responsibility to Scholarship and Science":

> ...anthropological researchers are subject to the general moral
> rules of scientific and scholarly conduct: they should not
> deceive or knowingly misrepresent (i.e., fabricate evidence,
> falsify, plagiarize), or attempt to prevent reporting of miscon-
> duct, or obstruct the scientific/scholarly research of others
> (American Anthropological Association, 1998).

Though social science organizations do not present methods for teaching students how to avoid plagiarism, they do offer definitions of what constitutes plagiarism. With these guidelines in hand, social scientists should have the beginnings of a foundation upon which to begin to address the best ways to instruct their students about ethical research practices.

Education and Libraries

Founded in 1857 as the National Teachers Association (NTA) by educator Robert Campbell, The National Education Association (NEA) has worked to advocate for public education from preschool through graduate school. Membership is open to teachers on all levels at public institutions. Retired educators and college students studying to become teachers may also join the organization. Though there seem to be no official policy statements on plagiarism, the NEA does provide resources for teachers on the topic. National Education Association's *Advocate Online*, published online eight times a year in the Higher Education section of the NEA Web site, examines hot topics in the field. The December 2000 issue (NEA, 2000) includes a discussion of "cyber-cheating" and presents helpful information on how honor codes can help to discourage plagiarism. It also provides a list of excellent publications about academic cheating and preventing and detecting plagiarism. A search for plagiarism on the NEA Web site will lead to many helpful links to information about technology and student cheating and even a report of a Kansas teacher who resigned when the local school board did not support her decision to punish students who plagiarized a major report (NEA, 2002).

The National Association of Secondary School Principals, NASSP, in December 1998 issued a legal memorandum, "The Internet, Students' Rights and Today's Principal" (NASSP, 1998). It explores legal implications associated with student Internet use. Separate sections cover copyright law and the Internet, author's rights, and fair use. A sample acceptable use policy, including a statement on plagiarism, will help high school administrators and professionals who provide computer and systems support in secondary schools to formulate such a policy for their own school districts.

Professional organizations that focus on higher education have issued their own statements on academic integrity and fraud and misconduct in research. The Association of American Universities, founded in 1900, is composed of 62 major research universities ranging from Ivy League schools to land grant institutions. In 1988, the organization published "Framework for Institutional Policies and Procedures to Deal with Fraud in Research" (Association of American Universities, 1988). Though it was formulated to have policy in place to deal mainly with scientific research sponsored by outside agencies, it can serve as a model for what should be included in policies that deal with academic dishonesty. The document defines research fraud in detail, outlines the process for handling allegations, and proceeding with an inquiry.

The Association of American Colleges and Universities (AACU) represents institutions engaged in the process of undergraduate liberal education. More than 900 accredited institutions ranging from research universities to liberal arts colleges to community colleges work together through the organization to promote quality liberal education. In the AACU "Statement on Liberal Learning" (AACU, 1998), its members assert, "we cultivate a respect for *truth*" and "we experience the benefits of liberal learning by pursuing intellectual work that is *honest*, challenging, and significant" (AACU, 1998). Though no official policy on academic integrity seems to exist, the association's position was put forward in *CQ Researcher's* excellent issue, "Combating Plagiarism." Debra Humphreys, the association's vice president of communications and public affairs, commented on the importance of integrity in a liberal education:

> Academic honesty is the cornerstone of college learning and liberal education and, indeed, is a continuing problem that colleges face.... Problems related to plagiarism on campus paralleled problems in the larger society, such as newspaper plagiarism scandals and illegal file sharing of music and movies (Hansen, 2003: 775).

One of the AACU's most outstanding resources for educators is The Center for Academic Integrity, a consortium of 320 institutions whose students, faculty, and administrators share information about academic integrity and promote its importance. Affiliated with the Keenan Institute for Ethics at Duke University, the Center sponsors an annual conference, a newsletter, a listserv, and an excellent Web site (www.academicintegrity.org/index.asp) with links to helpful how-to resources for starting a program at your own institution, member institution honor codes, an assessment guide, and information about the center's Fundamental Values Program. This program is described in the center's publication, "The Fundamental Values of Academic Integrity." The publication defines five elements of academic integrity and discusses why it is an essential component of higher education. Plagiarism is addressed specifically thorough this directive, "All must show respect for the work of others by acknowledging their intellectual debts by proper identification of sources" (Center for Academic Integrity, 1999). At its publication in 1999, this statement was distributed to colleges and universities. One copy is available free for download from the center's Web site (www.academicin tegrity.org/fundamental.asp).

As early as the beginning of the 1990s, professional organizations concerned with technology in higher education began to address issues of ethics and computing. The "Bill of Rights and Responsibilities for Electronic Learners" (American Association of Higher Education, "Ethics and Technology") is a result of the Ethics and Technology Initiative of the American Association for Higher Education. Dr. Frank W. Connolly, recently retired professor of computer science at American University, was the impetus behind this document created in 1993. Its principles have stood the test of time and are still valid despite the rapid changes in technology since then. The document addresses the rights and responsibilities of individuals and institutions with regard to electronic learning and intellectual ownership. With regard to the responsibilities of institutions of higher learning the bill of rights states in Article IV, Section 4: "Institutions...shall train and support faculty, staff, and students to effectively use information technology. Training includes skills...to understand the ethical and legal uses of the resources" (American Association of Higher Education, "Ethics and Technology").

The American Library Association (ALA) is the oldest and largest library association in the world. With more than 60,000 members, the organization "promotes the highest quality library and information services and protects public access to information" (ALA, 2003a: vii). Two divisions, the American Association of School Librarians (AASL) and the Association of College and Research Libraries (ACRL), have resources concerning honesty in research. The AASL advocates for library media services for children and has issued a guide for school library media specialists. The "AASL Resource Guides for School Library Media Program Development" includes a bibliographic section on copyright with citations to articles especially relevant to use in elementary and high school libraries (ALA, "AASL Resource Guides").

The ACRL, with more than 12,000 members, "...enhances the effectiveness of academic and research librarians to advance learning, teaching, and research in higher education (ALA, 2003a: 83). ACRL has developed "Standards for College Libraries" that aid in assessing the effectiveness of academic libraries and librarians. Plagiarism is addressed under "Instruction":

> Information literacy skills and bibliographic instruction
> should be integrated into appropriate courses with special
> attention given to intellectual property, copyright, and plagia-
> rism (ALA, 2000).

In addition, the organization has long been concerned with information literacy and developing lifelong learners. As a result of this responsibility, ACRL produced "Information Literacy Competency Standards for Higher Education" and promotes use of these standards in higher education. Their recommendations are very clear. Standard Five states:

> The information literate student understands many of the economic, legal, and social issues surrounding the use of information and accesses and uses information ethically and legally (ALA, 2003b).

Furthermore, Outcome 2F of the standard asserts:

> Demonstrates an understanding of what constitutes plagiarism and does not represent work attributable to others as his/her own (ALA, 2003b).

Thus, it is apparent that educators, administrators, and librarians on all educational levels, from primary through graduate school, have a wide range of excellent policy statements and tools available from professional organizations in their field to guide them through the process of creating ethics codes and training students about academic integrity.

Science and Engineering

Scientific and technical organizations have long been concerned with the ethics of research because of the use of animal and human subjects and because the falsification or misappropriation of information could have dire consequences for the advancement of science and for society in general. This section will cover only official statements and policy on plagiarism in the scientific and engineering community. It does not attempt to be all-inclusive, but concentrates on major government organizations concerned with scientific research and with a selection of professional societies that govern individual fields in science and engineering.

The National Science Foundation (NSF), an agency of the federal government founded in 1950, has as its mission the initiation and support of scientific and engineering research through grants and contracts as well as to strengthen research and education programs. The National Science Foundation's Office of the Inspector General (OIG) "reviews and investigates all allegations of misconduct in science" (NSF, "An Overview"). The National Science Foundation defines research misconduct as "fabrication, falsification, plagiarism, or other serious deviation from accepted practices" (NSF, "An Overview"). Plagiarism is defined as "the appropriation of another person's ideas, processes, results, or word without giving appropriate credit" (NSF, "An Overview"). The OIG has an outreach program directed at administrators, researchers, and students involved in federally supported research. It sponsors seminars that use actual cases to encourage discussion of ethical choices and makes presentations at professional society conferences to inform the community it serves. There is also a toll-free hotline for reporting allegations of misconduct.

The National Institutes of Health (NIH) comprises 27 centers and institutes in the areas of medical and behavioral research ranging from the National Cancer Institute, established in 1937, to one of the newest, the National Center on Minority Health and Health Disparities, begun in 1993. The institute's Office of Extramural Research has issued a policy titled "Ensuring Integrity of Scientific Research" that stresses the importance of integrity of research in science and includes plagiarism in its definition of scientific misconduct (NIH, 2000). The National Institutes of Health also has a detailed policy that governs their Intramural Research Program that includes a definition of plagiarism (NIH, 1991).

The National Academy of Sciences (NAS) was created by an act of incorporation signed by President Abraham Lincoln in March 1863. Today, experts in all areas of science, medicine, technology, and engineering give their time to study crucial issues in these areas and to advise the government and the general public. Its publishing arm, the National Academies Press, makes more than 3,000 books available free online. "Integrity in Scientific Research: Creating an Environment that Promotes Responsible Conduct" is available for viewing online (NAS, 2002). The document spells out what is expected:

> Researchers will not report the work of others as if it were their own. This is plagiarism. Furthermore, they should be honest with respect to the contributions of colleagues and collaborators (NAS, 2002).

It also recommends instruction for future researchers include professional ethics training and topics such as "plagiarism, honorary authorship, data selection, and graphic design" (NAS, 2002).

Professional organizations in the sciences have professional codes of conduct. For example, the American Chemical Society expects its members to follow "The Chemist's Code of Conduct," approved and adopted in 1994. It states:

> Conflicts of interest and scientific misconduct, such as fabrication, falsification and plagiarism are incompatible with this code (American Chemical Society, 1994).

Another professional organization committed to fostering intellectual honesty is Sigma Xi. This organization is the international honor society for science and engineering and it actively promotes integrity in science and sponsors educational programs on scientific integrity. Two excellent publications are available for purchase from the society, *Honor in Science* for graduate students and *The Responsible Researcher: Paths and Pitfalls* for faculty and administrators. It covers expectations and issues for undergraduate through faculty, deans, and department chairs. More information about the society and its policies is available at its Web site (www.sigmaxi.org).

An exceptional source for ethics information in engineering is The Online Ethics Center for Engineering and Science at Case Western Reserve University (www.onlineethics.org/) The center was established in 1995 under an NSF grant. The project is directed by Caroline Whitbeck, Professor in Ethics at Case Western Reserve University. A distinguished roster of experts from academia, professional societies, corporations, and the government serve as advisors to the center. The Web site section entitled "Responsible Research" (www.onlineethics.org/reseth/index.html) contains links to essays on research ethics, scenarios, and cases to use in student faculty discussions, educational resources including materials that can be used in courses, and an extensive list of reference materials on research integrity. The Online Ethics center is required surfing and studying for anyone involved in teaching science and engineering students.

Conclusion

There are other excellent resources that educators can turn to for information about guidance in teaching information ethics. The "Ten Commandments of Computer Ethics" is a farsighted and useful document that has relevance for anyone who uses computers. Since it was presented by Ramon C. Barquin at the Computer Ethics Conference in 1992, countless schools have used it. Commandment 8 is clear and to the point, "Thou Shalt Not Appropriate Other People's Intellectual Output" (Computer Ethics Institute, "Ten Commandments").

The Computer Ethics Institute is a project of the Brookings Institution. According to the Brookings Web site, the Brookings Institution is "an independent, nonpartisan organization" whose mission is to "analyze emerging issues and to offer practical approaches to those issues in language aimed at the general public" (Brookings Institution, "About"). Practicing what it preaches, the organization is governed by its own "Statement on Integrity of Research," adopted on June 25, 2003 (Brookings Institution, "About").

Those of us who face the daily rewards and challenges of working with students to teach them the ethics and methodology of scholarly research and writing are fortunate to be able to tap the resources and recommendations of professional and scholarly organizations for guidance. Educators, librarians, researchers, and students have a wealth of essential and useful information to guide them in properly crediting the work and ideas of others. Professional organizations in the humanities, social sciences, education, and the sciences have created excellent style manuals, Web sites, guidelines, ethics codes, and policy statements that clearly define academic honesty and present practical, easy to use tools for teaching and learning about the ethical use of information.

Works Cited

American Anthropological Association. 1998. "Code of Ethics." Available: www.aaanet.org/committees/ethics/ethcode.htm.

American Association of Higher Education. "Ethics and Technology Initiative." "Bill of Rights and Responsibilities for Electronic Learners." Available: www.luc.edu/infotech/cease/bill-of-rights.html

American Chemical Society. 1994. "The Chemist's Code of Conduct." Available: www.chemistry.org/portal/a/c/s/1/acsdisplay.html?DOC=membership%5Cconduct.html.

American Historical Association (AHA). 2003. "Statement on Standards of Professional Conduct." Available: www.theaha.org/pubs/standard.htm.

American Library Association (ALA). "AASL Resource Guides for School Library Media Program Development." Available: www.ala.org/PrinterTemplate.cfm?Section=resource guides&Template=/ContentManagement/HTMLDisplay.cfm&ContentID=15782.

———. 2000. "Standards for College Libraries 2000 Edition." Available: www.ala.org/ala/acrl/acrlstandards/standardscollegelibraries.htm

———. 2003a. *ALA Handbook of Organization 2003–2004,* Chicago: ALA.

———. 2003b. "Information Literacy Competency Standards for Higher Education." Available: www.ala.org/ala/acrl/acrlstandards/informationliteracycompetency.htm.

American Psychological Association (APA). "About the Manual: Who Uses APA Style?" APA Style.org. Available: www.apastyle.org/whouses.html.

———. "Ethical Principles of Psychologists and Code of Conduct." Available: www.apa.org/ethics/code2002.html#8_11.

———. 2001. *Publication Manual of the American Psychological Association.* Washington, DC: American Psychological Association.

Association of American Colleges and Universities (AACU). 1998. "Statement on Liberal Learning." Available: www.aacu.org/about/liberal_learning.cfm.

Association of American Universities. 1988. "Framework for Institutional Policies and Procedures to Deal with Fraud in Research." Available: www.aau.edu/reports/FrwkRschFraud.html.

Bartlett, Thomas. 2003. "Historical Association Will No Longer Investigate Allegations of Wrongdoing." *Chronicle of Higher Education* 49, no. 37: A12.

Brookings Institution. "About the Brookings Institution." Available: www.brook.edu/index/about.htm.

Center for Academic Integrity. 1999. "The Fundamental Values of Academic Integrity." Available: www.academicintegrity.org/fundamental.asp.

Computer Ethics Institute. "Ten Commandments of Computer Ethics." Available: www.brook.edu/dybdocroot/its/cei/overview/Ten_Commanments_of_Computer_Ethics.htm.

Council of Writing Program Administrators. 2003. "Defining and Avoiding Plagiarism: The WPA Statement on Best Practices." Available: www.ilstu.edu/~ddhesse/wpa/positions /WPAplagiarism.pdf.

Gibaldi, Joseph, editor. 2003. "Chapter 2: Plagiarism." In *MLA Handbook for Writers of Research Papers*, 66–75. New York: Modern Language Association.

Hansen, Brian. 2003. "Combating Plagiarism." *CQ Researcher* 13, no. 32: 773–796.

Modern Language Association (MLA). "About the MLA." Available: www.mla.org/about.

———. "Statement of Professional Ethics." Available: www.mla.org/resources/documents/ rep_profethics/repview_profethics.

National Academy of Sciences (NAS). 2002. "Integrity in Scientific Research: Creating an Environment that Promotes Responsible Conduct." Washington, DC: National Academics Press. Available: www.nap.edu/books/0309084792/html.

National Association of Secondary School Principals (NASSP). 1998. "The Internet, Students' Rights, and Today's Principal." Available: www.principals.org/services/legalmem_1298.cfm.

National Education Association (NEA). 2000 (December). "Advocate Online." Available: www.nea.org/he/advo00/advo0012/issues.html.

———. 2002 (May). "NEA Today." Available: www.nea.org/neatoday/0205/rights.html.

National Institutes of Health (NIH). 1991. "Policies and Procedures Relating to Possible Scientific Misconduct in the IPR at NIH." "NIH Policy Manual." Available: www1.od.nih.gov/oma/ manualchapters/intramural/3006/main.html.

———. 2000. "Ensuring Integrity of Scientific Research. National Institutes of Health Office of Extramural Research." Available: http://grants2.nih.gov/grants/policy/emprograms/overview/ integsci.htm.

National Science Foundation (NSF). "An Overview of the National Science Foundation's Office of Inspector General: Educational and Outreach Programs." Available: www.oig.nsf.gov/out-reachprograms.pdf.

CHAPTER 13

Plagiarism Busters: Free (and Not-So-Free) Web Resources for Plagiarism Detection

Eileen M. Stec

and

Dr. Mallika Henry

Introduction

Instructors in the academic environment encounter students daily who struggle with using words. These students may be searching for documents in the library and not know the key words to use for their search, or they may be struggling to write essays for their classes and not realize the extent to which they are giving up their own agency in using the words of others. The problem of appropriating the words of others comes up daily—how to use the right words in the right way, without relying too heavily on the words that are already available. A simple Google search on any phrase in a student essay, for example, can yield thousands of hits, although no real plagiarism has occurred.

The authors of this chapter are an instruction librarian and a writing instructor. Both authors work extensively with undergraduate students at a large university. As an instruction librarian, Ms. Stec became intrigued with how students viewed this dilemma—or did they recognize it as a dilemma at all?

Following extensive testing, it was clear that students do understand the basics of plagiarism. During her first year teaching, she required students to complete an online tutorial on plagiarism and academic integrity. She was alerted by the server administrator that someone from the dormitories had run a program attempting to locate the certificate of completion page that proved fulfillment of the assignment. Students were cheating on the ethics assignment! Designing the script to locate the certificate took some ingenuity and time to develop. It would have been simpler to work through the 25-minute online tutorial. Clearly, a human dynamic was at work having little relationship to the complexity of the assignment. Ms. Stec grew to appreciate the teaching faculty's frustration regarding the amount of energy and time it takes to prove instances of plagiarism. Though students should be made aware of a university's policy on cheating, education is not the answer to this problem.

Software publishers offer tools to educators in the form of plagiarism detection software. Librarians test electronic products regularly in their collection development function. It seemed natural and logical to join a writing instructor to determine if the software proved as reliable as it was promoted to be. It was time to test the tools.

Dr. Henry is a writing instructor. According to Dr. Henry, she experiences instances of plagiarism constantly. Henry reports that some of her students seem to evince the attitude: "if someone else says it better than I do, why not just use what he says?" Other students become frustrated because of their writing problems and resort to deliberate cheating. Some students become somewhat infatuated with the readings and perhaps unconsciously blend others' words and ideas into their own. Many of these small instances can be corrected through education. But when these small instances become large ones—when a student has her husband do her work, or buys a paper, or simply appropriates passages from an existing text, and turns it in as a major assignment—teachers need to find tools to make their tasks easier.

Most schools have rules that protect students from being wrongly accused of plagiarism. The task of proof lies with the instructor, who usually does not want to inflate the issue beyond its merits. However, the instructor has a right to uphold her own standards, and the obligation to honor the honest work that other students turn in. Tools have been appearing, and with the Internet as difficult to regulate and as permissive an environment as it is, people use these tools sometimes without knowing the pitfalls. In this chapter, the authors have tried to find available plagiarism detection tools and tested the most reputable one— as so many of the others have disappeared in the time it has taken to undertake this chapter. We present you with a finding that is not very encouraging, but it may help others avoid some mistakes.

What Kind of Cheating Do Students Admit to?

Donald McCabe is a leader in contemporary research on student cheating in U.S. colleges. In 1990–1991 McCabe found that over 67 percent of students studied self-reported cheating behavior at least once, and approximately 19 percent had cheated five or more times. The most frequent kind of cheating was the "failure to footnote sources in written work", while next in frequency was "collaboration on assignments when the instructor specifically asked for individual work." Students also admitted to "copying from other students on tests and examinations, fabrication of bibliographies, helping someone else cheat on a test, and using unfair methods to learn the content of a test ahead of time" in decreasing order of frequency (McCabe 1992.)

How Do Students View Their Own Behavior?

McCabe's work has demonstrated specific rationalization or neutralization techniques students employ in order to suspend their sense of ethics and protect their self-esteem (Sykes and Matza, 1957). Students feel victimized and project responsibility for their cheating onto others; believe that no one is harmed by their ethical lapses; retaliate against an unfair teacher by cheating; cheat because they see others receiving preferential treatment; and experience loyalty toward a person or group more strongly than toward the university or honor code (McCabe, 1992).

From an educator's point of view, most of this reasoning is likely to be attributable to already weak students. Anecdotal evidence and discussions with other educators point to the fact that students who feel victimized, who see their teachers as unfair, or who project responsibility onto others are often students who are rather marginally committed to their education. But another ethical issue is present: that of a hierarchy of loyalties. The foundational work in moral education by Laurence Kohlberg, which established a stage theory of moral development in which right and wrong correspond to broad social rules, has been critiqued by Carol Gilligan, who has suggested that girls as well as underprivileged young people prioritize *care of others* over social norms (Gilligan, 1982). She hypothesized that the breaking of social rules (*issues of justice*) was less important to these populations than the injunction not to turn one's back on a friend in need—her *ethic of caring*. Gilligan's work, though somewhat contradicted by further research, has opened up the conversation about ethical norms for different members of society. This prevalence of highly subjective ethical scales gives even more urgency to the need for widely discussing ethics and scholarly responsibility in the university setting. The fact that the Internet has changed the nature of student research, as well as of borrowing, buying, and pirating, should be seen as a strong motivation for universities to take up the challenge of holding frequent public discussion of honor codes and other systems of integrity. This is an issue McCabe treats in considerable depth (McCabe and Treviño, 2002).

The Role of Education

To a considerable extent, students are already aware of rules of plagiarism and academic integrity but continue to engage in behavior that violates these rules. In a study conducted at Rutgers University, several hundred students scored above 90% on questions about the nature of plagiarism (Stec, 2003). However, their scores were lower in the category McCabe refers to as "appealing to higher loyalties." Students were asked the following question: "Your best friend from high school has a business selling research papers. He is using the proceeds to support his new baby. You agree to sell a couple of papers to your college friends, but don't use any of the papers yourself." Students failed to recognize that this situation represented an ethical lapse, whereas they could recognize the lapse in other questions regarding purchase of research papers and in failing to document sources appropriately. Students were less clear about the issue of having someone else edit their papers and whether it was acceptable to substitute a replica print citation for an online publication if the student was unsure how to write a citation for an online item (Stec, 2003). These results can be seen as pointing to a broad situation of ethical relativism and the need for universities to articulate clearly enforceable standards for honesty in scholarship.

The salient results from this study lead to the conclusion that most students do understand the major aspects of cheating but are not necessarily motivated to correct their own behavior. The study demonstrates that students continue to download material from the Internet without citations and to copy material from other students. One obvious solution is to create enforcement mechanisms, necessitating tools for detecting plagiarism in student work.

Plagiarism Detection Software

Where Have All the Free Trials Gone?

The authors intended to test several software packages using free trials available as recently as October 2003. At that time, Plagiserve was a free service; EduTie and Eve2 both offered free trials. Currently, EduTie posts a discontinued service notice, and Plagiserve announces it has been sold. Both sites direct the user to a new company, MyDropBox, where free trials are only available to institutions. WordCHECK has discontinued its free demo. Glatt Plagiarism Services does not offer a free trial; CopyCatch only offers a free trial to United

160

Kingdom academic institutions. An interested customer may view a demonstration of Turnitin but not submit her own paper. Findsame has disappeared from the Web, its former URL available for sale. Table 1 indicates the availability and cost of the remaining services for the individual user.

Figure 13-1. Entry Level Pricing for Software Package as of January 29, 2004	
Software	**Cost**
Turnitin www.turnitin.com	No prices listed
MyDropBox www.mydropbox.com	Individual Membership, $89.90 per year
Eve2 www.canexus.com	$19.99 for unlimited use
WordCHECKsystems www.wordchecksystems.com	$149 academic price
Glatt Plagiarism Services www.plagiarism.com	Plagiarism Screening Program, $300
CopyCatch www.copycatch.freeserve.co.uk/	No prices listed

The authors had access to Turnitin through their university license. Therefore, it was the only software that could be tested first-hand.

Certain software was beyond the scope of this chapter. The authors only investigated software used for essay writing and research papers. Applications like Jplag and MOSS (Measure of Software Similarity) are used to review computer programs for stolen code (Simmonds, 2003). Those applications were not included in the research.

Controversies

According to the LeMoyne College Electronic Plagiarism Seminar, there are "by conservative guess, at least tens of thousands of sites available from which students can download papers and assignments, so no comprehensive list is possible" (LeMoyne2003). In fact, paper mills may be connected with plagiarism detection services in some cases. The *Chronicle of Higher Education* (Young, 2002) has reported that two online services, PlagiServe.com and EduTie.com, seem to be "fronts for paper mills" according to Louis Bloomfield, a physics professor at the University of Virginia. Bloomfield stated: "It is entirely possible that papers you submit to those services will later be sold to other students." Particularly suspect, we believe, are those plagiarism services being offered free of charge. This practice can be seen as very tempting for any company that is collecting student papers. In any case, legal issues may be raised about the collection and use of student papers online, as students thereby lose complete control of the use of their work. This dilemma questions the very use of plagiarism detection services, as companies that store copies of student research papers and use them for comparison with other student papers thereby increase the value of their databases without compensating students for their work.

Research Results

In a 2001 report sponsored by the Joint Information System Committee (JISC), 40 United Kingdom post-secondary faculty participants tested several plagiarism services using staff-authored essays. The most highly rated for detection abilities were CopyCatch with Turnitin and Eve2 tied for second place. It should be noted, however, that CopyCatch only detects evidence of collusion among class papers, Eve2 only searches the Internet for cut & paste evidence, and Turnitin does both. CopyCatch and Turnitin were also tested with essays acquired from companies selling research papers. Both had good detection rates, with CopyCatch slightly higher. Because CopyCatch does not search the Web, how the company obtained these results is unclear. These faculty also hold the view that students use more illicitly copied material from textbooks and theses than from the Internet (Bull et al., 2001). Turnitin had more detection functionality than either of the other two services under review.

Both Turnitin and MyDropbox have features that allow students to upload their papers, checking themselves for plagiarized material. Eve2, WordCHECK, and CopyCatch do not have provisions for student submission. Turnitin compares submitted work against its database of Web pages and the growing database of previously submitted student papers. Our tests showed that the application posed considerable problems. The first trial consisted of submitting a paper written by one of the authors, freely available on the Web. The software returned a report that the paper was free of plagiarism, which was obviously incorrect as the paper had been obtained online, albeit by its own author. When the paper was copied and pasted into the Turnitin window, the title and author's name were inadvertently included. When the same paper was submitted a second time without the identifying information, the report cited massive plagiarism and correctly identified the URL hosting the original work.

It was unclear if the report picked up the plagiarism from its own database (as Turnitin had already obtained the paper with the first submission) or if it correctly located the Web address it was supposed to find.

For the second trial, a recent article from the *D-Lib* online journal was submitted. The report indicated 10% of the text submitted matched the original article from *D-Lib*. There was no acknowledgment that the entire article was copied. Again, this was a major oversight and a strong signal that Turnitin cannot trace important instances of plagiarism. Several student papers were submitted. The results appropriately highlighted several phrases that originated from Internet sites. However, all the significant passages were footnoted and referenced correctly by the students—thus; these were not instances of plagiarism, though they were detected as such. Turnitin does not compare footnoted passages with a paper's listed citations. This means that the use of Turnitin can incorrectly implicate honest students.

We found that Turnitin was unable to detect papers from the "Invisible Web," articles that require navigating registration or passwords. Royce found that Turnitin could not trace material lifted from Usenet discussion groups or from journals in subscription databases. It did not work well with paraphrased material, and it does not look for further matches once it finds a single match, making it possible to skip the actual occurrence of plagiarism if the first instance is a correctly cited quote. "Turnitin," wrote Royce, "does not find plagiarism. What it does is find sequences of words in submitted documents which match sequences of words in documents in its database, or sequences of words in documents on the Internet." But it does not find the latter in any consistent manner. Turnitin's strengths are its mechanical search ability, not always thorough enough to detect plagiarism, and its growing database. However, John Royce reports "it seems enough for a school to announce that it has subscribed to Turnitin for its levels of suspected plagiarism to fall" (Royce, 2003).

Recent Enhancements

As of this writing, Turnitin is partnering with WebCT course management software to make submissions simpler. ProQuest is also allowing Turnitin to search articles from its databases: ABI/Inform, full-text Periodical Abstracts, and Business Dateline. This begins to address the faculty's need to identify plagiarized material from the journal literature. MyDropBox also indicates on its Web site that it compares submissions to published works in "password-protected electronic document databases;" however, it does not list the databases (www.mydropbox.com). The company also is partnering with

Blackboard course management software for simpler access to detection services. CopyCatch is in trials with a new product allowing students to check their own work for plagiarism during the writing process.

Free Software

Instructors still have search engines, such as Google, available to them. In a test using the same author's paper used with the Turnitin trial, five different sentences or phrases were searched, and each and every time Google, Yahoo, Teoma, and Vivisimo located the original article. Bearing in mind that search engines cannot crawl and search subscription journal databases, nor understand the nuances of the search phrase, they match patterns quite well on the free Web, and remain the simplest and most direct instrument for detection.

Students Tested

The students whose papers were tested were enrolled in a 200-level writing course on writing research essays. These students had agreed to have their papers used for research, having signed a form at the beginning of the semester that asked their permission to use their work for "nonprofit scholarly research and training projects." In addition, they had been advised verbally that the research involved would be related to plagiarism detection. Whereas the usual method for detecting plagiarism employed by instructors of this course had been a simple Google search on any suspect phrase, the university's recent purchase of Turnitin prompted its use for this study. This pilot study largely confirmed what many instructors had already found to be true, that most students enrolled in these courses do not engage in plagiarism. This is likely to be due to the pedagogical approaches used to teach these courses, discussed in another chapter in this volume, "Communicating Honesty: Building on the Student/Teacher Relationship" (Henry 2004).

Conclusion: Successes and Limitations of the Tools

A new offense on the plagiarism playing field is emerging. Researchers at Cornell University are developing software that can paraphrase whole sentences ("Software Paraphrases Sentences," 2003). What may emerge is cheating comparable to steroid-enhanced performance in competitive sports. Students will no longer simply copy and paste sentences from a Web page; rather, they can produce bulked-up paraphrases instead of writing their own.

From an educator's point of view, this generation of plagiarism detection tools has limited value. Though students may become somewhat intimidated just by knowing that their instructor is using plagiarism detection tools, the fact can just as easily destroy an atmosphere of trust and alienate students, who may then be more careful in plagiarizing. In this case, existing tools have very little value, as they do not detect plagiarism from hard-copy texts, from most databases, from documents a few keystrokes away from the surface of the Web, or papers that must be purchased. Students can also use slight paraphrasing to elude plagiarism detection tools. Given the existing state of the art, it would seem far more useful to invest time in requiring students to go through a gradual drafting process whereby educators can trace the development of their students' work in a transparent manner. Until this software develops in a more imaginative fashion, it seems of very limited usefulness to educators.

Plagiarism Detection Web Sites

CopyCatch: www.copycatch.freeserve.co.uk/

Turnitin: www.turnitin.com

Eve2: www.canexus.com/eve/

WordCHECK: www.wordchecksystems.com

Glatt Plagiarism Services: www.plagiarism.com

MyDropBox: http://mydropbox.com

Works Cited

Bull, Joanna, Carol Collins, Elisabeth Coughlin, and Dale Sharp. 2001. "Technical Review of Plagiarism Detection Software Report." Available: http://online.northumbria.ac.uk/faculties/art/information_studies/Imri/Jiscpas/docs/jisc/luton.pdf.

Gilligan, Carol. 1982. *In a Different Voice: Psychological Theory and Women's Development.* Cambridge, Mass.: Harvard University Press.

LeMoyne College Electronic Plagiarism Seminar. October, 2003. Available: www.lemoyne.edu/library/plagiarism.htm.

McCabe, Donald L. 1992. "The Influence of Situation Ethics on Cheating among College Students." *Sociological Inquiry* 62 (August): 365–374.

McCabe, Donald, and Linda Klebe Treviño. 2002. "Honesty and Honor Codes." *Academe.* Available: www.aaup.org/publications/Academe/02JF/02jfmcc.htm.

Royce, John. 2003. "Has Turnitin.com Got It All Wrapped Up?" *Teacher Librarian* 30(Apr): 26–30.

Simmonds, Patience. 2003. "Plagiarism and Cyber-Plagiarism: A Guide to Selected Resources on the Web." *College and Research Libraries News* 64(June): 385–389.

"Software Paraphrases Sentences." *Technology Review*, December 8, 2003. Available www.technologyreview.com/articles/rnb_120803.asp.

Sykes, Gresham M., and Matza, David. 1957. "Techniques of Neutralization: A Theory of Delinquency." *American Sociological Review* 22(Dec): 664–670.

Stec, Eileen M. 2003. Unpublished research.

Young J. R. 2002. "Anti-plagiarism experts raise questions about services with links to sites selling papers." *Chronicle Daily News,* March 12. Available http://chronicle.com/daily/2002/03/2002031201t.htm (accessed July 22, 2003).

CHAPTER 14

Where to Go for What They Need to Know: Style Sheets, Writing Guides, and Other Resources

Robert J. Lackie

Introduction: Web Resources for Citing, Research, and Writing

As I read the plethora of articles in magazines and on Web sites about preventing academic dishonesty in writing and combating plagiarism in general within our high schools and colleges, I find that many articles do not distinguish between the different types of plagiarism that teachers and professors find in academic writing. True, downloading an entire paper from the Web is wholesale intentional cheating. However, many students—even above-average high school and college students—make mistakes while summarizing, paraphrasing, and quoting source materials and integrating these into their research papers. Many students that I have taught in past college freshmen English composition courses did not seem to have a lot of experience with generating, revising, and editing academic papers, much less actually researching ideas and attributing sources used.

Fortunately for today's educators and students, there are many free interactive and user-friendly resource and tutorial sites available on the Web that can greatly assist educators in teaching research and academic writing skills to high school and college students. However, as the coverage and content of the Web summarily advances and transforms, it is becoming increasingly difficult and time consuming for many teachers and librarians to find efficiently those accurate and reliable education sites—sites that make teaching and learning about research and academic writing easier and more enjoyable. This chapter will serve as a specific resource guide to those quality sites for the intended audience of high school and higher education English faculty, instruction librarians, and their students. The topics to be covered will include Web-based style guides and online tools, concentrating on Modern Language Association (MLA) but also providing guides to other frequently used citation and documentation styles. In addition, this chapter will introduce free quality research and writing sites that provide guidelines for researching and constructing exemplary papers and that address the quandaries of how, when, and why to cite sources.

Teaching Good Writing Skills:
Web Resources for Citing Sources

As you can imagine, figuring out how to cite the various types of sources integrated into a research paper is not what most students describe as a fun activity. In fact, some of the most frequently asked questions that I receive from anxious and/or frustrated students (whether I am teaching an English class, leading a library instruction, or conducting a reference interview at the library reference desk) deal with how to properly cite and document a source for a paper. Obviously, students struggle with generating "Works Cited" pages and in-text parenthetical citations, trying to formulate correct formatting, punctuation, and so forth, for all of their attributions. It certainly can be time consuming and even overwhelming for many as they attempt to read and interpret the most common, current style handbooks and manuals, such as the *Modern Language Association Handbook* (6th edition, 2003), the *Publication Manual of the American Psychological Association* (5th edition, 2001), and *The Chicago Manual of Style* (15th edition, 2003) guidebooks, even though all have been updated, significantly improving upon previous editions. This is where the Web is advantageous, providing Web-based frequently asked questions (FAQs), interactive tools and tutorials, additional citation examples, and general assistance with the published style manuals.

The Modern Language Association (MLA; www.mla.org/style), American Psychological Association (APA; www.apastyle.org/), and The University of Chicago Press/*Chicago Manual of Style* (CMS; www.chicagomanualofstyle.org/) all supply excellent accompanying Web sites to the latest published editions of their handbooks/manuals, containing especially useful online FAQ sections. However, although I have found all of them to be valuable, they still do not answer many of the questions we frequently entertain from students regarding proper documentation—nor do they provide enough detailed and/or diverse examples. Conducting a search on a major Web search engine will yield an overabundance of help sheets, guides, and explanations, but examples found on some sites contradict those on other sites, or the examples and explanations are now incorrect as they follow outdated versions of the published style guides. This is especially true for sites detailing MLA and CMS guidelines, as both of these organizations published new editions in mid-2003.

Because all students must learn when and how to cite properly borrowed words and ideas from the works of others, my goal for this section of the chapter is to highlight Web sites (other than the official organizations' sites mentioned above) that now provide us with the best online assistance in order to help students (and other interested parties) with proper documentation of sources. Following are brief abstracts to a few of the best free, quality documentation sites on the Web that provide ample examples, explanations, tools, and handouts concerning the proper use of a variety of documentation styles, especially MLA.

Research and Documenting Sources

(http://owl.english.purdue.edu/handouts/research/index.html)

Brought to us by Purdue University's Online Writing Lab (OWL), this site is highly recommended by many experts and evaluative Web directories. This section of their site not only provides clearly written instructions and extensive explanations for citing sources using MLA and APA styles, but it also lists many other discipline-related resources for documenting sources, linking to official and explanatory sites for each when available.

Citation Style for Research Papers

(www.liunet.edu/cwis/cwp/library/workshop/citation.htm)

This is the Schwartz Memorial Library at Long Island University's citation style general resource site that compares MLA as well as APA, CMS, Turabian, and the American Medical Association (AMA) style manuals. I like the color coding used within the clearly written annotations, as well as Web page author Robert Delaney's "own style" (he created it, not following any particular style) for clearer examples of citing Internet resources.

Online! A Reference Guide for Using Internet Sources, Update 2003

(www.bedfordstmartins.com/online/citex.html)

Probably the site I visit most often for citing electronic sources, this accompanying Web site for *Online! A Reference Guide for Using Internet Sources*, published by Bedford/St. Martin's, details in Chapters 5 to 8 how to cite and document Internet sources using MLA, APA, CMS, and Council of Biology Editors (CBE). It has an excellent FAQ, too.

Citing Sources and Avoiding Plagiarism

(www.lib.duke.edu/libguide/citing.htm)

Linking to Part 7 of Duke University Libraries' superb online Guide to Library Research, this section details how to cite sources and prepare a works cited page for MLA, APA, and Turabian styles, as well as providing strategies for avoiding plagiarism.

Research and Documentation Online

(www.dianahacker.com/resdoc/index.html)

This is a companion Web site for the book *Research and Documentation in the Electronic Age* by noted textbook author and professor of English Diana Hacker. I found this site to be useful not only for the up-to-date guidelines and advice presented for documenting print and online sources using the MLA, APA, CMS, and CBE styles, but also for the sample papers provided in Adobe PDF for each of the four styles.

In addition to the style manual guide sites described above, free interactive citation generator tool sites exist on the Web. A few fairly well-known interactive MLA bibliography citation generators can be found at the Oregon School Library Information System (OSLIS) site and Damon and Debbie Abilock's NoodleTools site. At both Web sites, you choose a citation source located on the interactive page, fill in the fields as described with your citation information, and each of the free tools will create and let you view your citation in the proper MLA style format. Of the two sites, the NoodleTools' section seems to be updated most frequently, but both are kept current.

OSLIS Citing Sources

(http://oslis.k12.or.us/secondary/howto/cited/index.html)

This link takes you to the secondary school level page containing the Citation Maker they designed to help simplify the sometimes difficult task of creating a MLA works cited page. OSLIS also has a specific MLA citation generator geared for the elementary school student.

NoodleTools Quick Cite!

(www.noodletools.com/quickcite/)

This free MLA citation generator tool is used often by elementary students and teachers for quick simple MLA citations. I use it because it is up-to-date, user-friendly, and useful for teaching someone not familiar with the MLA style how to put together a citation (provides different format examples). The comprehensive formerly free NoodleBib software is now available for a small fee to create advanced MLA works cited and APA references lists. Other free tools and teacher resources exist on the NoodleTools main page (www.noodletools.com/) that are worth taking the time to explore.

Teaching Good Writing Skills:
Web Resources for Research and Writing

In addition to steering our students toward excellent, free Web-based citation and documentation guides, we should also provide our students with supplementary quality research and writing assistance resources for use inside and outside of the classroom. While perusing a very comprehensive and useful annotated listing of articles and Web sites regarding plagiarism (www.Webminer.com/plagiarism), recently compiled and updated by Sharon Stoerger at the Office of the Vice Chancellor for Research, University of Illinois at Urbana-Champaign, I noticed that many highlighted plagiarism prevention strategies such as educating students on the meaning of plagiarism and providing interactive quizzes and other resources to assist students to research properly and write academic research papers. In an article on plagiarism prevention, Rebecca Moore Howard (2002), noted author and expert on plagiarism, stresses real pedagogical reform as a key plagiarism prevention strategy, but she indicates that current working conditions may be preventing some professors from finding the time to prepare genuinely meaningful and useful writing assignments, teach the research process, and incrementally respond to their students' writing drafts. I must say that schoolteachers often tell me this is intensified for them because of the myriad of demands placed upon them in areas ranging from the cognitive to the affective domains. Fortunately, educators from all academic levels do not have to "reinvent the wheel" when it comes to assignment redesign and research writing support because just as the Web provides help in the form of style guides and tools that can successfully be used inside and outside of the classroom, the Web also provides excellent support materials and interactive sites that can help us ensure that good teaching takes place along the way.

Obviously, many high school and college students are comfortable with and frequently surf the Web. Therefore, encouraging them to use the Web as an additional guide to research and writing—rather than for intentional theft of papers—should not be a difficult task for us. However, although many students may be well versed in locating certain types of information on the Web—or using it to communicate with their friends—they may not be aware that it can be a very valuable resource for information retrieval and practice with research and writing strategies. And finding those accurate and reliable academic writing "hidden gem" sites can be difficult and time consuming. Therefore, to save time for all concerned, we should be ready to direct our students to the best free online support material and interactive sites on the Web for researching and writing academic papers. Then, as we conference with our students, look at drafts, and discuss the assignment progression with our students to determine if more assistance with research and citing is required, we have tools immediately at our disposal to assist us in teaching good writing skills. Here are a few of my preferred research and writing sites, freely available on the Web, that can help prevent plagiarism from becoming a reality for novice and/or frustrated writers:

Research and Documenting Sources

(http://owl.english.purdue.edu/handouts/research/ index.html)

Mentioned earlier in this chapter for its style manual assistance, Purdue University's OWL also has highly cited sections on Writing Research Papers, to include A Step-by-Step List, Plagiarism, Quoting, Paraphrasing, Summarizing, and more.

The Writers' Workshop

(www.engl.niu.edu/comskills/)

This award-winning site, brought to us by Northern Illinois University, is a great resource for high school and college instructors, students, and tutors. It is broken down into Students' Resources, Tutors' Resources, and Instructors' Resources sections, offering very useful writing resources and quizzes for students to test themselves. The Students' Resources section has some particularly helpful info on Grammar and Mechanics, Plagiarism, Quotations, and the MLA style for citing resources.

A+ Research and Writing for High School and College Students

(www.ipl.org/div/aplus/)

Created by the highly-respected Internet Public Library, this is one of the best student-friendly explanatory guides to writing research papers on the Web, to include Step by Step Research and Writing, Learning to Research in the Library and on the Web, and an annotated list of online resources for research and assistance with Paraphrasing, Summarizing, Plagiarism, and Using Quotations.

Nuts and Bolts of College Writing

(www.nutsandboltsguide.com/)

Created by Professor Michael Harvey of Washington College, Maryland, this comprehensive writing guide site is one of the most popular on the Web for students and teachers, covering the beginning stages of writing to the polishing of the finished product. Because this guide is meant for students and teachers in all types of college courses, not just research writing and literature courses, it also provides detailed help guides to common documentation styles of APA, CMS, and CBE, in addition to MLA.

Guide to Grammar and Writing

(www.ccc.commnet.edu/grammar/index.htm)

Secondary and higher education English teachers, tutors, and instructors will find this site, maintained by English Professor Charles Darling from Capital Community College, Hartford, Connecticut, especially helpful as it is chock full of instructional materials. It contains numerous interactive quizzes on grammar, copious PowerPoint presentations and guides on English usage, and a sizeable number of recommendations on writing essays and research papers—all provided free to the general public. The Principles of Composition and the annotated Online Resources for Writers sections of the site are valuable for students and teachers alike.

Additional Help with When and Why to Cite Sources

Although I believe that high school and college faculty and their students will find my recommended online style guides, interactive tools, and online research and writing sites to be handy and practical, sometimes more in-depth help is needed to help us educate ourselves and/or teach others how to better avoid plagiarism. Particularly pleasing tutorial sites and unique online workshops on plagiarism prevention are freely available on the Web—resources that offer additional discussions and lessons for educators to help them assist students in understanding and avoiding the perils of practicing plagiarism.

Synthesis: Using the Work of Others

(http://departments.umf.maine.edu/~library/plagiarism/)

This detailed antiplagiarism tutorial site from the University of Maine at Farmington's Writing Center details issues surrounding plagiarism, including what it is, why we should care about it, why it is difficult to avoid, what we can do to prevent it, and a practical interactive plagiarism game. In addition, this site provides information on copyright; assistance on citing and giving credit for papers, presentations, and Web sites; and, conveniently, another interactive game, this time on copyright infringement.

The Plagiarism Court: You Be the Judge

(http://library2.fairfield.edu/instruction/ramona/ plugin.html)

This excellent tutorial site by Reference and Educational Technology Librarian Ramona Islam of the Fairfield University DiMenna-Nyselius Library provides a Macromedia Flash movie with voice-overs as a part of the plagiarism avoidance lesson, ending with a short 10-question interactive quiz. I think students and educators will find this tutorial stimulating and effective, and if Flash is not to your liking, they also offer two HTML versions of the tutorial.

Cybercheats: Plagiarism and the Web

(www.stevegarwood.com/classes/cybercheats/ default.htm)

Steve Garwood, librarian and part-time lecturer at Rutgers University's School of Communication, Information and Library Studies, provides an instructive and engaging PowerPoint presentation on plagiarism, using "Timmy's Tragic Tale" as the centerpiece for the lesson. The entire site, to include the presentation, class Web site, and informative bibliography (all available free-of-charge), is worth exploring and sharing.

Plagiarism Workshop

(http://mail.nvnet.org/~cooper_j/plagiarism/)

Northern Valley Regional High School (Demarest, New Jersey) Media Specialist Janice Cooper designed this carefully planned and comprehensive workshop and lesson plan for high school students, providing them with an introduction to plagiarism, copyright, and fair use. This site leads students to many online resources and demonstrates several techniques (paraphrasing, quoting, citing) that they can employ to help avoid committing plagiarism.

Conclusion

I am sure that it is no surprise to those of you reading this chapter that excellent free educational Web sites exist to help us to conduct our own research, to write our educational reports and academic papers, and to attribute properly our sources. As librarians and educators, more than likely, our experience and education has significantly assisted us in becoming more adept at research and writing. But current reports and articles, such as the latest interesting and comprehensive *CQ Researcher* issue on plagiarism, indicate that plagiarism has become one of our society's most important and controversial topics, inside and outside of our educational systems. You will read in that issue that plagiarism detecting companies and their services, such as the Turnitin.com plagiarism detection system, are starting to become household names within many educational institutions (Hansen, 2003). The advent of the Web seems to have had a somewhat negative impact on the development of proficient research and writing skills for some high school and college students, as they use it to scarf someone else's ideas and words instead of conducting authentic research. Therefore, just as we must diligently provide explanations, strategies, tips, and resources for our students to cultivate good quality research and writing skills, we should also endeavor to guide regularly and teach our students about the issues surrounding plagiarism and how to avoid it by properly citing and documenting attributions within their speeches and papers.

We only have so much face-to-face time with students within our classrooms and libraries, so we need to direct our students to those free, excellent supplementary resources and tutorials on the Web to help them to develop more proficient research, writing, and documentation skills. Because of the expanding and constantly changing aspect of the Web, it does make our job as teachers and librarians a bit more difficult to efficiently and effectively locate those highly rated online tools and sites that make teaching, learning, and research easier. But those accurate and reliable sites do exist, and they can help us to develop a curriculum that will prepare our students for future research and writing opportunities, while possibly giving them an exciting addition to the traditional English composition and rhetoric curriculum.

My goal for this chapter was to have it serve as a specific resource guide to those quality Web sites enabling and facilitating the research and academic writing processes. I suggest that you periodically review the recommended Web resources for citing, researching, and writing that are contained within this chapter. I propose that you check out some of the online workshops and presentations, experiment with some of the tutorials and quizzes, and play around with the various citation generators and interactive research and writing guides. Then, bookmark your favorites and share them with other educators and students. I believe that they will sufficiently provide additional tools and guidelines for helping you to better teach others how to research and construct exemplary papers. Additionally, I believe they adequately address the quandaries of how, when, and why to cite sources.

Just remember that not all sections of every recommended site may be totally up to date for each type of information provided, so evaluate accordingly. According to the Council of Biology Educators, the CBE Manual is undergoing major revisions (Council of Biology Educators, 2004). Be advised that it may take a while for some sites to update their information regarding that style manual. However, I meticulously chose and recommended the resource sites for their general currency, accuracy, ease of use, low cost, and interactivity, as well as my belief that owners of the sites will strive to keep the information and materials as up to date as possible or lead you to another site that does a better job at providing the best citing, researching, and writing assistance. Many Web sites with outdated information on citation guides, for instance, did cite the Turnitin.com service that I mentioned above. I was pleasantly surprised after following one of the links to find that iParadigms's

175

Turnitin.com site (www.Turnitin.com/research_site/e_home.html) houses an excellent, free, comprehensive plagiarism prevention/research resource section for educators and students—I particularly found their FAQ subsection poignant and their Important Terms listing useful. I hope that you also find value in their resource section, as well as within the many recommended tools and sites presented in this chapter.

Works Cited

Abilock, Damon, and Debbie Abilock. "Quick Cite! NoodleTools." Noodle Tools, Palo Alto, CA. Available: www.noodletools.com/quickcite.

American Psychological Association. 2001. *Publication Manual of the American Psychological Association,* 5th edition. Washington, DC: American Psychological Association.

American Psychological Association. "APA Style." Available: http://apastyle.org.

Cooper, Janice. "Plagiarism Workshop." Northern Valley Regional High School, Demarest, NJ. Available: http://mail.nvnet.org/~cooper_j/plagiarism/.

Council of Biology Educators. 2004. "Publications: Scientific Style and Format, Seventh Edition. Reston, Virginia." Available: www.councilscienceeditors.org/publications/ssf_7th.cfm.

Darling, Charles. "Guide to Grammar and Writing." Capital Community College, Hartford, Connecticut. Available: www.ccc.commnet.edu/grammar/ index.htm.

Delany, Robert. "Citation Style for Research Papers." Schwartz Memorial Library, Long Island University, Brookville, NY. Available: www.liunet.edu/cwis/cwp/library/workshop /citation.htm.

Department of English. Writers' Workshop. Northern Illinois University, DeKalb, IL. Available: www.engl.niu.edu/comskills.

Garwood, Steve. "Cybercheats and the Web." Available: www.stevegarwood.com/classes/ cybercheats/default.htm.

Gibaldi, Joseph. 2003. *MLA Handbook for Writers of Research Papers,* 6th edition. New York: Modern Language Association of America.

Hacker, Diana. "Research and Documentation Online." Bedford/St. Martin's. Available: www.dianahacker.com/resdoc/index.html.

Hansen, Brian. 2003. "Combating Plagiarism." *CQ Researcher* (September 19): 773–796.

Harnack, Andrew, and Eugene Kleppinger. 2003. "Online!: A Reference Guide for Using Internet Sources. Update 2003." Bedford/St. Martin's. Available: www.bedfordstmartins.com/online /citex.html.

Harvey, Michael. "Nuts and Bolts of College Writing." Hackett Publishing. Available: http://www.nutsandboltsguide.com.

Howard, Rebecca Moore. 2002. "Don't Police Plagiarism: Just Teach!" *Education Digest* (January): 46–49.

iParadigms. "Turnitin Research Resources." Available: www.Turnitin.com/research_site/ e_home.html.

Islam, Ramona. "The Plagiarism Court: You be the Judge." DiMenna-Nyselius Library, Fairfield University, Fairfield, CT. Available: http://library2.fairfield.edu/instruction/ramona/plugin.html.

Lawton, Kelly A., Laura Cousineau, and Van E. Hillard. "Guide to Library Research: Citing Sources and Avoiding Plagiarism: Documentation Guidelines." Duke University Libraries and The University Writing Program, Durham, NC. Available: www.lib.duke.edu/libguide/citing.htm.

Modern Language Association of America. "What Is MLA Style?" Available: www.mla.org/style.

Online Writing Lab. "Research and Documenting Sources." Purdue University, West Lafayette, IN. Available: http://owl.english.purdue.edu/handouts/research/index.html.

Oregon School Library Information System, Oregon Public Education Network, Albany, OR. "Secondary How To: Citing Sources." OPEN Clearinghouse. Available: http://oslis.k12.or.us/secondary/howto/cited/index.html.

Schwartz, Kathryn L. "A+ Research and Writing for High School and College Students." TeenSpace@The Internet Public Library, School of Information, University of Michigan, Ann Arbor, MI. Available: www.ipl.org/div/aplus.

Stoerger, Sharon. "Plagiarism." University of Illinois at Urbana-Champaign, Urbana-Champaign, IL. Available: www.Web-miner.com/plagiarism.

The Chicago Manual of Style, 15th edition. 2003. Chicago: University of Chicago Press.

———. "Chicago Manual of Style—Q and A." Available: www.chicagomanualofstyle.org.

Writing Center/Mantor Library. "Synthesis: Using the Work of Others." University of Maine at Farmington. Available: http://departments.umf.maine.edu/~library/plagiarism.

CHAPTER 15

High-Tech and Low-Tech: A Survey of Methods for Teaching Intellectual Honesty

Leslie Murtha

Introduction

The task of teaching students to value academic integrity and to understand and apply the rules of scholarly attribution is one that is shared by the entire education community. In recent years, many organizations have turned to digital learning tools to help them in this task. Like textbooks, workbooks, and other assignments, online teaching tools extend the classroom beyond its physical walls and scheduled times.

Online resources have both advantages and disadvantages as teaching tools. An obvious advantage is continuous accessibility at all times and in most places. In addition, digital tools increasingly provide opportunities for developing learning materials that use multimedia and pedagogy based on active learning. The equally obvious disadvantage of online teaching tools is that access is limited by the availability of computers, electricity, and Internet access. Somewhat less obvious are the costs of production and maintenance of the materials. It is axiomatic that tools that take the most advantage of the unique characteristics of digitally delivered instruction are the most expensive to develop and maintain and require the most expenditure on the part of the user for equipment and connection speed. Another disadvantage that may easily be overlooked is the challenge posed by the needs of learners with disabilities. Because the features that aid one disabled user may constitute barriers for another, creating online learning tools that are accessible to all members of a learning community requires considerable thought and care.

In this chapter, a wide variety of teaching and learning tools relating to plagiarism, academic integrity, and scholarly documentation are reviewed. These tools may serve as examples or models for educators who are interested in developing online tutorials on this topic for their own communities. Because they often refer to institutional policies, most of these tutorials are not suitable as classroom resources outside their own institutional context, but some are generic enough to be used by other communities. Some employ cutting-edge technology, whereas others are examples of relatively low-cost, low-tech approaches to online instruction. The reviews deal with content, style, creative or effective use of technology, design, and pedagogical strategies.

The resources reviewed here were discovered by means of extensive searching and citation chasing. Sources searched include PRIMO (formerly the Internet Education Project Database), the Educator's Reference Desk, LOEX Clearinghouse for Library Instruction, and the directories and search indices of Google, Yahoo!, and Altavista. The tutorials represent the work of libraries, writing programs and centers, offices of judicial affairs, academic departments, and individual faculty members. Most, but not all, are directed at undergraduate students. Surprisingly, only one tutorial was identified that was developed for the use of students of high school age or younger. Many more resources were found than could be included in this chapter, and so the resources included have been selected as either representative of a particular approach to teaching, or a particular format, or because they provide examples (good or bad) of the use of technology or pedagogy. The reviews have been grouped according to the level of technology employed, but readers are reminded many of the resources could readily be adapted to a higher or lower level of technology.

High-Level Technology

The development of the tutorials in this category requires a high level of technological expertise, such as programming or multimedia skills.

Plagiarism Court: You Be the Judge

Islam, Ramona. 2002. Fairfield, Conn.: DiMenna Nyselius Library, Fairfield University.

(http://library2.fairfield.edu/instruction/ramona/plugin.html)

This tutorial is presented as a courtroom scenario. Participants enter through animated pillars, where they receive a briefing on plagiarism. Lesson

objectives are set out, followed by a definition of plagiarism, and an enumeration of the consequences of plagiarism, both within and outside the university. The remainder of the lesson consists of tips on documentation, note taking, quoting, paraphrasing, and citation styles. The lesson is followed by a 10-question quiz, in which participants select multiple-choice answers, designated "objections." Correct answers are objections sustained; incorrect answers are objections overruled. Feedback is presented for each answer, explaining the basis of the judgment.

The tutorial provides simple, straightforward examples of plagiarism and excellent tips on note taking. The examples and explanations of appropriate use of quotations and paraphrasing are well done. The tutorial is designed in Macromedia Flash, but two additional versions are available: one with graphics and text and one with text only. The Flash version is very pretty, with highly professional animated graphics. This viewer found some of the animations to be rather distracting, but not enough to detract significantly from the whole. Unfortunately, the same is not true of the use of sound, which consists of chapter heading announcements, atmospherics, and a demo that is incomprehensible and virtually inaudible. Another problem with this version is that there are links to related information embedded in the pages, but if a user clicks on a link, leaving the Flash presentation, it is impossible to return to the point of departure. In order to continue with the tutorial, it is necessary to start the Flash presentation over from the beginning. Although not as pretty, the HTML versions of the tutorial provide almost equally effective instruction.

LOBO, The Library Online Basic Orientation: Using Resources

Boyer, Josh, Kim Duckett, Cindy Levine, Megan Oakleaf, Darby Orcutt, May Chang, David DeFoor, Rob Main, Eric Pauley, Tom Zack, Deborah Hooker, Rachel Lutwick-Deaner, and Patricia Lynne. n.d. Raleigh, N.C.: North Carolina State University Libraries.
(www.lib.ncsu.edu/lobo2/)

This is a chapter in LOBO, the online tutorial of the North Carolina State University Libraries. LOBO, in both its previous and current incarnations, has long been recognized as an exemplary online learning resource. LOBO is extraordinary in the way in which it embeds the student's current research assignment in the learning material. This chapter deals with defining and explaining plagiarism, integrating sources into text, and the process of citation. Language is direct, but not simplistic, and the graphics and layout are well designed. Questions requiring thoughtful answers are placed at strategic points and added to a worksheet that can be printed out. The worksheet preserves information about the student's project, thus supplying research support, and could also be turned in as part of an assignment. This chapter also features an NCSU-developed citation builder. LOBO is based on PHP and JavaScipt.

Copyright & Plagiarism Tutorials: Plagiarism-You can Avoid it...An Interactive Tutorial for Students

Buehler, Marianne. 2003. Rochester, N.Y.: Wallace Library, Rochester Institute of Technology.

(http://wally.rit.edu/instruction/dl/cptutorial/)

This tutorial consists of a preliminary exercise, a 15-minute streamed PowerPoint presentation, and a final exercise. A transcript of the presentation is available. The tutorial sets plagiarism in the context of copyright, and the greater part of the content deals with explaining and defining copyright, public domain, fair use, and copyright infringement. The explanations are, for the most part, clear and useful, though sequencing is sometimes conducive to confusion. This approach of associating plagiarism with copyright infringement provides students with an authoritative argument that extends beyond academia, but it also bypasses some important issues in academic writing. The tutorial actually deals very little with the issues that are most apt to confuse students, such as quotation, paraphrase, and collaboration. It provides few guidelines or examples, compared to other resources. The final "exercise" is in fact not an exercise, as it requires no activity whatever on the part of the student; it is merely a single good example of inappropriate and appropriate usage of paraphrase and summation. A link to additional practice resources is provided, but the link is broken, and the page referred to could not be located on the library site.

Plagiarism

Bowman, Vibiana, and John Gibson. 2003. Camden, N.J.: Paul Robeson Library, Rutgers University.

(http://library.camden.rutgers.edu/robeson/cddev/channel1.html)
(http://library.camden.rutgers.edu/robeson/cddev/channel2.html)
(http://library.camden.rutgers.edu/robeson/cddev/channel3.html)
(http://library.camden.rutgers.edu/robeson/cddev/quiz.html)

This tutorial, still in experimental stages, parodies popular television shows as a means of teaching students about plagiarism. The tutorial consists of three very short segments of instructional material, employing RealVideo and JavaScipt, and a short quiz, driven by Macromedia Flash and Macromedia Shockwave. Playing on the first "channel" is a 2-minute presentation that mimics an educational program for young children, defining and explaining plagiarism. The second "channel" provides examples from a student-written paper, showing where errors have been made in failing to attribute material from other sources. This segment is very short, with only two examples, and unfortunately, the size at which the video clip is displayed makes the examples somewhat difficult to read. The third "channel" is a parody of a popular game show and provides an introduction to the quiz that follows. The quiz consists of five questions. Each question provides a clip from a student paper and asks the viewer to decide whether or not the passage needs a citation. Answers must be checked before the viewer can move on to the next question, and immediate feedback is provided. Although very short in comparison with some of the other tutorials examined here, this one is an interesting example of the creative use of streaming audio and video to engage students using the context of their own culture.

Plagiarism and Academic Integrity at Rutgers University

Stec, Eileen, Scott Hines, Anthony Joachim, and the faculty and staff of the Mabel Smith Douglass Library. 2001. New Brunswick, N.J.: Rutgers University Libraries.

(www.scc.rutgers.edu/douglass/sal/plagiarism/intro.html)

Originally designed for the first year class of Douglass College, this tutorial takes the form of a series of eight short skits around a single plot line. The story involves students facing typical dilemmas and uncertainties about academic integrity while in the process of researching and writing a paper. Two cartoon characters represent the "voice of reason," pointing out the potential consequences of unethical behavior. The scenes are interspersed with interactive quizzes, in which a scenario is presented to the user, who is asked how he or she would behave under the stated conditions. Immediate feedback is given in response to the answer the student selects. Issues covered include the citing of common phrases, theft and vandalism of library resources, purchasing or ghostwriting of papers, reusing previously submitted papers, and the difference between editorial assistance and contribution to content. The standard of ethical conduct is derived from the policy on academic integrity of the New Brunswick campus of Rutgers University.

The tutorial provides entry-level students with a good overview of some major issues in academic ethics. It does not deal extensively with the mechanics of avoiding plagiarism and completely sidesteps the issues of citation formatting, paraphrasing, and quotation. The colorful graphics make for an attractive piece, and a small but diverse cast presents situations with which students may readily identify. Although the interactive quizzes are in a multiple-choice format, they require some reflection, and the feedback is thoughtful. Dialog is presented in a sidebar as text for users whose computers are not activated for sound. The cast is drawn from the faculty and staff of the library, and the acting is adequate, but not polished. The tutorial requires the Macromedia Flash player and is enhanced by sound. A text-only version is available.

Understanding Plagiarism

Frick, Theodore. 2002. Bloomington, Ind.: Department of Instructional Systems Technology, School of Education, University of Indiana Bloomington. (http://education.indiana.edu/~frick/plagiarism/)

This site consists of two related tools designed for graduate students in the School of Education at the University of Indiana Bloomington.

What is Plagiarism at Indiana University?

Frick, Theodore. 2001. Bloomington, Ind.: Department of Instructional Systems Technology, School of Education, University of Indiana Bloomington. (http://education.indiana.edu/~frick/plagiarism/index2.html)

This lesson consists of a short introductory explanation of the concept of plagiarism, followed by a 10-question quiz covering a variety of errors in citation. Students are asked to identify plagiarized materials and select the correct explanation of why the text constitutes plagiarism. Feedback is given in pop-up windows driven by JavaScipt. Wrong answers prompt the student to try again until the correct answer is chosen. The questions are well designed, and the feedback for correct answers provides a thoughtful explanation of why the selection is correct.

How to Recognize Plagiarism

Boling, Elizabeth, Meltem Albayrak-Karahan, Joseph Defazio, and Noriko Matsumura, 2002. Bloomington, Ind.: Department of Instructional Systems Technology, School of Education, University of Indiana Bloomington. (www.indiana.edu/~istd/)

This tutorial is required of all students in the Department of Instructional Systems Technology. Students are encouraged to repeat the tutorial as often as necessary in order to gain a complete understanding of the practice of crediting sources (Boling et al., 2002). The tutorial focuses on common errors in documentation but does not attempt to teach the mechanics of citation. It consists of seven sections. The first two define plagiarism and institutional policy at the University of Indiana. The second two sections provide a brief overview of the practice of citation and links to articles and other resources containing details of plagiarism cases. The next and most substantial section consists of writing examples. Each example consists of a sample from an original publication, a plagiarized version, and a "correct" version of a reference to the publication. Five examples demonstrate different types of word-for-word plagiarism, and another five demonstrate inappropriate paraphrasing. Students then can take a practice exercise before beginning the final test.

The tutorial is composed primarily in plain text with a small number of diagrams. The practice exercise uses simple HTML, but the test is based on a PHP script, and cascading style sheets are used throughout. The tutorial with practice exercise can be completed in 25 to 35 minutes, but the test requires close reading and would probably require another 20 to 30 minutes or more from a novice user. The strength of the tutorial is in the large number of examples of common errors in citation, with accompanying explanations. A small caveat: the designation of the second version as "correct" tends to imply that there is only one acceptable version of the text; the corrected version might better have been labeled "appropriate" or "acceptable." The tabular layout of the examples makes comparison easy, but reading would be easier if the tables were somewhat wider. Both the practice exercise and the test are well constructed, but they are not very well matched pedagogically. The practice exercise asks students to determine whether or not a passage has been plagiarized; the test, which is significantly more demanding, requires them to identify the specific type of error committed.

VAIL Tutor

Virtual Academic Integrity Laboratory [VAIL]. 2003. Adelphi, Md.: Center for Intellectual Property, University of Maryland University College. (www-apps.umuc.edu/forums/pageshow.php?forumid=3)

The VAIL Tutor is a product of the Virtual Academic Integrity Laboratory, which serves as a portal for finding information about academic integrity for both students and instructors. The tutorial, which is just one of the many resources available from VAIL, is directed at students, and consists of four modules accompanied by a glossary and an extensive online quiz. Module One focuses on social and philosophical aspects of academic integrity, including a discussion of the lack of consensus in academic policies and the need to be familiar with local institutional policies. The second module consists of 10 "tips" on avoiding plagiarism and approaching research projects in an ethical fashion. The third module covers details of documentation, including issues of common knowledge, paraphrasing, quotation, summary, and documentation styles. Excellent examples are provided as well as links to a very extensive guide to citation. The final module deals with plagiarism policies.

The tutorial is based on Macromedia Flash and makes excellent use of the platform. The graphics, animation, and music are slick and professional, and rollovers provide examples and extensions of the topics under discussion. Vocabulary definitions and external links are displayed in a secondary window. The content of the tutorial is relatively demanding, forcing students to deal with ambiguities and contextual issues. This tool is definitely geared to a college-level audience and makes no concessions, either in content or in style, to underprepared students. Surprisingly, given the overall quality of the product, its greatest weakness is in the editing. There are a few noticeable typos, and in the second module, the navigation buttons proceed through the text in what appears to be reverse order; in Module Three, one of the illustrated examples is totally illegible. The quiz, although it is accessible throughout, can only be submitted at the end of the tutorial. Feedback is provided for about 75% of the questions, and some of the questions are worded ambiguously.

Plagiarism and Honor

Ruggiero, Cheryl. 1996–1999. Blacksburg, Va.: Department of English, Virginia Polytechnic Institute and State University.
(www.english.vt.edu/%7EIDLE/plagiarism/plagiarism1.html)

This tutorial was designed as part of a suite of materials developed to support and extend classroom teaching in the composition class for first-year students at Virginia Tech (Swenson et al., 1998–1999). The tutorial consists of five sections followed by a self-test and a short project on honesty in writing. The university's honor code forms a framework for the instructional material. The introduction is unusual in that it features thoughtful presentations about the issue of plagiarism written by a teacher and a student. The introduction is followed by a definition of plagiarism, with explanations. The next section features examples of plagiarized and properly attributed texts. These are among the best examples reviewed; the tabular layout and use of color make the explanations exceptionally clear.

The remaining two sections consist of an introduction to the honor code, and a guided tour of the Web site where the code resides. These are followed by a 20-question self-test. The exercise is intended as an open-book quiz; both the tutorial and the honor code remain open in other windows. All questions are multiple choice, testing retention (or ability to find again) of the material covered in the tutorial. Upon submission, students get feedback about their score and the correct answers to all questions. Students may retake the quiz as many times as necessary but must get all questions correct to move on to the next step. The final section of the tutorial, which is password-protected, consists of a short writing assignment that students submit to their instructors via e-mail (Swenson et al., 2000).

The tutorial is well designed, with interesting graphics and lively text. The layout and use of colored text enhance the content, though they would provide problems for students with visual challenges. The instructional material is presented as HTML with graphics, and the self-test is driven by WhizQuiz, a proprietary server-side application developed by the Information Systems and Insect Studies Lab at Virginia Tech.

Intermediate-Level Technology

The tutorials in this category require a relatively advanced level of knowledge of Web design. They employ such elements as cascading style sheets, JavaScipt, and cookies.

Avoiding Plagiarism: Tutorial

Lewis-Clark State College Library. 2003. Lewiston, Idaho: Lewis-Clark State College.

(www.lcsc.edu/library/ILI/Module_2A/Tutor1.htm)

This tutorial forms a part of a suite of online learning resources developed by the Information Literacy Institute at Lewis-Clark State College. It consists of four sections of instruction followed by a brief review. The first section introduces basic concepts in academic integrity and incorporates a short quiz asking students to identify various types of violations of the student code of conduct. The second section covers the basic concepts of citation, and the third addresses paraphrase and quotation, with some well-designed examples. The final section deals with the basics of copyright. This resource does not cover any details of creating citations or reference lists, but those topics are the focus of a companion module. The tutorial, which employs cascading style sheets, is visually attractive, with nice graphics and good navigation tools. The conversational tone and clear language are well geared to novice researchers, and the examples reflect typical student writing behaviors. There is an online quiz available, but it requires a WebCT login and thus was not available to the reviewer.

Avoiding Plagiarism

Online Writing Laboratory. 1995–2004. West Lafayette, Ind.: Department of English, Purdue University.

(http://owl.english.purdue.edu/handouts/research/r_plagiar.html)

This is a slightly different approach to providing instructional material online. The "tutorial" is basically an online handout providing students with decision support about documenting sources. It is available in two printable forms as well as being formatted to display well on the Web. The Web-optimized version employs cascading style sheets and JavaScript, which presumably serve to facilitate maintenance but are not essential for the user interface.

A number of institutions have made "handouts" available in this fashion; this is a good example. It deals nicely with some of the finer points of academic culture with which students are apt to struggle and provides a good diagram of types of plagiarism. Basic rules are explained, and tips for developing good documentation habits are provided. The tutorial concludes with a very nice exercise, which would be a good classroom assignment, but unfortunately, in its current form, provides students with no mechanism for getting feedback. This resource does not include examples or instruction on the practice of quotation or paraphrase, which are available in a separate resource from the Online Writing Lab.

Plagiarism

San Jose State University Library. n.d. San Jose, Calif.: San Jose State University.

(http://130.65.109.143/plagiarism/index.htm)

This tutorial concentrates on issues of citation, paraphrase, and quotation. It consists of short pages of text, illustrated with cartoon-style graphics, and a terminal quiz. The introduction includes a link to the university's policy on academic dishonesty and a definition of plagiarism, with examples of common instances. Common knowledge exemptions are explained. The following section deals extensively with paraphrasing, with excellent examples of unacceptable practices, and changes that would make the sample acceptable. The next section deals with reading and constructing citations, and includes graphical illustrations of library catalog and typical index citations, accompanied by renditions in Modern Language Association (MLA) and American Psychological Association (APA) format. Finally, there is a short section on plagiarism detection services. A 15-question quiz, in PDF format, rounds out the tutorial, which can be completed in 15 to 30 minutes. The feature that places this tutorial in the advanced technology category is the registration form at the beginning, which enables the tracking of users and the compilation of statistics. The form employs JavaScript to collect and store information about each student; guest users may bypass the form. The tutorial also employs PHP programming.

This is a nicely designed tutorial. The graphics are colorful and witty, but not bandwidth-intensive, and the text is well laid out. Navigation is simple and straightforward. The content is somewhat narrow and touches only briefly on some of the most egregious forms of plagiarism, but concentrates on helping students to avoid careless or accidental misconduct. The issue of paraphrasing, with which many students struggle, is nicely covered. The quiz is, for the most part, somewhat simplistic, but it provides a good reinforcement for the information covered in the tutorial. Its primary weakness is that it provides no form of feedback nor any information about how to receive feedback. This is unimportant if

188

it is used as part of a class assignment, but a definite disadvantage when used independently. It is possible that this is a feature of the guest version of the tutorial, and the problem may be eliminated in the student version.

Plagiarism 101: How to Write Term Papers
Without Being Sucked into the Black Hole

Starr, Karen, and Trudi Jacobson. 2002. Albany, N.Y.: University Libraries, University at Albany, State University of New York.

(http://library.albany.edu/usered/plagiarism/)

This is a short (13 page) tutorial intended for undergraduates at SUNY Albany. It consists of three sections plus additional resources and a list of references. The introduction defines plagiarism and discusses some of the issues and consequences relating to intellectual dishonesty. The underlying assumption of this resource is that students (and others) plagiarize in response to social and academic pressures and personal insecurities. The second section provides suggestions on planning research projects and about the process of learning. Several typical scenarios are posed to the students as ethical dilemmas. The section ends with a short writing assignment; clearly, the tutorial would best be used incorporated into a writing course. The last section of content is labeled "Citation Practice: Crediting your sources," but actually consists of a short true/false quiz followed by a very brief discussion of electronic documents, some minimal guidelines, and a bullet-point summary.

The approach taken by this tutorial is interesting in that it encourages students to examine their ideas about cheating and sloppy work and acknowledges the existence and legitimacy of the pressures and fears that they face. The solution posed is to plan carefully and to get an early start, which, of course, is an excellent prescription for better work all around, not just avoiding the temptation to cheating or carelessness. It is, however, open to question just how valuable this advice is likely to be at the time when the students are engaged in the tutorial. Tutorials on plagiarism are most often positioned near the end of a sequence of lessons on research and writing, and judging by its position in the list of online tutorials on the university library's Web site, this is no exception. By the time this tutorial is assigned, it seems likely that it will already be too late for students to pay any heed to the advice to begin their research early.

Visually, the tutorial is attractive, with plenty of white space and original artwork. The navigation is easy, and the text is written at a level that is easily understood by most first-year students. The technology is straightforward HTML, except for the quiz, which is driven by JavaScipt. Immediate feedback is provided in a pop-up window for each question answered. The questions are posed in such a way that they could require students to transfer learning from one situation to another, but in fact, the answers are based entirely on the previous text, and so are really measuring recall. Wrong answers prompt the user to try again; this would be a more effective teaching strategy if there were more than two possible selections.

Student Resources on Academic Integrity and Plagiarism

Texas A&M University Libraries. 2003. College Station, Tex.: Texas A&M University.

(http://library.tamu.edu/tamulib/content/renderer/children/0,2875,1724 _1001620,00.html

This tutorial consists of 10 sections covering topics relating to academic integrity. Definitions or academic dishonesty are provided from the university's book of student rules. Plagiarism is defined and its relation to copyright explained. Tips are provided on the process of documentation, and additional guidelines are provided for international students. The final content section provides examples of plagiarized and correctly documented and paraphrased or quoted texts. Although they appear as lists, the examples are clearly laid out and easily understood.

A nice feature of this tutorial is the two-part exercise with which it concludes. The first exercise is a 20-question quiz requiring students to recall information covered in the tutorial. The second exercise is another 20-question quiz in which students must transfer their learning to apply to the situations outlined in the questions. A couple of the questions are somewhat ambiguous, or the answers somewhat poorly matched, but overall, it is an excellent exercise. Feedback about the score is provided when an exercise is submitted, but no information is included about which questions were missed or what the correct answer would be. The tutorial is composed in HTML with cascading style sheets, and the quizzes employ JavaScipt.

Faculty Resources on Academic Integrity and Plagiarism

Murphy, Karen, Cynthia Anderson, Rhonda Blackburn, Mike Buckley, Charles Gilreath, Arthur Hobbs, Wendi Arant Kaspar, Darcy McMaughan-Moudouni, Debbie Pipes, Jim Snell, and Elizabeth Tebeaux. 2003. College Station, Tex.: Taskforce Subcommittee of the Educational Workgroup on Plagiarism, Texas A&M University Libraries.

(http://library.tamu.edu/vgn/portal/tamulib/content/renderer/children /0,2875,1724_709708,00.html)

This site is an excellent resource for novice instructors to learn about issues in academic integrity and strategies for promoting conscientious and meticulous writing. Included on this site are: definitions of dishonest practices, with an emphasis on plagiarism; an examination of factors that contribute to academic dishonesty; tips for structuring classes and creating assignments to promote appropriate behavior; tips on detecting plagiarism; and guidelines for dealing with suspected cases.

Plagiarism and How to Avoid It

Gardner, David. 1999–2004. Hong Kong: The English Centre, University of Hong Kong.

(http://ec.hku.hk/plagiarism/)

This five-part tutorial was developed for students at the University of Hong Kong, both at the undergraduate and graduate levels. The language is simple (but not simplistic) and conversational in tone. The first section introduces the idea of plagiarism. The second covers the basics of quotation and paraphrase and includes examples. The third provides students with guidelines for bridging the space between their own ideas and material gathered from other sources. The fourth section covers the construction of in-text references and a works cited list, including some examples of online sources.

An unusual feature of this tutorial is the self-test at the end. Two passages of "scholarly" text are presented, and then students are asked to review five examples of student writing and determine whether or not plagiarism has been committed. However, unlike many of the tutorials reviewed here, Gardner has not employed radio buttons and a true/false format. Each student must submit a short written answer, explaining what is wrong and how it could be corrected. Students submit their answers and can then view Gardner's comments on the example. This is a very good example of an authentic assessment embedded in a digital learning tool. The tutorial employs JavaScipt and active server technology. The content can be covered in 25 to 45 minutes, but the self-test requires close reading and could take as long as an hour, depending on the efforts and reading ability of the student.

Synthesis: Using the Work of Others (Antiplagiarism Website)

Roberts, Teresa, and Shelly Davis. 2004. Farmington, Maine: Writing Center, and Mantor Library, University of Maine at Farmington.

(http://departments.umf.maine.edu/~library/plagiarism/index.html)

This tutorial consists of four sections addressing various aspects of academic integrity and the idea of intellectual property. The first section defines plagiarism, with reference to the university's Code of Academic Integrity. The second provides tips for doing research and note taking and also covers quotation, paraphrase, and summary. The third covers the process of citation, and the fourth looks at copyright issues. The tutorial includes two interactive quizzes, asking students to recognize correctly plagiarism and copyright violation.

This tutorial is unusual in that it is the result of collaboration between the library's instruction program and the staff of the university's Writing Center. The benefit of this collaboration can be seen in the seamless blending of suggestions for conducting research and incorporating resources into composition. Another feature of this resource is that it addresses questions about documenting sources in presentations other than the standard research paper. Because many courses now demand that students exhibit oral presentation skills, this is an important and neglected area in the teaching of scholarly attribution. The quizzes are unusual in that, although they are designed in a true/false format, some have no correct answers. The ambiguity and context-sensitive nature of documentation is acknowledged in this way, but it may be somewhat confusing to beginning researchers. Some design features of the tutorial are nicely done; the layout contains lots of white space, and all of the links open in a separate window, including feedback in the quizzes. However, there are certain navigation problems; in some places, one progresses to the next page by following links at the bottom of the text, whereas in others it is necessary to go back to the sidebar menu. It is possible to get caught up in spiraling links and skip over whole sections. The tutorial employs JavaScipt to run the quizzes and selected visual effects.

The Nuts and Bolts of College Writing: Evidence

Harvey, Michael. 2003. Chestertown, Md.: Washington College. (http://nutsandbolts.washcoll.edu/plagiarism.html)

This resource is a precursor of and companion to a book of the same name, published by Hackett Press. It is designed to teach college students the process of writing and is intended to address issues of writing across the curriculum. The chapter on evidence covers strategies for searching the Internet followed by an introduction to plagiarism and citation, a lesson on quotation and paraphrase, and extensive sections on the use of four common style manuals. The section on Web searching is nice, though somewhat dated, and incorporates information on citing Web resources. The following section gives simple but clear explanations of the ideas of plagiarism and citation. The section on quotation and paraphrase is one of the best of any reviewed for this chapter, because it teaches approaches to good writing, rather than mere mechanics. The sections covering individual style manuals provide students with guidance for picking out the most important things to which novices should pay attention. The tool is nicely laid out, although some pages seem to have been formatted for an unusually large screen, and the pages are lively and attractive. Nuts and Bolts has no interactive elements, but the author notes that upgrades to the site are in the works and requests feedback from instructors about the usefulness of online quizzes and other interactive elements. The site employs cascading style sheets and JavaScript.

Almost Low-Tech

The development of the resources in this category requires some advanced knowledge of HTML coding and the use of some additional applications.

Plagiarism-The Cheating Disease: Student Tutorial & Teacher Toolkit

Hinrichs, Stephanie. 2002. Blackwater, Queensland, Australia: Blackwater State High School Resource Centre.

(www.blackwatshs.qld.edu.au/index_plagiarism.htm)

This lively and colorful tutorial is designed for students in high school. Plagiarism is framed by the concept of cheating, which can be presumed to be more familiar to secondary school students. An interactive quiz at the beginning gives students the opportunity to test their understanding of the rules of documentation. The following text examines the temptations of electronic text, some of the reasons for and potential consequences of plagiarism, with tips and basic information about the rules and processes of documentation. The focus of the tutorial is ethical behavior, rather than on teaching the mechanics of citation. Designed in vivid colors with large fonts and a plethora of animated graphics, this site seems busy and crowded to an adult reader, but may well appeal to a secondary school audience. One significant drawback is that the preliminary quiz provides the same feedback for every correct or incorrect answer. This is initially confusing, and then rather boring for the user, and misses the opportunity to discuss the ethical issues posed by each question more specifically.

Citing Responsibly: A Guide to Avoiding Plagiarism

Committee on Academic Integrity. 2002. Washington, D.C.: George Washington University Law School.

(www.law.gwu.edu/resources/citing.asp)

Here is another unusual approach to providing online instructional material. This 15-page handbook is available in PDF format and provides guidelines for adhering to the policy of the law school on plagiarism. As it is intended for law students, the document itself has a very legal flavor, but without the police state mentality that seems to pervade the UC Davis tutorial reviewed below. Plagiarism is defined, and penalties outlined. Basic citation rules are provided, along with tips and examples. Two unusual features of this tutorial are the sections on citation in early drafts and on issues for students from other countries.

Academic Integrity

Office of Student Judicial Affairs. 1999–2003. Davis, Calif.: University of California Davis.

(http://sja.ucdavis.edu/a-i.htm)

This site consists of four sections addressing different aspects of academic integrity. The first section discusses the concept of academic integrity, with appeals to individual conscience, as well as academic and social consequences. The second section deals with issues of plagiarism. Plagiarism is briefly framed in the context of scholarship and the UC Davis Code of Academic Conduct. A definition is provided, along with a brief discussion of ethical issues. A very simplistic explanation of the process of citation is included and amplified by some guidelines and examples of proper quotation and paraphrase. The third section deals with issues of collaboration, and the fourth provides instructors with guidelines for promoting academic integrity and deterring cheating.

Not surprisingly, given its origins, this resource is more concerned with laying down the law than with giving students extensive guidance in learning to adhere to academic standards. The definition of plagiarism goes into great detail as to the meaning of "work" and "sources" but is followed by an explanation of citation that takes account only of books as sources and only of MLA as a style format. The examples of plagiarized and properly composed and documented text are adequate, but not extensive. A unique aspect of this site is that it discusses issues of collaboration, an area that causes considerable confusion for students. Unfortunately, although the section is well thought out, with good examples and explanations, it focuses only on unauthorized collaboration and leaves the reader with the sense that UC Davis places more emphasis on constructing and enforcing a set of rigid rules than on encouraging learning.

The resource is designed in straightforward HTML with a few simple graphics. It is easy to navigate, though the layout of the two principle sections is initially somewhat confusing. For the first three sections, the target audience is students; the fourth section is designed for instructors and rendered in PDF format (other sections are also available in PDF). The switch in target audiences is not apparent from the top level. It is only after the PDF document is opened that the change in approach may be detected. Clustering material that is meant for instructors along with material intended for students seems, in this instance, self-defeating. Instructors are less likely to find the material intended for them, and students can see exactly what their teachers know about detecting cheating.

The Lemonade Tutorials: Plagiarism

Dorn, Sherman. 1997–2003. Tampa, Fla.: Department of Psychological and Social Foundations, College of Education, University of South Florida. (www.coedu.usf.edu/~dorn/Tutorials/plagiarism/plagiarism.htm)

This witty tutorial takes a low-tech approach to teaching the ethics of academic writing. Consisting of four short chapters, the tutorial takes a student-centered approach to explaining the philosophical and practical issues relating to

194

plagiarism in the classroom. Dorn addresses the common excuses and questions of students with thoughtful, concise explanations of the principles and mechanics of submitting work that meets academic standards. Issues covered include intellectual piracy, fraud, cultural differences, verbatim regurgitation, paraphrase and quotation, and defense against unjustified suspicions. Tips on documentation, paraphrasing, and note taking are included, and additional resources are recommended.

The tutorial is almost entirely plain text, with no graphics or illustrations, but it is engaging and funny as well as forthright and pointed. Students are likely to appreciate the humor and the equitable approach as well as the information and explanations. Dorn provides links to stories about intellectual dishonesty and articles about concepts in academic integrity. The one serious flaw in the tutorial is that the links have not been maintained; it is disappointing to find that some of the material is not accessible. As a guide for student research, it is somewhat idiosyncratic; Dorn's approach to documentation is practical, rather than nitpicking, but students who complete the tutorial will have few doubts about what is expected of them. A bonus is an outrageously funny satiric song, accessible from the opening page, which requires the RealOne Player.

Low-Tech

The resources included in this category require only a moderate facility with HTML coding for development.

Plagiary and the Art of Skillful Citation

Rodgers, John. 1996. Houston, Tex.: Department of Immunology, Baylor College of Medicine.

(www.bcm.tmc.edu/immuno/citewell/)

This nine-part tutorial is designed for graduate students of the Baylor College of Medicine. It appears to be designed to accompany a lecture on the ethics of science that forms part of the curriculum of the required course Introduction to Graduate Research. It is an unusual work in that it concentrates on the philosophical issues of plagiarism and scientific ethics and has little to say about the mechanics of citation or other practical issues. Definitely written at a graduate level, it provides some thought-provoking material for the consideration of fledgling scientists and some practical advice on documenting sources during the course of research. Unfortunately, the resource has not been kept up to date; some of the links are broken, and there are references to obsolete software packages. The navigation is circumlocutory, and page layout is problematic, but the content is unusual.

How Do I Write this Paper: Citation

Writing and Tutorial Center. 1999. Brooklyn, N.Y.: Pratt Institute. (www.pratt.edu/wtc/writing/citation/right.html)

This tutorial, which forms part of a suite of materials on writing, is an object example of a poorly designed product. The problems with this tool are legion. The tone is patronizing and overly vernacular, as if directed at an audience much younger than college age. The content covers definitions of plagiarism, the practice of documentation, and various aspects of composition, but in such a way to provide students with very little real information about the process of documentation in academic writing. The navigation is awkward, and some of the internal links are broken or circular.

Conclusion

The tutorials reviewed here provide much food for thought to anyone who is interested in developing online instructional materials on the topic of plagiarism. One can explore the possibilities of multimedia, get ideas for incorporating active learning or developing authentic assessment, or find creative low-tech, low-cost solutions to the challenge of providing instruction online. Some provide fine examples of good visual or structural design, whereas a few have defects in these areas that may equally be educational to a novice developer. A wide range of pedagogical approaches is used, including lecture, drama, role-playing, coaching, and Socratic dialogue. In style, they range from conversational to didactic, from humorous to scolding. They are directed at students working at many different levels, and a few are intended for instructors.

In terms of content, the one constant factor is, of course, an emphasis on the ethics of academia. Some focus on the research process, some on citation mechanics, some on composition, and some on philosophical issues. Many concentrate on commonly misunderstood areas such as quotation, paraphrase, and use of Web resources. A few address issues of cultural or disciplinary differences. Surprisingly, only one tutorial was found that covers documentation of sources in oral or other nontextual presentations, though several address the use of nontextual sources. Another topic that has largely been ignored is that of group work or collaboration, an area that is rife with confusion for students. One tutorial deals with unauthorized collaboration, but no one has provided any guidelines for students in situations where group work or discussion is either approved or assigned.

Developing online instructional material on the topic of plagiarism can help us to communicate to students the importance of academic integrity. By making materials available online, we can provide instruction at point of need and across disciplinary lines. We can design material to suit multiple learning styles and take advantage of the characteristics of multimedia. The developmental process is also fertile ground for cross-campus collaboration. It is important to remember, though, that online tutorials are not a panacea for the problem of plagiarism; they will not, by themselves, solve this or any other problem in teaching. Tutorials will be most effective in combating plagiarism in an environment where they are simply one manifestation of a culture that articulates a high value for academic integrity.

Works Cited

Boling, Elizabeth, Theodore Frick, Meltem Albayrak-Karahan, Joseph Defazio, and Noriko Matsumura. 2002. "How to Recognize Plagiarism." Bloomington, Ind.: Department of Instructional Systems Technology, School of Education, University of Indiana Bloomington. Available: www.indiana.edu/~istd/.

Swenson, Karen, Cheryl Ruggiero, Len Hatfield, and Randy Patton. 1998–1999. "Project Abstract—Phase one. In Integrating Diverse Learning Environments [IDLE]: Writing and Critical Thinking in Traditional and Digital Domains." Blacksburg, Va.: Department of English, Virginia Polytechnic Institute and State University. Available: www.english.vt.edu/~IDLE/menu/abstract.html.

———. "IDLE 2000: Modules." 2000. Blacksburg, Va.: Department of English, Virginia Polytechnic Institute and State University. Available: www.english.vt.edu/~IDLE/menu/modules.html.

CHAPTER 16

And in the End: An Annotated Bibliography of Resources, Media, and Other Teaching Tools

Patience L. Simmonds

Introduction

Plagiarism is a big deal. It is a big problem for educators and librarians, and quite recently it has been very worrisome for people in the commercial world too. Plagiarism and the other issues associated with plagiarism like cheating, academic dishonesty, academic integrity, honor codes, and so forth, have been the topics of discussion in many communities. Students in high schools, colleges, and universities are often targeted as the people who are responsible for committing most of the acts of plagiarism and cheating. The Internet has contributed to the problem of plagiarism and its antecedents, but plagiarism existed long before the birth of the Internet. What the Internet has done is to make more visible the immense number of resources available for people interested in the topic of plagiarism and the sources they can use to define, deter, prevent, detect, and educate people about plagiarism.

When one begins a search on the topic of plagiarism, one is confronted with an extraordinary large number of resources on the topic. Resources on the topic of plagiarism include books, magazine and journal articles, products to detect and prevent plagiarism, plagiarism and antiplagiarism software, and network and cable television programs. The purpose of this chapter is to provide the reader with an annotated bibliography to use for further research regarding the topics discussed in this book. There are thousands of books and periodical articles on the issues of plagiarism and cheating among students discussed from many angles. Educators who are concerned about this plagiarism issue and academic integrity have approached the problem from various sides. There are resources targeted at students, teaching faculty, and administrators in general. The perennial nature of the plagiarism problem has also contributed to the difficulty of having a single all-rounded definition of plagiarism that would be understood by all students without exception. Most of the sites examined have the basic definition of what they perceive plagiarism to be, and the more it is defined, the more educators and librarians have to strive to make students understand and stop committing plagiarism and academic dishonesty. The available resources on plagiarism and other forms of cheating listed here are aimed at discussing what plagiarism is, how people commit plagiarism, what the authors think contribute to plagiarism, and what in their opinions can be done to deter, prevent, detect, and halt this fast-moving "plague" called plagiarism.

Web Sites on Plagiarism: Definitions, Explanations, and Statements

Avoiding Plagiarism from the Glendale Community College Site

(www.glendale.edu/library/libins/icweb/Handouts/Plagiarism.htm)
This site defines plagiarism for the students and provides a list of relevant terms which the student should know help them recognize what plagiarism is and how to avoid it. There is also information on what and how to quote, how to paraphrase, what to cite, when to cite, and how to cite.

Avoiding Plagiarism: Mastering the Art of Scholarship

(http://sja.ucdavis.edu/avoid.htm)
This handout from the University of California Davis Student Judicial Affairs provides guidelines for avoiding plagiarism within the UC Davis code of academic conduct and presents examples of ethical scholarship. It also provides examples of proper citation of sources for the students. The handout is also available in PDF (portable document format).

DePauw University Writing Center

(www.depauw.edu/admin/arc/writing_center/plag.asp)
This DePauw University guide defines and describes for the students what plagiarism is and presents guidelines to watch out for when "using sources in essays." It lists four types of plagiarism, "direction detection," "borrowing from

other students," "vague or indirect citation," and "mosaic plagiarism," which they define as "The writer does not copy the source directly, but changes a few words in each sentence or slightly reworks a paragraph, without giving credit to the original author. Those sentences or paragraphs are not quotes, but are so close to quotes that that they should be quoted or, if they have been changed enough to qualify as a paraphrase, the source should be cited." The site also provides reasons why student plagiarize and suggests ways for students to avoid committing plagiarism.

Documentation Guidelines

(www.lib.duke.edu/libguide/citing.htm)

Duke University Libraries has guidelines available for students for citing sources and avoiding plagiarism. They contain sections for citing sources within the student's paper and how to assemble a list of works cited in a paper. The purpose of this site is to educate students about plagiarism and the consequences of plagiarism and to give them strategies for avoiding it. The site allows the student to use the citation style they want to in text citation within their paper and presents them with an example of how to cite their sources. It also makes available the Duke University honor code, which discusses plagiarism and other academic misconducts and how to deal with them.

How to Avoid Plagiarism

(www.northwestern.edu/uacc/plagiar.html)

Northwestern University has academic integrity policies that apply to both undergraduate and graduate research. They provide strategies for students to avoid plagiarism.

How to Recognize Plagiarism: Indiana University

(www.indiana.edu/~istd/)

This site was developed by the Instructional Systems Technology (IST) Department, Indiana University at Bloomington. All IST students are required to take this tutorial, but it may be beneficial to other students and faculty who are interested in addressing issues of plagiarism. An overview, cases, examples, and even a test are covered.

Plagiarism: Definitions, Diagnoses, Preventions, and Cures for Students and Faculty at the University of Minnesota

(http://cisw.cla.umn.edu/plagiarism/)

The Center for Interdisciplinary Studies of Writing at the University of Minnesota provides links for faculty and students to detect and avoid plagiarism. In addition, links to the definitions of plagiarism and a bibliography of plagiarism articles are included.

Plagiarism: Definitions, Examples and Penalties from the Department of Chemistry at the University of Kentucky

(www.chem.uky.edu/courses/common/plagiarism.html#Examples)

This site includes the university definition of plagiarism, which is taken from the *Student Rights and Responsibilities Handbook*. It presents examples of plagiarism and shows procedures and penalties recommended if an instructor is confronted with acts of cheating and plagiarism.

Plagiarism Q & A

(www.ehhs.cmich.edu/~mspears/plagiarism.html)

This site is an excellent resource for students as well as faculty. It is broken into sections that help students understand plagiarism, its penalties, how to avoid it, how to paraphrase correctly, and more. Faculty members will the find the links for searching for plagiarized papers a helpful and possibly time-saving tool.

Plagiarism: What It Is and How to Avoid It

(www.montgomerycollege.edu/library/plagiarismintro.htm)

This site provides a tutorial that discusses what plagiarism is and how students can avoid it. It starts by defining plagiarism, provides examples of what constitutes plagiarism, and shows how and what sources should be cited. It gives examples of proper and improper paraphrasing and discussing plagiarism within the context of the Montgomery College Student Code of Conduct. The site also provides an evaluation and quiz section that, when completed and submitted, would earn the student an extra credit.

Plagiarism: What It Is and How to Recognize and Avoid It

(www.indiana.edu/~wts/wts/plagiarism.html)

"Plagiarism: What It is and How to Recognize and Avoid It" is based on the Student Code of Rights, Responsibilities, and Ethics Handbook of Indiana University (Bloomington). Topics include: acceptable and unacceptable paraphrasing; what is or is not common knowledge; and strategies for avoiding plagiarism.

Purdue Writing Lab

(http://owl.english.purdue.edu/handouts/print/research/r_plagiar.html)

The Purdue University Online Writing Lab has a handout on avoiding plagiarism. The handout "is designed to help writers develop strategies for knowing how to avoid accidental plagiarism." It contains information on actions that might be deemed to be considered as plagiarism and how students can avoid these by taking necessary precautions. The handout provides them with examples and suggestions for avoiding intentional and accidental plagiarism.

What Is Plagiarism?

(http://hnn.us/articles/514.html)

The History News Network staff has posted three definitions of plagiarism provided by the American Historical Association, Modern Language Association, and the American Psychological Association. One of the definition states that "plagiarism includes more subtle and perhaps more pernicious abuses than simply expropriating the exact wording of another author without attribution." The site encourages all scholars, especially students of history, to resist plagiarism.

What Is Plagiarism at Indiana University? Recognizing Plagiarism

(http://education.indiana.edu/~frick/plagiarism/index2.html)

This is a tutorial site that was developed by the School of Education's Instructional Systems Technology (IST) Department at Indiana University at Bloomington. The tutorial defines what plagiarism is for the students, provides an overview of what it is and how to recognize it, presents two types of text examples, one original and the other edited to show signs of possible plagiarism. After practicing the examples, the students can take a test on their knowledge of what plagiarism is and how they can recognize it and avoid it. Students are allowed to retake the tests until they get the required score and are given a confirmation certificate. Students are, however, not given a certificate until they score 100% on the tests.

What Is Plagiarism?/Avoiding Plagiarism

(http://tlt.its.psu.edu/suggestions/cyberplag/cyberplagexamples.html)

Aspects of plagiarism and cyber-plagiarism are discussed here at this Penn State site. These include examples of wholesale copying, cut and paste, inappropriate paraphrase, when to cite, and sample citation guidelines to help students cite their work. Links to other relevant sites that provide similar information on plagiarism are provided.

WPA Statement on Avoiding Plagiarism: Best Practices

(www.ilstu.edu/~ddhesse/wpa/positions/WPAplagiarism.pdf)

This statement defines what plagiarism is according to the Council of Writing Program Administrators and outlines strategies for avoiding plagiarism. It has sections devoted to students, administrators, and teaching faculty who are involved with writing.

College and University Statements on Plagiarism and Academic Integrity

Academic Integrity: A Guide for Students

(www.purdue.edu/odos/administration/integrity.htm)

"Academic Integrity: A Guide for Students" was written by Stephen Akers from the Office of the Dean of Students at Purdue University. This document states that "Purdue prohibits dishonesty in connection with any University activity. Cheating, plagiarism, or knowingly furnishing false information to the University are examples of dishonesty. It goes on further to show examples of academic dishonesty and tips on how to avoid committing them. As of spring 2002, Senate Policy 43–00 (Syllabus) requires instructors to provide a statement on Academic Integrity within a syllabus. This makes it possible for every student to be aware of where Purdue stands on academic integrity and academic honesty.

Academic Integrity at Penn State

(www.psu.edu/oldmain/prov/academicintegrity.htm)
(http://tlt.its.psu.edu/suggestions/cyberplag/)
"A Statement by the Council of Academic Deans" defines and outlines what academic integrity is at Penn State. It states:

> The primary responsibility for supporting and promoting academic integrity lies with the faculty and administration, but students must be active participants. A climate of integrity is created and sustained through ongoing conversations about honesty, trust, fairness, respect, and responsibility and the embodiment of these values in the life of the University.

The American University Honor Code

(www.american.edu/academics/integrity/code.htm)
The American University Honor Code provides definition of academic violations and outlines the adjudication of academic offenses. It also has a frequently asked questions (FAQ) section that answers pertinent questions both students and faculty may have. There are also quizzes to test students' knowledge about the academic integrity code and academic violations.

The Center for Academic Integrity

(www.academicintegrity.org/index.asp)
The Center for Academic Integrity is located at the Keenan Institute for Ethics at Duke University, and it "provides a forum to identify, affirm, and promote the values of academic integrity among students, faculty, teachers and administrators." The Center for Academic Integrity is a consortium of about 320 member institutions from U.S. and Canadian institutions, and their stated aim is "joining together to promote academic integrity." CAI has a list of academic institutions with sample honor codes. Membership to CAI is open to any educational institution for an annual fee of $350, and members enjoy certain privileges including being able to search the institute's database. Individuals can also apply for membership for a fee.

Sample honor codes from member institutions of the Center for Academic Integrity can be found at www.academicintegrity.org/samp_honor_codes.asp.

The George Washington University Code of Academic Integrity

(www.cs.seas.gwu.edu/academics/gwintegrity.html#_Toc420653047)

The George Washington University Code of Academic Integrity was established by the students, faculty, librarians, and administration of The George Washington University. The Code of Academic Integrity has jurisdiction over many of the schools within the university. It describes examples of common academic dishonest behaviors among students and shows how these behaviors can be reported and dealt with within the Code of Academic Integrity at George Washington University. This makes it a very powerful code because it binds all areas of the university community.

Plagiarism: A Library Guide for Faculty at the University of Chicago

(www.lib.uchicago.edu/e/reg/using/instruct/plagiarism.html)

"Plagiarism: A Library Guide for Faculty at the University of Chicago" examines plagiarism within the context of the university guides and policy statements. It defines plagiarism, and examines the role library instruction plays in preventing plagiarism.

Plagiarism and Antiplagiarism

(http://newark.rutgers.edu/~ehrlich/plagiarism598.html)

This is a discussion of what plagiarism is and shows how to avoid it. Suggestions include becoming familiar with "the details of the plagiarism policies of your university, college, department, course, and assignment." Individuals are also encouraged to know the penalties for plagiarism, the ins and outs of plagiarism as they are related to computers and the Internet, and copyright laws. The site also has a list of useful Web pages for detecting and deterring plagiarism.

Rutgers University Plagiarism Module

(www.scc.rutgers.edu/douglass/sal/plagiarism/intro.html)

Rutgers University has a library skill plagiarism module that is a mini-play that teaches students about proper citation, cheating, plagiarism, and so forth.

What Is Plagiarism?

(www.georgetown.edu/honor/plagiarism.html)

This is a section of the Georgetown University Honor Code for students and crafted by the Honor Council. Nine questions related to plagiarism and cheating are discussed and it provides sample statements often given by student who plagiarize; for example, "In my country/high school, using someone else's work is assign of respect" or "I don't have time to do it right."

Resources for Plagiarism Deterrence and Prevention

Cheating 101: Paper Mills and You

(www.coastal.edu/library/mills2.htm)
Kimbel Library has a "list of active Internet term paper and essay sites compiled as part of a Teaching Effectiveness Seminar on cheating, plagiarism and Internet paper mills." This site, by Margaret Fain and Peggy Bates with the help of other school librarians, was "designed to help faculty combat plagiarism in their classes," includes an alphabetical list of about 250 paper mill sites.

Cyber-plagiarism: Prevention and Detection

(http://tlt.its.psu.edu/suggestions/cyberplag/)
This site provides information and links to sources in the general news about plagiarism and academic misconduct and definitions and causes of plagiarism and cyber-plagiarism. Resources for plagiarism detection and prevention, sources of paper mills, are also identified here. Penn State policies about academic integrity and sample online quizzes that are aimed at educating students about academic honesty and academic dishonesty are also present.

Deterring Plagiarism: Some Strategies

(www.utoronto.ca/writing/plagiarism.html)
Margaret Proctor, Coordinator, Writing Support, at the University of Toronto created this site. She presents practical ways to deter plagiarism by "making assignments an integral part of the course, demonstrating the instructors' expectation for the course, and making the assignment a process rather than a one time exercise." The site has available resources and examples for students, instructional resources for students, advice and resources for faculty, and advice and examples from other universities.

Plagiarism Detection Programs and Software

CopyCatch

(www.copycatch.freeserve.co.uk/)
CopyCatch Gold is a U.K.-based program that can be used on a stand-alone or networked computer. It can be used "for detection, deterrence, investigation and instruction" and "handles all common document types automatically." The creators of CopyCatch Gold claim "100% accuracy in identifying shared material." It costs £250 per year for a single-user license.

Eve2 (Essay Verification Engine)

(www.canexus.com/eve/index.shtml)

The creators of Eve2 describe it as "a very powerful tool that allows professors and teachers at all levels of the education system to determine if students have plagiarized material from the World Wide Web. Eve2 accepts essays in plain text, Microsoft Word, or Corel Word Perfect format and returns links to Web pages from which a student may have plagiarized. Eve2 has been developed to be powerful enough to find plagiarized material while not overwhelming the professor with false links." Eve2 provides a full report "on each paper that contained plagiarism, including the percent of the essay plagiarized, and an annotated copy of the paper showing all plagiarism highlighted in red." Each professor who wishes to use Eve2 must purchase a one-time license of $19.95 for all essays submitted in his class. The license is not transferable from professor to another.

Glatt Plagiarism Services

(www.plagiarism.com)

Glatt Plagiarism provides services to "help deter plagiarism and encourage academic honesty." Glatt produces three types of plagiarism services: Glatt Plagiarism teaching program (GPTeach), a tutorial that teaches students what plagiarism is, shows them how to avoid it, and acts as a self-detection tool with a practice section on proper paraphrasing and proper citation. The second service is the Glatt Plagiarism Screening Program, which is a plagiarism detection procedure for teaching faculty. The last service, the Glatt Plagiarism Self-detection Program, is "a screening program to help deter inadvertent instances of plagiarism."

JISC

(www.jisc.ac.uk)

The Joint Information Systems Committee Plagiarism Advisory Service describes JISC as the "detection service [that] checks submitted work by students against material already available on the Internet and held in a central database. It then identifies where matches have been found. The color-coded originality report produced by the software provides an easily accessible method."

JPlag

(wwwipd.ira.uka.de:2222)

This is system that "finds similarities among multiple sets of source code files" and "can detect software plagiarism." The creator of JPlag also claims that "JPlag does not merely compare bytes of text, but is aware of programming language syntax and program structure and hence is robust against many kinds of attempts to disguise similarities between plagiarized files. JPlag currently supports Java, C, C++, Scheme, and natural language text." Use of JPlag is free but users must obtain an account by sending email to jplag@ira.uka.de and state the purpose for which they are going to use it.

Moss (A Measure of Software Similarity)

(www.cs.berkeley.edu/~aiken/moss.html)

This service is a tool used to detect plagiarism in programming language. Moss is "an automatic system for determining the similarity of C, C++, Java, Pascal, Ada, ML, Lisp, or Scheme programs." Currently, Moss is a free Internet service and is available to anyone who wishes to use it for educational purposes. In order to get a Moss account, one has to send email to moss@moss.cs.berkeley.edu. Commercial use of the program is forbidden.

MyDropBox.com

(www.mydropbox.com/)

MyDropBox.com identifies itself as the provider of "the world's leading technology to detect and prevent cases of Internet plagiarism." It is geared toward administrators, faculty, and students. Its "goal is to use technology to help reduce academic dishonesty and keep your classroom a level playing field for all students" It provides a 30-day free trial pilot to all academic institutions. MyDropBox.com checks a student-submitted document "against every possible source on the Internet" and does an "analysis of published works in password-protected electronic database." It also checks their customers' own database of submitted papers to prevent "peer-to-peer cheating." It also offers both individual and institutional licenses for purchase.

Plagiarism.org

(www.plagiarism.org)
(www.turnitin.com)

Plagiarism.org is the parent organization under which Turnitin.com operates. Turnitin.com claims to be "the world's leading online plagiarism prevention resource." Turnitin.com also claims it "has been helping millions of faculty and students in over 50 countries to improve writing and research skills, encourage collaborative online learning, ensure originality of student work, and save instructors' time—all at a very affordable price."

Products from Turnitin.com include a preventive tool that identifies unoriginal documents by students. Turnitin.com provides a 1-month free trial to prospective users, and it provides individual licenses to instructors and staff from departments and schools. The cost of Turnitin.com is determined by school or institution type, the license plan chosen, and total enrollment of the school.

The Plagiarism Resource Center at the University of Virginia

(http://plagiarism.phys.virginia.edu/)

This is a program that "examines a collection of document files. It extracts the text portions of those documents and looks through them for matching words in phrases of a specified minimum length. When it finds two files that share enough words in those phrases, WCopyfind generates html report files. These reports contain the document text with the matching phrases underlined." This is a free software designed by Professor Lou Bloomfield and cannot "search for a text that was copied from any external source unless you include that external source in the documents you give to Wcopyfind. It works on only purely local data-it cannot search the web or Internet to find matching documents."

Studies and Reports about Plagiarism

Academic Misconduct: Guide for Instructors, Dean of Students Office, UW-Madison

(www.wisc.edu/students/acad_misconduct_guide.htm)

This site includes UWS 14, the chapter in the UW System Administrative Code regulating academic misconduct. This document includes tips on preventing academic misconduct, a definition of academic misconduct, and description of the investigation process, penalties and procedures, and a student right to a hearing. It also has a sample format for an instructor to use if he suspects that a student has committed academic misconduct.

Cut-and-Paste Plagiarism: Preventing, Detecting and Tracking Online Plagiarism

(http://alexia.lis.uiuc.edu/~janicke/plagiary.htm)

This site, created and maintained by Lisa Hinchliffe, defines plagiarism and provides suggestions for preventing, detecting, and tracking down plagiarized materials. It also provides links to term paper mills.

History News Network: Plagiarism Cases

(http://historynewsnetwork.org/articles/article.html?id=504)

The History News Network (HNN) provides a thorough examination of the Stephen E. Ambrose plagiarism controversy. It examines various accounts of the controversy from many news reports and touches on the difference between sloppiness in research and deliberate copying of the work of other authors. The History News Network has links to other sites that discuss the Ambrose controversy.

Pearson, Gretchen. Electronic Plagiarism Seminar, Syracuse, New York: Noreen Reale Falcone Library, Le Moyne College, 2003

(http://lemoyne.edu/library/plagiarism/index.htm)

This site was created in December 1999 and was updated as recently as February 2004. It is a comprehensive and well organized site with a general bibliography on plagiarism and another bibliography on scientific misconduct. It provides definitions of plagiarism and tips on detecting and preventing plagiarism. There are guides for educators and students. The document stays current on news items from various news organizations about plagiarism cases. There are also sections on general strategies for preventing plagiarism, a section on ethics and honor codes, and writing strategies to help prevent plagiarism.

Plagiarism

(www.web-miner.com/plagiarism)

Sharon Stoerger is a librarian at the University of Illinois at Urbana-Champaign, and she prepared this comprehensive document. She examines selected articles relating to copyright and intellectual freedom targeted to instructors and students. She also discusses and provides links to topics such as plagiarism cases, plagiarism detection tools, term paper sites, and current articles on plagiarism cases in the news.

Plagiarism in Colleges in USA

(www.rbs2.com/plag.htm)

This long and very comprehensive document was prepared by Ronald B. Standler, who is an attorney and a consultant. He discusses plagiarism by students and faculty and legal cases involving plagiarism. Topics discussed in this document include law of plagiarism, trademark law, copyright law, and statutes and court cases involving the sale of term papers. He has practical ideas about how faculty can detect plagiarism. He provides information on actual cases involving plagiarism in colleges, cases against commercial institutions, and legal actions that have been taken against people who report plagiarism. He also provides information on cases where degrees have been revoked after cases of plagiarism or academic misconduct has been revealed after a student has graduated.

Plagiarism Stopper: A Teacher's Guide

(www.ncusd203.org/central/html/where/plagiarism_stoppers.html)

This is list on plagiarism and links to other sources was compiled by Jane Sharka with the help of some school librarians and other educators from across the United States. The list is targeted toward teacher to help them know "places to go for help with student plagiarism, how to identify it, what to do when it happens, how to prevent it." It includes detection tips on plagiarism and plagiarism prevention and training. It provides information about free detection tools and links to fee-based detection services. It also provides a current list of paper mills.

Student Plagiarism in an Online World

(www.asee.org/prism/december/)

This site, which is sponsored by the Society for Engineering Education, features resources and strategies to help detect plagiarism among students.

Paper Mills

Web sites that provide "research papers" to students promote plagiarism and other forms of academic dishonesty. Whether these so-called "research" papers are free or obtained for a fee, these sites do not help the students' academic growth one way or another. There are thousands of these sites that make it extremely easy to help these students commit plagiarism and outright academic theft. Teaching faculty, administrators, and librarians need to know what paper mill sites are available, what they offer, and which ones their students frequently use. Here are a few of the popular ones students use.

A 1 Term Paper

(www.a1-termpaper.com/)

This site claims to have a database of 20,000 prewritten and custom-written papers on all imaginable subjects on file and available for a fee. All prewritten papers are priced individually, but custom-written papers "vary from $19.95 to $35.00 per page, depending on difficulty of subject matter, library research required, time demands, etc."

Cheathouse.com

(www.cheathouse.com/index.php)

The articles available at Cheathouse.com are primarily in English, but there are also a few in Spanish, German, and Danish. Registration is required, but the papers are free. Essays are obtained from submissions to the site by other students. Cheathouse.com claims to have a total of about 12,500 essays. Even though it claims to provide free access to essays to students, students who want full access to Cheathouse.com and better quality research papers do, however, have to pay a specific amount weekly, monthly, or yearly. The most Cheathouse.com would charge a student for a full-year subscription is $49.95.

DirectEssays.com

(www.directessays.com/)

DirectEssays.com boasts of 101,000 high-quality essays and term papers. Paid members log in by using identification and password.

Fastpapers.com

(www.fastpapers.com)

This is a commercial service from which one can purchase essays and longer reports, all at the fixed rate of $9.95 per page. Fastpapers.com claims to have in their database more than 50,000 essays on many different subjects for sale for same-day delivery. There are many other paper mills like Fastpapers.com under the parent organization of the Paper Store.

Genius Papers

(www.geniuspapers.com/)

Genius Papers boasts of having more than 100,000 papers in its database and claims to "have done the research for you." "Genius Papers pricing policy is simple: A one-time fee of $19.95 gives you a full year of unlimited access to thousands of term papers, in addition to membership to the Academic Research Center." Members log in to obtain "unlimited access to the database of thousands upon thousands of papers."

SchoolSucks.com

(www.schoolsucks.com/)

SchoolSucks.com provides free term papers. Students do, however, have to register to be members and log in to access the free paper. For more detailed custom-written papers, students are charged substantial fees. An article on the topic of television and school violence written between 1992 and 1993 with 52 citations, 25 pages, and 16 sources cost $136.

Using Search Engines for Plagiarism Detection

There are a few search engines on the Internet that are very capable of detecting Internet plagiarism. Sometimes, all you have to do is take a few of the words from the text you think has been plagiarized and follow the instructions the particular search engine gives for detecting plagiarism. Here are a few of the engines, which can be used effectively to detect plagiarism.

Dogpile.com

(www.dogpile.com)

For a search in Dogpile, enclose your search in quotation marks. Dogpile will search for phrases by using various search engines including Google.

Google.com

(www.google.com)

The advanced search feature in Google can be used to determine if a section of a document has been plagiarized. If you enclose 10 or fewer words in quotation marks and search in Google, the search engine should come up with similar phrases in documents on the Web. Google will search for stop words to find similarities.

Internet Essay Exposer

(www.mattclare.ca/essay/)

In order to search for possible plagiarism in an essay using Internet Essay Exposer, select "Web Search" and insert one or two sentences between the quotation marks provided. This service checks about 10 search engines, and the user can select which search engines he prefers.

Selected Books

Harris, Robert. 2002. *Using Sources Effectively: Strengthening Your Writing and Avoiding Plagiarism.* Los Angeles, Calif.: Pyrczak Publishing.

Harris discusses tips and strategies for citing sources and giving proper credit in a very effective and easy to follow textbook. The content and descriptions are clear and easy to understand. It teaches students to learn how not to plagiarize.

Harris, Robert A., and Vic Lockman. 2001. *The Plagiarism Handbook: Strategies for Preventing, Detecting, and Dealing with Plagiarism.* Los Angeles, Calif.: Pyrczak Pub.

In the book *The Plagiarism Handbook: Strategies for Preventing, Detecting, and Dealing with Plagiarism*, Harris tackles the causes of plagiarism and cheating and the many types that are available. He offers materials and suggestions to help students deal with the issues related to plagiarism prevention, detection, and the means of handling policy issues on the institutional and administrative level. There are sample definitions, policies, quizzes, and activities, and reproducible handouts. Harris uses cartoons to illustrate his points and makes available about 24 reproducible handouts that can be used for teaching and discussion and presents faculty with practical ways to handle the many issues related to plagiarism and cheating. The book is well organized, and the material is treated in a way that makes it easy to understand and apply the strategies Harris suggests.

Lathrop, Ann, and Kathleen E. Foss. 2000. *Student Cheating and Plagiarism in the Internet Era: A Wake-up Call for Educators and Parents.* Englewood, Colo., and London: Libraries Unlimited; Eurospan.

Lathrop and Foss's book "is organized as a practical guide for educators and parents who want to reduce cheating and plagiarizing." The book includes "strategies to counter both high-tech and more traditional and "low-tech" cheating and plagiarism in K-12 schools, electronic plagiarism, how parents can be "vigilant, informed, and involved," integrity, ethics, character education, and definition of plagiarism. The authors present tools for writing without plagiarizing, alternatives to writing assignments, and online sites for reports and research papers. It has references to print and online resources and has a collection of articles at the end of the chapters to promote further discussion of the issues. The topics in the book are well laid out, and the authors provide a thorough treatment of the issues.

Markman, Roberta H., Peter T. Markman, and Marie L. Waddell. 2001. *10 Steps in Writing the Research Paper,* 6th edition. Hauppauge, N.Y.: Barron's.

The authors of this book describe it as a "succinct, easy-to-follow guide [that] gives students clear directions for writing papers in virtually all academic subjects." The authors also "describe how to determine a subject, formulate and outline a provisional thesis, prepare a bibliography, take notes from sources, write a draft, and then revise and edit the paper, bringing it to its final form. Added advice includes avoiding plagiarism and making the most of library resources."

Pattison, Tania, Trent University, and Academic Skills Centre. 2002. *Avoiding Plagiarism: A Guide for ESL Students.* Peterborough, Ont.: Academic Skills Centre, Trent University.

An introduction to the subject of plagiarism is presented. The author explains the differences between deliberate or intentional plagiarism and unintentional, accidental, or plain sloppy research. There are strategies to show students how to do research and to learn proper paraphrasing and summarization. The book also includes strategies for proper documentation using examples from the APA style manual.

Yeshiva College. 1990. *Upholding Academic Integrity: Definitions of and Consequences for Cheating and Plagiarism.* New York: The College.

This is a booklet from the Yeshiva College Writing Center, and it defines and describes what plagiarism is for the student. The booklet also deals with academic integrity.

Selected Articles

Numerous articles have been written on plagiarism and other plagiarism-related topics. Articles selected and discussed here may give the reader a better and clearer understanding of what plagiarism is and what strategies can be used to prevent, detect, deter, and teach students not to plagiarize. This is only a selected list of the vast number of articles available on plagiarism.

Auer, Nicole J., and Ellen M. Krupar. 2001. "Mouse Click Plagiarism: The Role of Technology in Plagiarism and the Librarian's Role in Combating It." *Library Trends* 49, no. 3: 415.

The authors present a historical perspective on plagiarism and show how "views on plagiarism have changed over time." They discuss how the Internet has contributed to the increase in plagiarism. They list different types of plagiarism, "plagiarism by copying, by paraphrasing, and by the theft of an idea." Students and faculty attitudes about plagiarism are discussed, and the article also examines the role that the librarian can play in tackling the plagiarism problem. The authors suggest that librarians should be informed and make faculty aware of resources that can help tackle the issues related to plagiarism.

Austin, M. Jill, and Linda D. Brown. 1999. "Internet Plagiarism: Developing Strategies to Curb Student Academic Dishonesty." *Internet and Higher Education* 2, no. 1: 221–233.

Austin and Brown contend that the "use of computers have made dishonesty easier." It is easy for student to "cut and paste" ideas from other peoples' work and claim it as their own. It is equally difficult for faculty to "document these sources to know whether the information is legitimate. Their article discusses the responsibilities of university administration to prevent plagiarism, the responsibility of educating students about academic plagiarism, and discussing plagiarism with students.

Bowden, Darsie. 1996. "Coming to Terms: Plagiarism." *English Journal* 85, no. 4 (April): 82–85.

Bowden discusses intentional and unintentional plagiarism and how these can be resolved through "explanation and instruction." The author touches on the origin of the term "plagiarism" and the traditional Western view of language as connecting with authorship, the concepts of authorship, and how "concepts of individual authorship inevitably affect how much help can be given to students, especially in writing centers where primary work involves writers helping other writers, predominantly through some form of collaboration." The article explains clearly the dilemma of plagiarism and collaboration among college students and recommends that the instructor provide a handout that defines plagiarism, explaining the university's policy on academic dishonesty, and noting sources that will assist the students in using the Internet for research in appropriate way.

"Combating Plagiarism." 2003. *CQ Researcher* 13, no. 2 (September 19).

CQ Researcher presents a comprehensive overview of plagiarism in its September 19, 2003, issue "Combating Plagiarism," including a thorough treatment of plagiarism and other plagiarism-related issues. Topics examined include a general overview, pros-cons of plagiarism, a chronology of plagiarism, bibliographies to enable further research, and a list of contacts.

Gardiner, Steve. 2001. "Cyber cheating: A New Twist on an Old Problem." *Phi Delta Kappan* 83, no. 2 (October): 172–174

The growing problem of cybercheating is discussed in this article, and the author shows how he uses search engines on the Web to track down sources that his students had copied word for word. He used engines such as AltaVista, Google, Yahoo, Netcrawler, and, more recently, Dogpile. Gardiner also provides a list of term paper sites to make faculty aware of some of the places where their students are getting their "research" papers. He also recognizes how the Internet can be a good tool for research if used properly.

Klesser, Kate. 2003. "Helping High School Students Understand Academic Integrity." *English Journal* 92, no. 6 (July): 57–66.

The article recommends that teachers educate high school students about academic integrity before they make the transition to college. She suggests that professors in academic institutions should be invited to discuss with high school students what academic integrity is and that it is important to be fully knowledgeable about what academic integrity is or is not.

McCabe, Donald L. 1996. "What We Know about Cheating in College." *Change* 29, no. 1 (January/February): 28.

McCabe tackles the issue of cheating in college and how the presence of academic integrity on a college campus can deter cheating. He examines various researches on cheating in colleges among college students. He touches on tests that the teaching faculty gives to students and the collaboration among students that often leads to instances of cheating. McCabe discusses the need to "change student attitudes about cheating and their resulting behavior." He also recommends changing faculty attitude by emphasizing the "sense of campus community."

Minkel, Walter. 2002. "Web of Deceit." *School Library Journal* 48, no. 4: 50.

The article "Web of Deceit" highlights the problem of plagiarism in the high school. Christine Pelton, a high school teacher, was embroiled in this controversy when she flunked 28 of her sophomore students for cheating. She was forced to give up her position when her community attacked her actions against the students and when she failed to get the support of the school principal and the town sheriff. The article recommends discussing academic integrity with students in high school by helping them know how to define it, recognize it, cite it, and properly credit other people's work.

Owens, Trevor. 2001. "Learning with Technology: Plagiarism and the Internet: Turning the Tables." *English Journal* 90, no. 4 (March): 101–104.

Owen discusses how the Internet as a technological tool that can be used to combat plagiarism. He shows how one can select a document and use some of the Internet detection resources to tell whether that particular document has been plagiarized. He uses examples from texts taken from Martin Luther King Jr.'s books and speeches.

Pincus, Holly Seirup, and Liora Pedhazur Schmelkin. 2003. "Faculty Perceptions of Academic Dishonesty: A Multidimensional Scaling Analysis." *The Journal of Higher Education* 74, no. 2 (March/April): 196–209.

What faculty thinks about academic dishonesty (cheating and plagiarism) is the topic of his article. The authors discusses what plagiarism encompasses based on an analysis of research that he conducted. The results of their research indicated that "faculty perceives academically dishonest behavior in two dimensions: seriousness and papers versus Exams." The authors "recommend that policies be made more explicit as to differential sanctions."

Simmonds, Patience. 2003. "Plagiarism and Cyber-plagiarism." *College and Research Libraries News* 64, no. 6 (June): 385–389.

This article, which appeared in the June 2003 issue of *College and Research Libraries News*, is s selected guide to plagiarism resources on the Web. This guide was created by Patience L. Simmonds, and it offers a definition and statements on plagiarism, links to plagiarism detection and prevention sites, academic integrity sites and honor codes, and links to sites that sell term papers.

Willis, Dottie, J. 2001. "High Tech Cheating: Plagiarism and the Internet." *Kentucky Libraries* 65, no. 4 (Fall): 28–30.

The author examines how technology has "dramatically changed the teaching and learning process in twenty-first century classrooms." This article defines plagiarism and shows how flagrant plagiarism is in the American society.

Young, Jeffrey R. 2001. "The Cat-and-Mouse Game of Plagiarism Detection." *The Chronicle of Higher Education* 47, no. 43: A26–27.

The article describes how colleges and universities provide professors with Web detection tools to tackle the problems of plagiarism and describe how professors should be vigilant.

Audiovisual Resources

Cahn, Steven M. "Ethics in Academia." 1 videocassette, 28 minutes, 1996.

In this video "Ethics in Academia," Steven Cahn discusses ethical issues in academia, fairness in grading, the tenure system, and plagiarism.

Crook, Bob, Bruce Deck, Dallas TeleLearning, and PBS Adult Learning Service. 2003. "Critical Challenges in Distance Education: Cheating and Plagiarism Using the Internet." 1 videocassette, ca. 90 minutes.

This is a video presentation from the teleconference "Critical Challenges in Distance Education: Cheating and Plagiarism Using the Internet," which took place April 3, 2003. This is a presentation of the PBS Adult Learning Service. The video is approximately 90 minutes long, and it is about cheating and plagiarism, the role of the Internet in education, intellectual property, and plagiarism.

The video recommends that faculty involve themselves in all aspects of the student writing process, and offers solutions for cheating and plagiarism by showing the use of strategies such as teaching students to cite sources properly. It also encourages teaching faculty to be creative about assignments so they are not so predictable

Davis, Stephen F., and Austin Peay State University. 1993. "Cheat Your Heart out Plagiarism in the 90's." 1 videocassette, 65 minutes.

This video was made by the Austin Peay University Media Center with the participation of Stephen Davis of Emporium State University. It is about cheating and plagiarism in education and is a presentation of cheating and the responsibility the institution has for upholding academic integrity. The video was created in 1993.

Egan, Clifton, Robert J. Rutland Center for Ethics, and Clemson University. 2002. "Academic Integrity Initiative Ethics Vignettes." 1 videocassette, 21 minutes 17 seconds.

The video is produced by the Robert J. Rutland Center for Ethics at Clemson University in South Carolina with the participation of director Clifton Egan. The video presents case studies of student ethics, college student cheating, and moral and ethical aspects in higher education. The viewer is presented with a series of six vignettes in the university setting. These include situations dealing with plagiarism, cheating, and other types of academic dishonesty. The vignettes are "Cheating 101," "The Café," "The Lab Report," "The Paper," "Dream," and "Professor." There is also a pamphlet that contains discussion questions.

Makley, Mary, Toks Olagundoye, Judy Boykin McCarthy, and Great Plains National Instructional Television Library. 1997. "Cheating Yourself: What's The Big Deal?" Two parts in 1 videocassette, ca. 25 minutes.

This video is about cheating and plagiarism in education. It makes it possible for students to realize that there are different types of cheating and that plagiarism is only one of these. Students are shown ways to recognize and understand what constitutes cheating, and they are presented with alternative ways to respond when they are thrust into circumstances that would force them to cheat or commit plagiarism. The video is in two parts. The first part is "Cheating Yourself" (14 minutes), and the second part is "Cheating Yourself—Plagiarism (11 minutes). The video is targeted to students from grades 5 to 12 but is appropriate for college students, too.

Naphin, Deirdre, Morley Safer, Lou Bloomfield, CBS Video, CBS News Archives, and CBS Worldwide. 2002. "Cheaters." 1 videocassette, 13 minutes.

The video "Cheaters" is a segment of the CBS *60 Minutes* television program that was originally aired November 10, 2002. CBS reporter Morley Safer discusses the topic of cheating in colleges and universities. His interviews feature

Lou Bloomfield, a physics professor from the University of Virginia, and Donald L. McCabe, who is the founder of the Center for Academic Integrity. The video tries to find out why students cheat and also touches on sale of research papers on the Web. There is also a brief discussion about plagiarism detection software and how this can detect plagiarism in student papers.

Rather, Dan, Rob Klug, Barry Leibowitz, and CBS News. 2001. "Truth and consequences." 1 videocassette, ca. 43 minutes.

The video "Truth and Consequences" was first broadcast as an episode of the program *48 Hours*. This video is 43 minutes long, and the host of the program was Dan Rather with parts of the segment being presented by Rob Klug and Barry Leibowitz. The video treats the topic of cheating and plagiarism in the United States.

Rather, Dan, Erin Moriarty, B. Lagattuta, Steve Hartman, Harold Dow, Rob Klug, Barry Leibowitz, and CBS News. 2002. "Truth and Consequences." 1 videocassette, 44 minutes.

This is an in-depth look at cheating, honesty, and plagiarism in education. It examines honesty in people and asks people whether they would cheat and, under what circumstances, who they would cheat. This video is part of the CBS *48 Hours* television program that was broadcast May 31, 2002. Other correspondents in the video include Erin Morriaty, Bill Lagattuta, Steve Hartman, and Harold Dow.

Rehm, Diane, WAMU-FM and American University. 2002. "Plagiarism." 1 sound cassette, 59 minutes.

"Plagiarism" is a sound recording by Diane Rehm on the Diane Rehm Show The topic is on plagiarism in the United States and cheating in education. It is a 59 minute discussion with Diane Rehm and three panelists, Donald L. McCabe, James Sandefur, and Patricia Harned. The discussion is on plagiarism among high school and college students. The reasons why students plagiarize are discussed, and the relationship between the Internet and plagiarism are discussed. The use of plagiarism detection software is discussed. Roles and responsibilities of both students and faculty are also mentioned, and some penalties for plagiarism are also discussed by the panelists. The panel also discusses high-profile cases of plagiarism involving professional writers like Stephen Ambrose. Listeners were invited to phone in their questions on plagiarism.

Sanders, Bob Ray, Hope Burwell, William L. Kibler, Jessica A. Kier, LeCroy Center for Educational Telecommunication, Dallas County Community College District, and PBS Adult Learning Satellite Service. 2003. "Cheating and Plagiarism Using the Internet." 1 videocassette, 90 minutes.

The video is a teleconference on cheating in education and cheating and plagiarism on the Internet. This video was taped on April 3, 2003. It is an examination of what constitutes cheating and plagiarism. It touches on the importance of honor codes and the role faculty can play in requiring students to refrain from committing plagiarism, teaching them about plagiarism, and teaching them about proper ethical behavior. It presents effective strategies for detecting plagiarism and shows what methods can be used once plagiarism has been detected. Distinctions are made between what plagiarism and cheating are and what they are not. Interested persons can also listen to the audio version of the program at www.wamu.org/dr/shows/drarc_020218.html.

Wetherington, Kevin, Shannon McWhirter, and Jude Lee Routh for Educational Video Network, Inc. 2002. "Research Skills: How to Find Information." 1 videocassette, 22 minutes.

"Research Skills: How to Find Information" is a video about report writing, research methodology, information resources, and plagiarism. The video is divided into six sections: "What Is Research?," "Selecting a Topic," "Research Tools," "Organizing Research Information," "Plagiarism," and "Writing a Research Paper." The video is targeted to high school and college students. Too much emphasis is placed on the presence of the card catalog considering the fact that many students are now more familiar with the online catalog.

Wetherington, Kevin, Ronald Green, and Ellen Grassie for Absalom Productions and Educational Video Network, Inc. 2003. "Plagiarism: It's a Crime." 1 videocassette, 22 minutes.

This videocassette discusses intellectual property rights, copyright infringements, and plagiarism. It includes definitions of plagiarism and what happened when people plagiarized, why people plagiarize, types of plagiarism, and strategies that can prevent people from committing plagiarism.

Index

About the Editor

Vibiana Bowman, an assistant professor at the Paul Robeson Library, Rutgers—The State University of New Jersey, Camden, is also a reference librarian and the library's Web administrator. Her areas of research include bibliographic instruction, community outreach, Web accessibility, educational Web design, and information ethics. She has been published in various scholarly journals including: *Library Hi-Tech*, *Internet Reference Service Quarterly*, and *Urban Library Journal*. Ms. Bowman has been a presenter at local, state, and national library and information science conferences.

Active in various national and state professional organizations, Prof. Bowman is the chair of the Chapters Council of the Association of College and Research Libraries (ACRL); chair of the Teaching, Learning, and Technology Committee of American Library Association's Library Instruction Round Table; and is a past president of the New Jersey state ACRL Chapter.

About the Contributors

Nick Cvetkovic

An author, teacher, and speaker, Nick Cvetkovic is president of NBC Associates, Inc., a computer consulting firm incorporated in 1980. Mr. Cvetkovic has held a variety of leadership positions within the independent computer consulting and computer user group communities and has been a personal computer hobbyist since 1982.

Mr. Cvetkovic is a former national board member of the Independent Computer Consultants Association and is a past president of the Association of Personal Computer Professionals in the Philadelphia area. He is one of the pioneers of on-line subscribers and is the founding "wizop" for Compuserve's Computer Consultants Forum and currently the forum administrator for photography.

Michele D'Angelo-Long

Michele D'Angelo-Long has been a teacher for 15 years and has taught preschool, elementary school, middle school, high school, and college. She has a B.A. in political science and an M.A.T. She is certified to teach English, social studies and English as a second language (K-12) and is currently enrolled in an Ed.S. program for school psychology. Presently, Ms. D'Angelo-Long serves as composition coordinator at Rider University, where she also teaches freshman composition classes. Additionally, she supervises student teachers at The College of New Jersey. In the last decade, Ms. D'Angelo-Long has presented at numerous conferences in the areas of literature and education and, most recently, academic integrity. She currently sits on Rider's University Academic Policies Committee on Academic Integrity.

John B. Gibson

John B. Gibson is the instructional technology specialist for the Paul Robeson Library at Rutgers—The State University of New Jersey, Camden. Mr. Gibson creates the programming and visual designs for Web-based materials used in information literacy instruction. He is also computing administrator for the library, which includes a new high-tech digital lab. Mr. Gibson has been cited for his work in instructional design in a number of professional publications and has presented at local, state, and national library conferences.

Dr. Mallika Henry

Dr. Mallika Henry is an adjunct assistant professor at York College of the City University of New York and also teaches in the writing program at Rutgers University. Her publications include foundational work on teaching through drama, human rights education, and international affairs. Dr. Henry's research interests are in the multicultural origins of human rights, qualitative studies of educational strategies, and English literature. She specializes in the teaching of essay writing, critical thinking, and developing verbal skills. After years of working at the United Nations, where she wrote and edited for an international staff, Dr. Henry developed communication strategies for varied populations such as homeless mothers and graduate students. More recently, she has developed curricula for educating college students in human rights and international affairs. Dr. Henry has presented at conferences on education, critical consciousness, and human rights.

Frances Kaufmann

Frances Kaufmann is the client services librarian at the Seton Hall University Library in South Orange, New Jersey. Her responsibilities include management of the circulation, reserve, interlibrary loan, and stack services departments. She is also a liaison to SetonWorldWide, Seton Hall University's on-line degree program. Ms. Kaufmann's areas of interest include resource sharing, interlibrary cooperation, library services for distance education, academic integrity, and recruitment and diversity in the library profession.

Ms. Kaufmann is the president of the New Jersey Chapter of the Association of College and Research Libraries (ACRL) and a member of the VALE Resource Sharing Committee. She has presented at regional and state library conferences and has held poster sessions and roundtable discussions accepted for ACRL and the American Library Association. At Seton Hall, she is chair of the Training Task Team of the University Copyright Committee.

Ms. Kaufmann has held library positions at Montclair State University, the College of Saint Elizabeth, Columbia University, and the University of Pennsylvania. She has a B.A. from Pennsylvania State University, an M.L.S. from Drexel University, and is currently a candidate for an M.A. in History at Rutgers University.

Robert J. Lackie

Robert J. Lackie is an associate professor-librarian at Rider University in Lawrenceville, New Jersey, where he co-leads the library instruction program and serves as reference collection development librarian. He has taught various business communications, English composition, public speaking, and library and Web research courses and seminars and has provided hundreds of library instruction sessions within many academic disciplines. In addition, he served as Rider's faculty-in-residence from 1998–2002.

Active in various library and educational organizations, Mr. Lackie is currently a trainer/evaluator for the NJ Train-the-Trainer Group, programs co-vice president for the Trenton Area Chapter of Phi Delta Kappa International, and outgoing chair of the Association of College and Research Libraries of New Jersey User Education Committee. In April 2004, he was selected by the New Jersey Library Association as the "2004 Librarian of the Year," and in May 2004, he was chosen as a recipient of the "2004 Rider University Award for Distinguished Teaching." A frequent presenter at local, state, and national conferences, his scholarly interests include e-classroom theory and pedagogy, learning and teaching styles, curriculum development, student development and retention, librarian/teaching faculty collaboration, Web and database research methods, and information literacy/teacher training.

Leslie Murtha

Ms. Murtha is an instruction and information services librarian for the Rutgers University Libraries. She holds a B.A. in theater arts, an M.L.S. , and an M.Ed. in adult and continuing education, and is also an alumna of Immersion 01, the Association of College and Research Libraries (ACRL) immersion program on information literacy. She teaches classes in library research and the retrieval and use of information. Her research interests include adult learning and culture, educational theory in library instruction, and the use of technology in learning. Ms. Murtha is also active in professional associations relating to information literacy on the state, national, and international levels. She is the chair of the User Education Committee of the New Jersey Chapter of ACRL and active in the Instruction Section of ACRL. She is also a member of the Standing Committee of the Information Literacy Section of the International Federation of Library Associations and Institutions.

Dolores Pfeuffer-Scherer

Ms. Pfeuffer-Scherer, a recipient of the Allen Davis Fellowship in Public History, is a Ph. D. candidate at the History Department of Temple University, Philadelphia, Pennsylvania. She is currently an intern at the Atwater Kent Museum in Philadelphia and was previously the senior program coordinator for the Honors College, Rutgers University, Camden, New Jersey. Ms. Pfeuffer-Scherer was a presenter at the National Collegiate Honors Council Conference and her areas of research include American social and urban history, specifically relating to the history of childhood and youth in the early 20th century.

Luis F. Rodriguez

Luis F. Rodriguez is the associate dean of public services for the Sprague Library of Montclair State University. He is active in state, regional, and national library organizations. Mr. Rodriguez is a past president of the New Jersey Library Association College and University Section/New Jersey Association of College and Research Libraries Chapter and currently serves as the legislative representative for that group. He also served on the national task force that created the Strategic Marketing Initiative for the Association of College and Research Libraries (2002.)

Patience L. Simmonds

Patience L. Simmonds is an assistant librarian at the John M. Lilley Library, Pennsylvania State, Erie. Her responsibilities include reference and library instruction and her areas of research include user satisfaction, needs and expectations in academic libraries, instruction and service for adult learners, and reference service. Ms. Simmonds has published in various refereed journals including *The Reference Librarian*, *Information Technology and Libraries*, *College and Research Libraries*, and *Library Trends*.

Ms. Simmonds is a member of both the American Library Association (ALA) and the Association of College and Research Libraries' (ACRL) Instruction Section. She is also a member of LIRT (Library Instruction Round Table) and a past chair of the LIRT Publications Committee.

Laura B. Spencer

Laura B. Spencer is a reference librarian at the Paul Robeson Library, Rutgers—The State University of New Jersey, Camden. This means that she is paid good money to ask students to outline the contours of what they don't know. Coming to terms with this and other paradoxes is the primary driving force behind her scholarly activity. She is also a member of the Delaware Valley Chapter of ACRL. She has previously written on user expectations and behaviors in the electronic environment.

Eileen Stec

Ms. Stec serves as the instruction and outreach librarian at the Mabel Smith Douglass Library, Rutgers—the State University of New Jersey, New Brunswick. She teaches extensively and develops multi-media instruction materials, including the peer-reviewed "Plagiarism and Academic Integrity" tutorial at Rutgers University, which was included in Association of College and Research Libraries' *Primo* database. She has published in *Medical Reference Services Quarterly* and in the forthcoming book *Digital Resources and Education Libraries: Invention, Innovation, and Implementation,* as well as many non-refereed venues. Ms. Stec works closely with the School of Communication's Information and Library Studies program at Rutgers University providing instruction experience for a number of graduate students.

She has presented at state, national, and international information conferences and is an active member of the Teaching, Learning and Technology Committee of American Library Association's Library Instruction Round Table and the Information Literacy Committee of the International Federation of Library Associations and Institutions.

Dr. Robert E. Wood

Dr. Robert E. Wood is chair of the Department of Sociology, Anthropology, and Criminal Justice at Rutgers-Camden. His research has focused on issues of globalization and development, and includes two books and several dozen articles. He has been the recipient of several teaching awards, including the Provost's Award for Teaching Excellence and the Warren I. Susman Award for Excellence in Teaching at Rutgers, and the Outstanding Contribution to Instruction Award of the Communication and Information Technologies Section of the American Sociological Association. He has published articles on teaching in *Teaching Sociology, Syllabus,* and *Innovate: Journal of Online Education*.